MY FIRST FORTY YEARS

To Pat with
my deep friendship after
so many years of
singing together with my
best wishes for your happiness
in life always. —
Looking for many more
years of friendship and
singing. —
Much love David

MY FIRST FORTY YEARS

PLACIDO DOMINGO

WEIDENFELD AND NICOLSON   LONDON

*To Marta, who throughout half my life has been not only a wonderful
wife to me and an incomparable mother to our children, but also the
inspiration and on many occasions the guide in my career.*

First published in Great Britain by
George Weidenfeld & Nicolson Limited
91 Clapham High Street, London sw4

ISBN 0 297 78291 6

Printed by Butler & Tanner Ltd,
Frome and London

CONTENTS

ILLUSTRATIONS

In *La forza del destino* (*Foto Lieske*), *Tosca* (*Anne Kirchbach*), *Don Carlo* (*Foto Lieske*) and *Aida* (*Foto Lieske*), Hamburg, 1967-9

In *Roberto Devereux* with Beverly Sills, New York, 1970 (© *Beth Bergman*)

In *Don Carlo*, Milan, 1970 (*E. Piccagliani, Teatro alla Scala*)

In *Lucia di Lammermoor* with Joan Sutherland, Hamburg, 1971 (*photo: Klein, Teldec; Foto Lieske*)

In *Tosca* with Gwyneth Jones, 1971 (*Anthony Crickmay*)

In *I vespri siciliani* with Peter Glossop, Paris, 1974 (*Colette Masson*)

In *Otello*: Paris, 1976, (*Colette Masson*); Hamburg, 1975 (*Jurgen Kranich*)

In *Carmen*: with Teresa Berganza, Edinburgh, 1977 (*Alex Wilson*); with Elena Obraztsova, Vienna, 1978 (© *Foto Palffy*)

In *Werther* with Brigitte Fassbaender, Munich, 1977 (© *by Fotostudio*)

In *Samson et Dalila*, Orange, 1978 (*Studio Bernateau*)

In a German television production of *Otello* with actress Dietlinde Turban, 1978 (*Foto Felicitas Timpe*)

In *Cavalleria Rusticana* with Elena Obraztsova, Milan, 1981 (© *Lelli & Masotti, Teatro alla Scala*)

In *Pagliacci*: with Teresa Stratas, Munich, 1978 (© *by Fotostudio*); Milan, 1981 (© *Lelli & Masotti, Teatro alla Scala*)

In *Manon Lescaut* with Renata Scotto, New York, 1980 (*J. Heffernan, Metropolitan Opera*)

In *La traviata* with Ileana Cotrubas, New York, 1981 (*J. Heffernan, Metropolitan Opera*)

In *The Tales of Hoffmann*: with Ruth Welting, New York, 1982 (*J. Heffernan, Metropolitan Opera*); Salzburg, 1980 (*Oskar Anrather/Bildberichier; © Winifried Rabanus*)

In *Manon Lescaut* with Kiri Te Kanawa, London, 1983 (*Clive Barda/London*)

BETWEEN PAGES 148 AND 149
c. 1972

At home (in Teaneck, New Jersey) with Marta, Placi and Alvaro, 1969 (© *Beth Bergman*)

Holding Avaro, with Pepe, Placi and Marta, New York, 1971 (*Erika Davidson*)

Signing my Metropolitan Opera contract, with Rudolf Bing, 1968 (*Metropolitan Opera*)

A concert at the Kremlin, 1974

With Sherrill Milnes and Leontyne Price at a party given to launch our recording of *La forza del destino*

Rehearsing *Carmen* in Vienna, 1978, with Franco Zeffirelli, Carlos Kleiber and Elena Obraztsova (*Foto Helmut Koller*)

With Pope John Paul II, The Vatican, 1982 (*Arturo Mari* © *Servizio Fotografico*)

ILLUSTRATIONS

Listening to a playback of a recording of opera arias, with Carlo Maria Guilini
    and technician Hans Weber, Los Angeles, 1980 (*Robert Cahen*)
Karl Böhm presenting me with his own vocal score of Beethoven's 9th Symphony
    while recording the work in Vienna, 1980
With John Denver, Los Angeles, 1980 (*Robert Cahen*)
With Milton Okun, Los Angeles, 1980 (*Robert Cahen*)
With footballer Kevin Keegan, near London, 1980 (*Clive Barda/London*)
Los Angeles, 1980 (*Robert Cahen*)
With Richard Baker, Sir John Tooley, Kiri Te Kanawa and Bernard Levin, near
    London, 1980 (*Clive Barda/London*)
In front of the Paris Opéra, *c.* 1975 (*L'Express*)
With Federico Moreno Torroba, *c.* 1980 (*Erika Davidson*)
With Anthony Bliss, Marta, and James Levine at the Met after the opening of
    The Tales of Hoffmann, 1982 (*Metropolitan Opera*)
The Maestro: rehearsing *Attila* in Barcelona, 1975

COVER PHOTOGRAPHS
Front cover: photo of author, 1983 (*Robert Cahen*)
Back cover: in *Otello*, Paris, 1978 (*Clive Barda/London*)

Unless otherwise indicated, all pictures belong to the author's collection

The first forty years give the text

– found by the author in a Chinese fortune cookie just after he turned forty

I
MADRID AND MEXICO (1941-61)

At twenty I was far from being technically ready to make my debut as a lead tenor singing Alfredo in *La traviata*, a difficult role for me even today. But I did just that, in May 1961, in Monterrey, Mexico. That performance took a great deal out of me, and not just vocally: I had not yet learned to control my emotions on stage, and I remember that I was actually in tears during the final ensemble, when Alfredo sings 'No, you won't die' to Violetta.

Worse had happened towards the end of the second act, after my lines 'Someone is in the garden. Who is there?' A messenger is supposed to enter, asking, 'Signor Germont?'

'It is I,' Alfredo replies. The messenger continues: 'A lady in a carriage, not far from here, gave me this note for you.' The messenger leaves, and Alfredo reads the shattering news that Violetta has left him.

Unfortunately, on that evening the messenger forgot to appear, and there was no answer to my 'Who is there?' I had to think quickly. I looked around and answered my own question by singing 'No one.' Then I walked over to the table where Violetta had written her note in the previous scene; luckily there were still some sheets of paper lying on it. I picked one of them up, sang 'From Violetta!' and proceeded with the scene, as if she had simply left the letter for me to find. The incident taught me at the outset of my career that I had to be prepared for absolutely anything in this business!

But I would be misleading you if I were to give the impression that I simply leapt onto the stage, without any background or experience in the theatre, and knew instinctively how to cope with the most hair-raising situations. My parents have devoted their lives, too, to the musical theatre, first in our native Spain and later in Mexico, and I cannot remember a time when the stage was not an important part of my existence.

I am very strongly attached to my family and to the whole concept of family. It is an essential element in my life, and that makes me particularly sorry that I never knew any of my grandparents. Three of them had died before I was born, and my maternal grandmother passed away when I was an infant. My mother's family is entirely Basque in origin, while my father's side is half Catalan and half Aragonese. One of his grandparents came from Ibiza, and I imagine that if I were to go very far back I would discover some North African ancestry.

Both the Basques and the Aragonese are said to be stubborn, hard-headed. There is a characteristic story about an Aragonese who tells his friends that he can bang a nail into a wall using his head as a hammer. He sets to work and manages to drive it in an inch or two but no further. Why? There is a Basque on the other side of the wall who is using *his* head to keep the nail from coming through. This is a useful heritage for anyone who makes his career in the performing arts.

In my father's home town, Saragossa, in a well-known district called El Tubo – the Tube, or the Pipe – there is a restaurant called Casa Colás, owned by an elderly gentleman who worked there as a waiter when it belonged to my paternal grandmother. She sold it to him before she died. In my grandmother's day it was called La Viuda de Domingo – Domingo's Widow – because she had managed it since her husband's premature death. She was a woman of incredibly strong character who succeeded in raising her children and in running an establishment frequented by a not always polite clientele: in those days it was more a tavern than a restaurant. For a woman of her generation she was remarkably independent and even drove her own car as early as 1918. Her generosity was well known in the town: once she bought a winning lottery ticket and shared her prize money with her employees.

The eldest of three children, my father was only ten when his father died. He studied the violin as a youngster and then played in opera and zarzuela orchestras in Saragossa and elsewhere in Spain. His excellent voice was discovered, and he began to sing baritone roles in the zarzuelas. Many experts felt that he had distinct Heldentenor qualities and urged him to study the Wagnerian repertoire in Germany, but he was devoted to his family and did not want to wander far from home. He made a few records in his early days, and I find the timbre of the elder Plácido Domingo's voice uncannily similar to that of my own voice. His idol was Miguel Fleta, the great Spanish tenor who had sung Calaf in the world première of *Turandot* at La Scala. Fleta was famous for his facility in bringing a big sound down to a pianissimo, and my father used to imitate that style, although as a baritone. There was a wonderful sense of line, a beautiful legato and diminuendo, in my father's singing. Unfortunately, his career ended early. During a tour, he caught cold but nevertheless continued to sing, thus doing permanent damage to his voice. Fortunately zarzuelas have roles for character actors who sing very little, and my father could continue to perform and, by then, to direct his own company.

The zarzuela is to Spain what operetta is to Vienna – a popular theatrical form that mixes musical numbers with spoken dialogue. Zarzuelas run from one to three acts in length and may be serious, semi-serious or comic. The action usually takes place in one or another of the Spanish regions, and the plot is about everyday life and troubles and passions. I suppose that about ninety per cent of zarzuelas have happy endings, and even those that do not rarely end in real tragedy, with murders and the like. The composers of some of the shorter works were lazy: they would write precious little music and leave most of the piece as spoken dialogue. Still, the musical quality of some zarzuelas is very high indeed.

I owe my love of music to the zarzuelas I so often heard from the time I was a small boy. They fascinated me then and still do now, to a point. When one grows up, one unfortunately tends to see more clearly the defects in the things one loves. But just as in other art forms there are great, good, so-so, bad and terrible works, the same is true of the zarzuela. What used to disturb me most, when I was in my teens, was that the comic, secondary roles were usually given to people with terrible voices, and I would often leave performances during their numbers and come back for the serious singing.

Like my father, my mother, Pepita Embil, was a star of the zarzuela. She came by her talent naturally, since the Basques are known for their love of singing. In Spain they say that one Basque is a *boina* (beret), two Basques are a *juego de pelota* (handball game), and three Basques are an *orfeón* (chorus). Even without musical training, many Basques have wonderful voices for part-singing, harmonizing beautifully and with innate flair. My mother's father was a church organist who loved to play piano reductions of operas in his spare time; and her uncle, an archpriest, was renowned for his impressive, dramatic delivery of the Mass. He was a tall, imposing man who used to vocalize very carefully before chanting the liturgy; my mother believes that observing this uncle at work when she was a child is what developed her sense of theatre.

The coastal village my mother came from, Guetaria, is famous for its

3

seafood and also as the birthplace of Juan Sebastián del Cano (El Cano), who headed Magellan's expedition after that great navigator was killed and who was therefore among the first men to circumnavigate the globe. Balenciaga, the famous *couturier*, was also a native of Guetaria, which is located about thirty kilometres from San Sebastián. It was, in fact, as a member of San Sebastián's Orfeón Donostiarra that my mother first performed regularly as a vocal soloist. The chorus toured widely, and by the time my mother was eighteen she had appeared in London and at the Salle Pleyel in Paris. She remained in Paris to study with an Armenian singing teacher for a while and then returned to Spain to make her debut at Barcelona's Teatro Liceo, Spain's foremost opera house, in a Spanish opera. In that work she played the part of a girl called . . . Plácida!

But the zarzuela, which was then in its heyday, began to attract her, and early in 1940 she found herself performing in *Sor Navarra* by Federico Moreno Torroba. It was the first of many occasions when that man played an important role in our family's history. My father was also singing in that production, and that is how my parents first met and fell in love. There is a moment in *Sor Navarra* when the soprano declares her love for the baritone, and after three months of performing the piece together, my father and mother got married. 'You were so insistent!' my father still tells her. 'What else could I do but marry you?' Their wedding took place on 1 April 1940, when my father was thirty-three and my mother twenty-two.

A great number of zarzuelas were being written in those days, and although my mother was offered a contract to sing opera at the Teatro Liceo, she was so flattered to have composers writing zarzuelas for her and so happy with her success in the genre that she decided to give it all her attention. In those days zarzuela singers performed once or twice every weekday and twice or three times on Sundays. Many works were given a hundred or even two hundred performances, and as soon as a company stopped performing one zarzuela another was immediately mounted. My parents were proud of their work, yet in a sense they were stuck. Both voices were a great loss to the operatic world, where they would undoubtedly have met with success. When my mother was in her forties she would let me accompany her in arias from *Tosca*, *Turandot*, *Cavalleria rusticana*, and I am not speaking from prejudice in declaring that it is a great pity that she never became an opera singer. As late as 1963, when Marta and I began working with the Hebrew National Opera in Tel Aviv – and when I realized what kind of company it was – I was tempted to urge my mother to join us and start an operatic career. She was still in marvellous vocal shape.

I was born in a characteristic Madrid *barrio* (quarter), the Barrio de Salamanca, at Calle Ibiza 30 (now 34), on 21 January 1941. My father's brother Pedro (Perico), and his wife, Rosita, still live in that building, and every time I visit them I hit a high B-flat, since it was there that I certainly sang, or at least shrieked, for the very first time, and probably in an even higher register. The city of Madrid has put a plaque on the building saying 'Plácido Domingo was born here', and my sister, Mari Pepa (born in September 1942), and my cousin Jaime say that they always feel like writing 'So were we' on it. (Mari Pepa is what we call a *castizo* name – not just typically Castilian, but typical of Madrid, the heart of Castile.)

I do not remember the war years at all because I was only four in 1945, but I do know that despite Spain's neutrality there were food shortages – white bread and sugar, for instance – and that my parents used to look for those items wherever they were performing, to bring them back to us.

There is only one family story about my precocious musical sensitivity, and it involves my mother's brother Francisco, who is my godfather. Tío Francisco, called Paco, was a big man who used to smoke a lot, and I am told that when my mother was changing my nappies he would sometimes stand near by, putting tobacco in his pipe and singing a phrase from a Spanish song: 'Levántate, morenito, levántate resalao' ('Wake up, little dark-skinned boy, wake up and be lively'). For some reason, either that phrase or Tío Francisco's voice had a relaxing effect on certain muscles, and I more than once ruined his fresh tobacco. This was undeniably a reaction to music, but I leave it to others to decide whether it was positive or negative.

In those days we shared an apartment not only with Tío Perico and his family but also with their sister, Enriqueta, and her husband, Pascual. The only thing I remember from those times is going on some reckless bicycle rides with my cousin in the grassy, tree-lined centre strip of Calle Ibiza, a broad avenue. My parents used to close their eyes in horror. As Mother and Father were always travelling, Mari Pepa and I often stayed with our dear aunt, my mother's sister Agustina. We are all very close to this day. When I was five or six years old, we moved to a different apartment about two blocks from the old one, in the Calle Sainz de Baranda. (I recently read a book by the conductor Ataulfo Argenta [1913–58] and realized that he spent the last years of his life in the same building that our second home was in.) My first school, the Colegio Ibérico, was on the same street, which ends in the large and beautiful Parque del Retiro. There is a zoo in the Retiro, as well as a botanical garden, and plenty of space for running,

5

playing and bicycling. I remember the comfortable feeling of that constant rotation in my life – home, school, park, home, school, park, day after day.

Although my parents travelled a great deal, there was a wonderful feeling of unity when we were together. My father and uncle both have very active senses of humour and always loved teasing and playing with us children. I do not have many musical memories from those first years, but I did attend a few of my parents' performances. I clearly remember seeing my father in tails and sporting a distinguished beard as he sang the part of the elegant Caballero de Gracia in a classic short zarzuela, *La Gran Vía*.

On cold, wintry Madrid mornings we used to eat *churros* (a thin dough fried lightly in oil – crisp, hot), which we would dunk in hot chocolate. Exquisite! One of my greatest delights as a child was to see the vendor standing at the corner. I would run down to get the *churros* for everybody. My Aunt Rosita or my parents also sent me to the food shops, and one day I was even allowed to buy eggs. I felt so happy as I was coming home that I twirled my net bag around and around over my head. By the time I got home I realized that all the eggs were broken. I told my aunt that I had fallen, but she said, 'Oh, no you didn't! We were watching you from the window!'

Christmas Eve is called Noche Buena in Spain, and it seems to me that my sister and I never really slept on a Noche Buena. There was a tremendous, happy party each year, with all the family and many friends participating. Since my parents were theatre people, there would always be a masquerade – improvised rather than organized. For instance, we would be eating when someone would unexpectedly appear at the door masked and in costume. On Epiphany (6 January), Spaniards have a traditional celebration called Los Tres Reyes or Magos (the Three Kings or Three Magi) – the same festival that the Italians call La Befana. The three kings come and bring gifts for children, much as Santa Claus does at Christmas in other countries. We would write letters to the kings a month in advance, and on the eve of the holiday we had to go to bed very early. A meal was prepared for the kings, including desserts, and there were even three big pitchers of water – one each for the camel, the elephant and the horse. We would polish and set out our shoes. It was all magical. The next morning there was the joy of waking up and finding so many wonderful toys. My parents played the comedy very well: the food was eaten, the water gone, and there was always a letter from the kings warning us to behave well during the following year. The special feeling of wonderment for things theatrical became part of me very early.

Every summer we went to Guetaria, my mother's little village, which is so beautiful that it has been designated a national monument. None of its buildings may be altered. Each year the mayor used to re-enact El Cano's return: he would disembark from a boat, and afterwards there would be a celebration in which a bull would be let loose to run through the streets. When I was five or six, a little troupe – a cross between a circus and a vaudeville show – came to town: a volunteer was needed to play the bass drum, and I went up, to the great surprise of Aunt Agustina and my sister. That was my artistic debut.

I have few other specific memories of my childhood in Spain, but I do remember a day when one of the boys I used to go swimming with in Guetaria took a dive, hit an overturned row-boat in the water and was killed. That was my first experience of death, and it made a powerful impression on me. Another time I nearly choked to death when a plum stone stuck in my throat. My father immediately set out with me for the doctor's surgery; but half-way there, realizing that I was suffocating, he reached inside my throat and pushed the stone all the way down. That did not feel very good, but it saved my life, and obviously without damaging my vocal cords.

In 1946 Federico Moreno Torroba, the composer who was so closely linked with my family's destinies, formed his own zarzuela company and took it to Puerto Rico, Mexico and Cuba for two whole years. My parents were part of the company. That period is unclear in my mind, probably because I was very unhappy about their absence. Their tour ended in Havana, and the company then returned to Spain. My parents, who had fallen in love with Mexico and who had in turn been adored by the Mexican public, decided to take a short holiday there before going back to their country. Their Mexican friends and admirers received them so enthusiastically that my parents made up their minds to form their own company and remain there permanently. My sister and I were sent for, and, accompanied by Aunt Agustina, we sailed from Bilbao on the *Marqués de Comillas* in December 1948. The last thing I did before leaving Spain was to drink an *horchata*, a very refreshing beverage made from almonds and other ingredients. When I returned to Spain for the very first time seventeen years later, the first thing I did was to drink an *horchata*.

Nothing could be more beautiful for two small children than a month-long boat trip. There were twenty or twenty-five other children aboard, and we all had the time of our lives: eating in the dining-hall every day, attending

7

the film showings, watching the dancing, being naughty and playing on the top deck – it was all marvellous. (On 6 January, the day of the Tres Reyes, we children were very puzzled as to how the camel, elephant and horse had managed to get to us on the high seas, but as everything seemed to be in order, we believed.)

The ship called at a few ports in northern Portugal; then we went directly to the Caribbean, stopping at Curaçao, in Venezuela, in Puerto Rico, and finally at an unforgettable place I have never seen since: Cuba. The sensation of heat as the boat came into the harbour was unbelievable. We stayed three days in Havana. In recent years I have had invitations to perform there, and I hope that that will happen soon. I would not go there, however, without checking first with my Cuban exile friends.

On 18 January 1949, just three days before my eighth birthday, we arrived at Veracruz, Mexico. The ship had to wait at anchor in the harbour overnight while the immigration authorities examined everyone's documents on board, but my parents had arranged to come out in a small motor-boat to meet us. My father had grown a moustache, and as their boat pulled up alongside the ship, my sister began to shout at my father that she didn't like the way he looked! But, of course, the experience of seeing our parents again was overwhelming for both my sister and myself.

We drove from Veracruz to Mexico City, where my parents had settled. They were in the midst of a zarzuela season, and we children were put in an American school. My mother had had the idea of opening an exclusive shop that sold babies' clothing imported from Spain, but while we were waiting for the store and for the apartment we were to live in behind it to be made ready, we stayed with Esperanza (Pelancha) Vazquez, who was one of my parents' best friends, and my own, too, until her recent death. Her niece and two nephews lived there as well, and we all had a wonderful time together. After a few months the house and shop at Avenida de los Insurgentes No. 299, were ready for us. We later moved to an apartment a few blocks away and later still to an apartment in a very old, traditional Mexican building called Edificio Condesa. Except for a short period, I remained there until I was twenty-one.

Although I continued at the American-run Windsor School to the end of that first school year, I did not learn English. There was an English class, but I was there too short a time for it to have done me much good. The following year I began to attend the Instituto México, where, for purely non-academic reasons, I had a great time: I liked football very much, and we used to play two games nearly every day! Our teacher, Alberto Godínez, was so dedicated to the game that he would keep all of us who were in the team in his class year after year – assuming that we all deserved to be promoted – so we could remain in the same class. He even allowed us to begin peeling off our street clothes during the last minutes of each class, and we were ready to play as soon as the fifteen-minute breaks began. I was the goalkeeper. On average we played two or two and a half hours a day, and the team was so good that three professional players developed out of it, including José Luis González, who gained international standing and played for the national team in two World Cup championships. The two standard ambitions of Spanish boys are to be football goalkeepers and bullfighters. When I was about fourteen I once went with a friend to a small *tientas* (training ring) to try my hand. The bull I was given to fight was only the size of a large dog, despite which I was afraid that I would be hurt and that my parents might find out. It chased me and flung me to the ground, and I went back to being a goalkeeper.

At the same time I began to gravitate toward the performances that my parents' company gave. Every weekend – and sometimes even on week-nights, despite having to go to school the next morning – I went to the theatre where they were playing. Besides their regular season, my parents performed with a Spanish company, Cabalgata (Cavalcade), which used to give programmes that included a zarzuela number, a flamenco number and a poetry recitation, usually of poems by García Lorca. They once set up a singing and dancing competition for children, and I participated by singing a sort of flamenco song called 'Tani'. I was eight at the time and dressed in short trousers. I was also very fat, and my mother says that one of my ears got very red as I sang – something that happens once in a while to this day when I am over-heated or very tired or embarrassed. I won the competition and was given some books and a football as a prize. But there was another little boy who was crying because he had not won, so I gave him all my prizes. That was my debut in the Western Hemisphere. (At the Instituto México I always volunteered to sing when someone was required for a school assembly. My repertoire was limited to 'Granada', and the other kids were so accustomed to hearing me sing it that they called me El Granado.)

Sometimes, when children were needed for one of my parents' zarzuela productions, my sister and I were pressed into service. In that way I began to learn the basics of theatrical practice from the time I was small. I attended orchestra and stage rehearsals, watched the set and costume makers at work, and placed the music on the orchestra's music stands. Since my parents were their own impresarios, I also saw the harsher aspects of the theatre world. Nowadays I am lucky, because I just sing and get paid and the theatre is full, but my parents' company did not always play to full houses. My mother or father would peer into the auditorium before the curtain went up to see whether the evening was a bad one or a good one, and I have never forgotten either that insecure feeling or the realization that whatever happened, they were artists and had to give their best. Fortunately, however, we never had real financial problems.

Shortly after our arrival in Mexico, my sister and I began studying the piano with Manuel Barajas, a fine teacher. Twice a week we went to after-school lessons, and we worked hard. Pelancha's nephews took lessons from him, too. Usually our aunts would come round to pick us up afterwards; and if the sessions had not gone well, Barajas would shout, 'Aunts, upstairs!' – and they would have to go up to hear him scream at one or another of us. If he wanted to punish us for some reason, he would make us stand for thirty minutes or an hour with our arms outstretched, holding books. Thinking about it now, it seems rather a cruel practice, but at the time it appeared perfectly reasonable.

Aunt Agustina looked after more than our music lessons, because my parents often toured the provinces and even other Latin American countries. They once had to spend eight months in Puerto Rico, which was a long separation for us. Although our aunt was very strict, she was wonderful. It is natural, when taking care of other people's children, to feel an even greater sense of responsibility than if the children are your own. Agustina was especially exacting about punctuality, and when my friends would play catch with the bottles of milk I had bought at the market, I was as afraid of getting home a few minutes late as of possible breakage. She often went on dates on Wednesday evenings – we used to call them 'Ash Wednesdays' – when we would secretly invite friends over and misbehave just for the joy of misbehaving. I especially remember a bust that was kept on the piano: one of my friends would drop it from our third-storey apartment and another would catch it below. But I think of Aunt Agustina and of those days with the greatest love: she really was a second mother to us.

When I was fourteen years old Barajas became ill and died. My parents then faced the question of whether or not I was to be trained for a professional career in music. They decided to enrol me at the National Conservatory, where I studied both musical and academic subjects. I found the Conservatory difficult at first. I had admired and been accustomed to Barajas, and it took some time before I felt comfortable with my new teacher. But I believe in *la forza del destino*, in fate, and in my own case things have usually happened for the best. It is true that had my teacher not died, I probably would not have gone to the Conservatory and might therefore have avoided the personal upheavals that soon grew out of my new way of life. But if Barajas had lived, I would most likely have tried to become a concert pianist; and although I had great facility at the piano and could sight-read well and play in a naturally musical way, I doubt that I could ever have become an outstanding keyboard artist. Finally, had all these other developments not taken place, I would never have begun singing as early as I did.

When I entered the Conservatory I was a boy, with nothing in my head except football and the piano. I continued to love football, but it no longer played such an important part in my life. I liked both literature and mathematics very much, and I especially remember the elderly Spanish lady who taught mathematics. Although I did not mind playing tricks on cruel teachers, this one was such a fine person that the class's pranks on her always upset me. They used to mimic this poor woman's Castilian pronunciation. There is a great difference between the way the letters *c* (soft) and *z* are pronounced in Castilian Spanish and the way they are pronounced in Mexico and elsewhere in Latin America. In Mexico they are roughly equivalent to the sounds they would have in English, while in Castile they are pronounced like the English *th*. When I first came to Mexico I was teased for my pronunciation and got into a number of fights as a result. Later, like all children, I adapted to the local pronunciation; but whenever I am in Spain I revert naturally to Castilian pronunciation – and, as a matter of fact, when I am in Argentina, I start pronouncing their way, with a more singing quality and rather harsh double *l*s.

Strangely enough, although I was supposed to be getting more serious musical instruction at the Conservatory than I had received from Barajas, my lessons there were much less interesting. A friend of mine says that there is nothing like a conservatory to make people stop liking music. Instead of a concentrated hour every three or four days, as I had been accustomed to having with my private teacher, I now had twenty minutes here and twenty minutes there. My mind blocked and I lost interest, although I did receive training in other important skills and subjects such as solfège (sight-singing), harmony and the other elements of composition. My solfège teacher, a competent man, would be so upset when someone could not read a part correctly that he would begin to shout: 'Musicians! We really are mentally retarded! Physicists and chemists have to learn

11

thousands of complicated formulae, and all we have to worry about are our do-re-mi-fa-sol-la-si – and then *again* do, *again* re, *again* mi, the same seven notes over and over again!'

In fact, the Conservatory was then in its heyday, with Carlos Chávez, the famous composer and conductor, the star faculty member. Julián Carrillo, another professor, was a leading exponent of composition for the quarter-tone piano. Among my friends at the Conservatory was Eduardo Mata, who is now a well-known and successful conductor. He and I even composed a piece together, the Sinfonietta No. 1 in C. We would escape from our non-musical classes – biology, mathematics, or whatever – to work at composition and play four-hand piano music. Eduardo later participated in Igor Markevitch's conducting class at the Conservatory, which I attended as an observer. The three pieces Markevitch worked on were Tchaikovsky's Fourth Symphony, the Second Suite from Ravel's *Daphnis et Chloë*, and Britten's Variations on a Theme by Purcell (*Young Person's Guide to the Orchestra*), and those sessions stimulated my interest in the symphonic repertoire and in conducting.

Before long I began to notice the singers from the National Opera coming to the Conservatory for lessons or coaching sessions, and my curiosity was aroused. I observed several teachers' classes; the world of opera slowly began to fascinate me, although I had not then even begun to sing zarzuela with my parents.

The Instituto México, which I had attended for five years, was for boys only, and when the school day had ended, I had gone home. But at the Conservatory, classes were mixed, and lessons sometimes went on into the evening. There was a ready alibi for not always being home for supper. I do not agree, by the way, that having separate classes for boys and girls necessarily helps concentration. When there are members of the opposite sex in the class there is a correspondingly greater urge to do well, even if only to make a good impression. I became very interested in some girls at the Conservatory and eventually started going out with one of them – a piano student, like myself, who was two years older than I. By then I was making my first attempts at singing, and she would accompany me at the piano.

At the age of sixteen – and barely sixteen at that – I made up my mind to leave home and to live with this girl. We hid for a while in the home of one of her elder brothers, and soon afterwards we were secretly married. This dramatic episode had major consequences for me and is difficult to discuss even today. I attribute it to three factors. As my parents were so often away from home and so busy with their work, my father had never talked to me about life, nor was he aware of what was happening within me. I had assumed that what I felt towards my girlfriend was really love, and as I was an intense boy, I had decided that we had to marry. Then there was my aunt's strictness, which, however well I understand it today, did of course bother an independent-minded teenager. Finally, there was the simple fact of being in such an emotionally charged state at the most difficult moment of adolescence – in the right place at the wrong time.

My parents, who were in Europe with Pelancha, learned that I had left home. They came back to town, managed to find me and took me back home. I eventually persuaded my father that since I was married, I ought at least to be allowed to see my wife. With him I went to visit her and her family, and when it was time to leave I said to my father, 'Please, I feel I have to stay.' I remained there. Her parents found an apartment for us; we moved in, and she soon became pregnant. It did not take long for us to realize that the situation was completely impossible. We were so young, and we had no experience of life, of ourselves. But the baby, a boy, was born in June 1958, when I was seventeen, and we named him José (Pepe for short). That is why at the age of forty-two I already have a twenty-five-year-old son and a little grand-daughter.

My wife and I separated after less than a year together, although the divorce did not come through for another year after that. At the time it was all terribly harrowing for me. I had no idea how to cope with so catastrophic a predicament, and although I can now look back upon it calmly, I do still wonder how her parents, who were aware of what was happening, could have allowed their eighteen-year-old daughter to leave home with and then to marry a sixteen-year-old boy.

Once again, however, fate was kind to me in the long run. In a sense, getting married accelerated my career, because it meant that I had to find work, had to do anything to support my wife, our child and myself. Had I remained at the Conservatory, I might have become what we call a 'conservatory rat' – someone who learns to do everything proficiently but never develops into a real performer. Leaving it opened the way to new experiences and made me independent.

Looking back at the four years between my son's birth and my departure from Mexico, I am still amazed by the quantity and variety of my musical and theatrical work. My first engagement was as my mother's accompanist in a concert at Mérida, Yucatán, following which I performed with my parents' zarzuela company. By then I was familiar with most of their repertoire, and I felt comfortable singing as a baritone.

My parents had given me some informal singing instruction at home; later, at the Conservatory, I began to observe the voice classes more seriously than before. I never had a singing teacher as such, although I did audition for several teachers. One lady was very keen on the physiology of the voice. She would tell me that the epiglottis had to go this way, the glottis that way, the breathing apparatus was doing such-and-such, the forehead muscles did something else, the resonance was caused this way or that. . . . It was entirely theoretical and did not help my singing at all.

There was, however, one teacher whose class fascinated me. Carlo Morelli, a Chilean, was the brother of Renato Zanelli, a tenor who was great in the role of Otello. (Their real double-surname was Morales Zanelli. Morelli started his career as a tenor and became a baritone, while Zanelli started as a baritone and became a tenor.) I was curious about Morelli's classes because I knew that many of Mexico's best professional singers went to him for coaching. It turned out that rather than concentrating on vocal technique, Morelli dwelt on interpretation, and that interested me from the start. He was a mystic, a spiritist, and believed in mysticism as an aid to singing. I did not and do not share those beliefs, but I enjoyed his classes none the less. Morelli had a beautiful sapphire ring, whose gold band had the form of a two-headed serpent. When he was dying he asked his wife to give me that ring, and I wear it to this day.

It was in Morelli's class that I reached a high B-flat for the first time. By chance, that day the president of Mexico, Adolfo López Mateos, visited the Conservatory. He came to our class and I sang in the quartet from *La Bohème*. I was so pleased with my new B-flats that years later another class member – who happens to be my wife, Marta – told me that I had been screaming my head off in the presence of the president, and all because I was so proud of myself!

Every Monday evening during my Conservatory days and even later, a good friend of mine, Pepe Esteva, used to open his home for musical get-togethers – sessions that came to play an important part in my education. Pepe, who was a singer, came from an unusual, almost bizarre family that was devoted to music: his mother played the harp; his sister, the guitar; and his brother was a violinist who now conducts a Mexican orchestra.

As few as four or five or as many as twenty people would show up each Monday. We all brought things to eat from our own homes, and Pepe's mother would make coffee at various times during the gatherings, which began at 8.30 or 9 in the evening and went on until 2 or 3 in the morning. Everyone brought music to sing or play; and, although I did some singing, my main task was that of official pianist. I would arrive with an enormous stack of music under my arm, joking about not having prepared anything. With Pepe's brother I went through violin repertoire; with other musicians I played chamber music; and, above all, I accompanied singers.

Those evenings became quite an institution. Usually, several leading singers from the National Opera would turn up to perform for each other, discuss roles and chat about the famous singers of the day. Since some of them were rivals, a certain amount of competition went along with the fun. Julio Julián and Carlos Santacruz – tenors with marvellous high notes – were both regulars at the Estevas'. Julián had a beautiful voice and made a successful career for himself in Mexico well before I got started; Santacruz was a member of my parents' company, and I later conducted him in *La Chulapona* and *Luisa Fernanda*, both by our old friend Moreno Torroba.

I developed as a musician more through those weekly sessions than through any other activity of my early years. The amount of repertoire I devoured was impressive, and the experience taught me when and how to lead, when and how to follow, and a great deal about different musical styles and different types of voices. My participation in those sessions went on for at least three years; I found them so instructive and enjoyable that I look back on them with love and regret. I wish that I had time today for more informal music-making.

Despite my B-flats and other indications that I might be able to develop into a tenor, I continued to sing as a baritone in my parents' company. But the zarzuela baritone always plays around in the top register: the tessitura is definitely that of a high baritone. One season my father and I toured south-eastern Mexico with another company. I sang in the chorus, played the piano to bolster the small orchestra, recited dialogue and did whatever else was required from one performance to the next. While we were in Veracruz, which is where I had first landed in Mexico as a child and which is also Marta's native city, the company's regular tenor fell ill, and I was asked to replace him for one performance of *Luisa Fernanda*. Zarzuelas have real tenor parts with terrifying tessituras; there is no joking with them. It was a momentous occasion for me to be making my debut as a tenor.

That tour remains in my mind for another reason, too. I once arrived late for an important rehearsal, and my father slapped and reprimanded me in front of the whole company, to my great embarrassment. But he was absolutely right: I learned an unforgettable lesson about professionalism and punctuality in the theatre.

I continued as a baritone in my parents' company, singing many of the principal works of the repertoire: *La Calesera*, *El Balcón de palacio*, *Katiuska*, *Luisa Fernanda*, *Gavilanes*, and many others. We performed in Monterrey, Guadalajara, Mérida, Aguascalientes, San Luis Potosí and, in short, throughout the Mexican Republic. It so happened that on the day of Pope Pius XII's death we were in the most Catholic of all Mexican cities, Guadalajara. The mourning period that followed was doubly sad for my parents because few people attended our performances.

In those months, auditions were announced for the solo and chorus parts of *My Fair Lady*, which was being staged in Mexico for the first time – in Spanish, of course. It was to be essentially the same production that had been done in London and New York – the same choreographer, sets, costumes, and so on. I was engaged to do one of the drunkards, a friend of Alfred P. Doolittle, and also as an assistant conductor and assistant coach. The part of Professor Higgins was played by one of our greatest Mexican actors, Manolo Fábregas, but there was some difficulty in finding a leading lady. One day I was waiting for a bus with Pepe Esteva when another friend, a soprano named Cristina Rojas, happened to walk towards us. Cristina complained about being out of work, so we insisted that she come along and audition for the chorus, which was not yet complete. Her audition piece was an aria from *Madama Butterfly*. When she had finished singing, I saw people emerging from the wings in droves – a tremendous commotion! Immediately they began measuring her for shoes, hats, dresses and wigs, and she was engaged to sing Eliza Doolittle. Although I had hardly anticipated such an outcome, I was of course very happy for Cristina. She did the part excellently and with great success.

Incredible as it may seem, there was a performance of *My Fair Lady* every day and two on Sundays. We never had a day off. In all, I did 185 performances without interruption. When people perform the same show month after month they begin to go a bit mad, and they start playing pranks to relieve the monotony. Someone would be given a broken-legged chair to sit on and fall off; or there would be a knock at a dressing-room door, and the person who opened it would have a pitcher of water thrown at him – just before he had to go on stage. We once dipped the false moustache of Jorge Lagunes (the tenor who was singing the part of Karpathy, the Hungarian language professor) in a chemical that made it smell like excrement, which made Fábregas, in his dialogue with Lagunes, change the line 'this repellent Hungarian' to 'this odoriferous Hungarian'. We were all fined. I, too, was a victim often enough. In order to be a respectable drunkard I had to wear crude, worn-out clothes and shoes, but I then had to change into tails and very elegant shoes to sing in the chorus during the ball. One evening, as I began to change my shoes, I realized that they had been nailed to the floor – and with five nails each! It was impossible to pry them off quickly enough; I had to appear for the ball in horrible old clodhoppers, and of course I was fined for that, too.

There were many aspiring opera singers involved in that production, but I was only beginning to dream about opera at that time. It seemed fantastically remote, especially since I had not even heard many operas. I assumed that if I could develop my tenor tessitura, I would go on singing in my parents' company.

One of the chorus girls in the *My Fair Lady* production was an aspiring night-club singer, also named Cristina, whom I liked very much and often accompanied at the piano. I would sometimes play for her at bars, and I did the same for a baritone who was a member of my parents' company. He frequently sang at a cabaret, and when he would come out to perform the clientele would become very rowdy. 'Go away! We don't want to hear you!' they would shout. 'We want to see the girls!'

'Come on, guys,' he would plead, 'don't interrupt me. The sooner you let me sing my three songs, the sooner you'll see the girls.'

'All right, go ahead and sing, but we're not going to listen to you.' Someone yelled at me, 'And you, Maestro? How do you manage to sit there with your eyes closed, looking so inspired?' It was quite an experience to accompany someone in romantic songs while the audience roared, 'Finish, already! Shut up!' and much worse. But we both saw the humour of the situation and took it lightly.

Not long after *My Fair Lady* had closed, Evangelina Elizondo, a famous and very sexy Mexican star, decided to appear in a new production of *The Merry Widow*. I was engaged for the exciting job of coaching her, and also to sing the tenor role. In the more than 170 performances, I took the part of Danilo in about forty and that of Camillo in the rest. During one rehearsal there was a fire, which two of my colleagues and I managed to extinguish. We were rushed to the Red Cross clinic in an ambulance to be treated for smoke inhalation, and the driver went so fast through the streets of Mexico City that I remarked to my companions, 'Nothing happened to us in the fire, but we'll probably all be killed in the ambulance.'

In another musical – a detective story, *The Redhead* – I had a lovely, melodic number to sing, during which the leading lady always did everything wrong on stage, throwing everyone out of synchronization. The lead was sung by a fine Spanish artist, Armando Calvo, a good friend of my parents. One evening he was ill, and as I was his 'cover', I ought to have taken his place. Instead, the part was given to his brother, Manolo Calvo. This unprofessional behaviour upset me very much, and I left the show altogether. The director, Luis del Llano, who is now a very powerful figure with Channel 41 in the States, always used to say that he loved me like a father. I told him at the time that I thought he had behaved very poorly. Years later, however, I thanked him, because that incident, too, accelerated my growth and my independence.

Manuel Aguilar, a fellow Conservatory student whose father was an important Mexican diplomat in the United States, was always telling me that I was wasting my time in musical comedy. He arranged for me to audition at the National Opera in 1959. The two baritone arias I chose to sing were the Prologue to *Pagliacci* and 'Nemico della patria!' from *Andrea Chénier*. The auditioning committee told me that they liked my voice but that in their opinion I was a tenor, not a baritone. Could I sing a tenor aria? I did not know the repertoire at all, but I had heard some tenor arias. 'I could sight-read something,' I said. They brought me the music of 'Amor ti vieta' from *Fedora*; and, although I cracked on the A-natural, they told me that I really was a tenor and that they were going to give me a contract.

I was amazed and thrilled, especially since the contract was financially decent and I was only eighteen. The National Opera used to have both a 'national' season, which employed native artists, and an 'international' season, for which famous artists were brought in from all over the world to sing the leading roles and local singers were employed as comprimari (singers of secondary roles). I was taken on mainly as a comprimario for the international season and to help with the musical coaching of other singers. As a coach I worked on many operas, among them *Faust* and Gluck's *Orfeo*, in which I played the piano for the rehearsals of Anna Sokolow, the choreographer.

My first role was the small part of Borsa in *Rigoletto*, with Cornell MacNeil in the title role, Flaviano Labò as the Duke, and Ernestina Garfias as Gilda. It was an exciting day, and since my parents were in the theatre business, they had had the most beautiful costume made for me. Labò wondered where this upstart tenor had managed to get such a nice costume. A few months later I sang the more important part of the chaplain in the Mexican première of Poulenc's *Les Dialogues des Carmélites*.

The 1960 and 1961 international seasons gave me my first opportunity to work with such truly outstanding singers as Giuseppe Di Stefano and Manuel Ausensi. My roles included Remendado in *Carmen*, Spoletta in *Tosca*, Incredibile and the Abbé in *Chénier*, Goro in *Butterfly*, Gastone in *Traviata* and the Emperor in *Turandot*. Although the Emperor has practically nothing to sing, I was given a wonderful costume for the production; and Marta, whom I was getting to know better in those days, now enjoys reminding me of how proud I was to be so beautifully clad despite having such a small role. When I was engaged to sing the Emperor I had never even heard of *Turandot*, and I shall never forget coming into the rehearsal hall at the very moment when the chorus and orchestra were working on 'Perchè tarda la luna', the chorus to the moon. Perhaps if I were to hear them today I would notice that they were playing flat or not singing so well, but at that moment the music had the most profound effect on me. It was one of the most moving experiences of my life, the most beautiful thing I had ever heard.

Performing Spoletta, Incredibile and Gastone gave me the opportunity of singing near Di Stefano. Among all the tenors I have heard in person, he was the one who most impressed me. The beauty, warmth and passion of his voice, the excellence of his phrasing and, above all, his masterly delivery of every word were a great inspiration to me. Di Stefano made me realize that the sort of wonders I had heard in the recordings of Caruso, Gigli, Fleta, Bjoerling and other giants of the past could be achieved by living human beings. Marta and the other young women were absolutely crazy about Di Stefano, and during the third act of *Tosca* they used to stand in the wings, peering in and listening to his 'E lucevan le stelle'. I would come up from behind and put my arms around Marta, and she would get very angry and ask me who I thought I was!

Manuel Ausensi, the Spanish baritone who sang Gérard in *Chénier* and Scarpia in *Tosca*, had one of the greatest voices I have ever heard - warm, beautiful and elegant. In one performance of *La traviata* in August 1961, Ausensi, as Giorgio Germont, sang 'Di Provenza il mar' so beautifully that he had to repeat the aria in order to satisfy the public. That very much upset Di Stefano, the Alfredo, who was so displeased that he threatened not to go back out for the finale of Act II. After much talk, Ernesto de Quesada, an important concert agent, said, 'Well, Mr Di Stefano, what can we do? If you refuse to go out, this Domingo boy who is singing Gastone will have to take over for you. Fortunately, he made his debut as Alfredo in Monterrey a few months ago.' At that point Di Stefano changed his mind and finished the performance. But I am getting ahead of my story.

The Opera only occupied me for a few weeks every so often. During the year or so following my first appearances there, I worked at a great variety of other jobs. To begin with, I played the piano for a touring ballet company – the Ballet Concierto de México. They could not afford an orchestra, so together with a certain Mrs Cardus (whose daughter, a talented ballerina, later performed with the Marquis de Cuevas's company in France and then with the Stuttgart Ballet), I played two-piano arrangements of *Giselle*, *Les Sylphides*, *Don Quichotte*, *Coppélia* and *Swan Lake*. It was very difficult for me to concentrate on the keyboard when there were twenty or twenty-five lovely girls (forty or fifty legs!) so close at hand – especially since I seemed to be the only male around who was interested in them. But the company's discipline was very strict, so the Maestro was not allowed to fool around.

I was also one of the people most heavily involved with Mexico's cultural television station, Channel 11, from its inception. My own music programme consisted of excerpts from zarzuela, operetta, opera and musical comedy, all done to piano accompaniment. The first and constant task was to select performers, and I invited many of my friends from the National Opera's Academy to participate. The only one I did not invite was Marta, strangely enough, because she seemed so high and mighty that I thought she would not have been interested. Later, she confessed that she had been dying to take part. I then had to choose repertoire, secure costumes, wigs and make-up (sometimes borrowed from my parents' company), accompany most of the singers at the piano and do some of the singing myself. We did have our share of mishaps. During a performance of the Gilda-Rigoletto duet, the baritone's beard began to come unstuck without his being aware of it; I gestured at him from the keyboard and he gave me the most puzzled looks, while his beard dangled ever more precariously. And tenor Rafael Sevilla, in the duet from Boito's *Mefistofele*, lost half a moustache, which is worse than losing a whole beard. The programme even contained a phone-in musical quiz; and Marta, using a pseudonym – the Great Opera Lover – once won a score of *La serva padrona*.

Through my girlfriend, Cristina, I became involved in another television series, this one dedicated to the theatre. We had participated together in an acting class taught by Seki Sano, a Japanese theatrical expert, and there we met a certain Constantin, who had interesting ideas about the stage. I helped to bring him in as drama director for the station, and under his guidance we performed plays by Pirandello, Benavente, García Lorca, Cassona and even Chekhov - whole works, not excerpts. I played only secondary roles, because most of my time was occupied by the musical programme, but it was good training for me all the same. Seki Sano himself made an oustanding director, and Constantin taught me to study the background of whatever part I was doing, in accordance with the Stanislavsky method. One must think about the psychological make-up of every character one interprets, not just through his words but also by considering what his family background would have been, his manner, his bearing, and so on. But my most important job for the drama series was selecting background music. I listened to an enormous amount of recorded music, especially symphonic repertoire, and during the broadcasts I had to monitor the musical volume level. There was almost no way to rehearse: everything was done on the spot, rough and ready.

Those two television series ran for twelve to fifteen weeks a year, and I believe that I was involved in them for two years.

Two of Mexico's best-known actors, Enrique Rambal and Rafael Banquells, got together to direct a zarzuela season whose highlight was *Doña Francisquita*, in which my parents participated. I was hired to train the chorus for that production; I worked hard and was proud of the results. Zarzuela choruses customarily sing with an open-throated sound. The members make no attempt to cover their voices or to blend with each other. Teaching them to sing like a real chorus was a great opportunity for me and an effective spur to my thinking about voice production and conducting. Assisting in coaching the chorus for *My Fair Lady* was also very instructive for me.

Not everything in my life was work, and I particularly remember my very full Sundays, which were always spent among friends. After Mass, we would dash to the soccer games and then sit down to an enormous lunch. Fortunately the stadium was just 300 yards from the Plaza de Toros, because after lunch we invariably went to the corridas. When the bullfights had ended, we would remain in the area, eating unimaginably delicious *tacos*, and then arrive at the theatre at 10 p.m. for the third and last of my parents' Sunday performances. (The others were at 4 and at 7.30.)

Among my many friends in Mexico City was one boy whose family was quite well off and who would throw big parties, at which he and I would sing together. Afterwards we sometimes went to some of the city's forbidden houses. One day we visited one where he knew the madam quite well, and we both sang and had a sort of social evening there.

In addition to working in opera, zarzuela, ballet, musical comedy and television, I made my first contact with the recording industry. In those days there were two singers of popular music, César Costa and Enrique Guzmán, who were particularly well known in Mexico, and I did some arranging for them. Most of the time I simply copied what I heard in the original American versions and figured out how to adapt the arrangements to our resources. Once in a while I even sang. There was one song that went, 'Put your head on my shoulder, ah-ah-ah-ah', and on that record – Mexican version, of course – I sang the 'ah-ah-ah-ah'! It was a bit of a leap from the descant in 'Put Your Head on My Shoulder' to Alfredo in *La traviata*, but that was my life in those days.

That *Traviata* in 1961 was, by the way, only one – albeit the most important one for me – of a number of early appearances I made in Monterrey. That performance had been organized in Mexico City, but most of the others took place under the auspices of a local impresario named Daniel Duno. He ran his opera seasons on a shoe-string budget, enticing singers by reminding them that 'the climate is great – lots of sun'. I had already sung secondary parts there in 1960: Pang in *Turandot*, Gastone in *Traviata* with Di Stefano, Cassio in *Otello* with Salvatore Puma, and Remendado in *Carmen*, again with Di Stefano. The pay was so low that it was hard to get by at all, but I managed through a funny combination of circumstances.

My mother had a brother, Sebastián, who was an adventurer, a world traveller (he recently died). Once, when I was about eleven, he came to Mexico, bringing with him a friend, a fellow Basque whose first name was Domingo (or Xtomin, in Basque). Xtomin remained in Mexico, married a Spanish woman and settled in Monterrey, where he opened a restaurant – and that, of course, is how I survived when I performed there. Most of my meals were provided gratis by Xtomin, and even on the long train journey back to Mexico City, Manuel Aguilar (who was managing the tour) and I ate our way through a pile of sandwiches and other goodies given to us by Xtomin – a good thing, too, because by the time I got home I did not have a penny in my pocket. Xtomin still has a pension in Monterrey, and I always stop in for a visit whenever I perform there.

Today, when people ask me how I manage to hold up under my extremely heavy work load, I answer that I became accustomed to intense activity very early in my life and that I love it now as I loved it then. The economic rewards were practically non-existent, but we did the best we could artistically. We all learned a great deal and managed to enjoy ourselves, too.

II
FROM MARTA
TO THE MET (1961-8)

A few months after the *Traviata* in Monterrey, I made my debut in the United States, singing the secondary role of Arturo in *Lucia di Lammermoor* with the Dallas Civic Opera. The Lucia was Joan Sutherland. Nicola Rescigno, a conductor under whose direction I had sung in Mexico, had been the one to recommend me to Dallas.

What impressed me most on that first visit to the States was the country's wealth. Although I did not then understand English, I was amazed by what I saw on television – especially on the quiz shows, where money, furs and cars were given away. It also amazed me that a big car was sent to bring me to the rehearsals, and that even members of the chorus owned cars. Everyone treated me very well, in an especially friendly way.

Rescigno had always complained that there was too little preparation at the opera in Mexico, too much improvisation. He had said that the Dallas season was much better organized, and that proved to be true, as a rule. But at one rehearsal only two days after my arrival, I was 'marking' my part (singing half-voice) when one of the other singers said, 'Plácido, at the pre-dress rehearsal we sing full voice.' I had not realized that we had already reached the pre-dress rehearsal, and I was a little surprised – and much amused – to find that the total amount of rehearsal time was not quite as great as I had anticipated.

It was marvellous for me to be able to sing with Sutherland, although I was not yet completely aware of the Sutherland phenomenon. She had only recently found her true path, thanks to the influence of her husband, Richard Bonynge, who got her to concentrate on the extremely dramatic coloratura repertoire. I was absolutely astounded by Joan's technique and delighted by her and Richard's simplicity and kindness. The principal tenor in that production was Renato Cioni, and – more important for me – Ettore

Bastianini was singing Enrico. It was the first and last time that I appeared with him, because he died when my career was still in its infancy. He had a wonderful sound – the baritone sound par excellence.

During the 1961-2 season I sang another Arturo, this time in New Orleans, with Gianna d'Angelo as Lucia, and a Pinkerton in *Madama Butterfly* in Tampa, Florida. An important production for me was a *Lucia* in Fort Worth, Texas, in which I sang Edgardo for the first time, opposite Lily Pons, who, at the age of fifty-eight, was singing her very last Lucia – a role she had first sung opposite Beniamino Gigli. She was a sweet, adorable person to work with, and I am glad that a pirate recording of that performance exists. Perhaps some youngster who sings with me fifteen or twenty years from now – if I am able to go on that long – will tell another youngster in 2040 that he or she sang in 2000 with Plácido Domingo, who sang in 1962 with Lily Pons, who sang in 1931 with Gigli, and so on. The line could probably be traced all the way back to Rubini or Malibran, and I like the idea of the continuity.

While I was participating in that production, *Otello* was being performed in nearby Dallas. I wished then, and wish even more now, that I had been able to sing in it. Ramón Vinay, who had begun his career as a baritone and had later, as a tenor, been the great Otello of his time, was starting a new career as a baritone in the role of Iago; Mario Del Monaco, who died while this book was being written and who was the great Otello of his day – and one of the greatest of all time – was indeed singing Otello; and I would have been the Cassio. There would have been three Otellos, past, present and future, on stage at the same time. I did at least manage to attend a performance. At the end of the third act, when Iago sings 'Ecco il leone!' ('Behold the lion!') and puts his foot on the head of Otello, who has swooned, it occurred to me that Vinay might just step a little too hard. . . .

I like the Otellos of both Vinay and Del Monaco, in different ways. Vinay's I know from the recording conducted by Toscanini, and I admire the interpretation enormously, while with Del Monaco it was the vocal power that was most impressive. I learned a great deal from listening to both recordings, and I did once sing Cassio to Del Monaco's Otello. That was in Hartford, Connecticut, on 19 November 1962; it was the last time I sang a small part and my last performance before embarking upon my great Tel Aviv adventure. One of the reviews, I recall, said, 'Not a comprimario, this gifted young man, but a rising star.' But I have not yet related many other interesting things that happened to me before that performance.

*   *   *

One of my greatest pleasures in writing this book has been to think back to the time when Marta and I were getting to know each other, falling in love and planning our future.

I had known Marta Ornelas for some time before we became seriously interested in each other. I certainly was not her cup of tea! When we first met, she was studying with the great Mexican mezzo-soprano Fany Anitúa, who had been an important singer at La Scala and elsewhere for many years – a great Amneris, Azucena and Dalila. I used to see Marta when she came to the Conservatory for her lessons, but at that time we met only casually and briefly.

She saw me as an undisciplined, not very serious boy, and the story of my early, unsuccessful marriage did not help my image. I was then spending quite a bit of time with another girl – Cristina, the *chanteuse*. Like most boys of my age, I greatly enjoyed the company of girls, but I went from one to another – a date with this one and a date with that one. Before Cristina, for example, there had been a dancer who had performed in *The Merry Widow*.

In order to spend more time with Cristina, I played the piano for her in bars and at auditions. But she was an intelligent girl, and she used to say to me, 'Plácido, I don't think I am good for your career, because you spend too much time with me. You have to dedicate more time to working at serious music.' Once she added, 'You know, you should marry someone like Marta Ornelas – she would be good for you.'

'What? You must be out of your mind!' I told her. 'She doesn't like me at all, and I'm not interested in her.'

That was the truth. I was no more taken with Marta than she was with me. She was too sophisticated for me in those days, and the fact that she drove to the Conservatory in a Mercury with an automatic transmission did not alter that impression. I later learned that Marta drove that car in order to help her father, who had had a partial loss of vision, but at the time I did not know that. Her voice teacher at the Conservatory was an Austrian, Ernest Roemer, who emphasized the Strauss repertoire and the lieder of Schubert, Schumann, Wolf and Brahms. This, too, made me think of Marta as someone removed and excessively refined, since I was completely absorbed in the Franco-Italian operatic repertoire, not to mention zarzuela and musical comedy.

'Love at first sight' definitely did not describe our case, but perhaps that made it all the more wonderful when we began, slowly, tentatively, to become involved with each other: besides being beautiful in itself, it was also a surprise – something neither of us had imagined would happen.

The first time Marta began to think that perhaps I was not such a hopeless character was during a rehearsal of *La traviata* at the National Opera, which she happened to attend. The stars of the production were Anna Moffo and Di Stefano, and I had the part of Gastone. We were doing the gambling scene; some of the other comprimari were missing, and I automatically began to sing the missing parts. Marta was impressed. She realized then that I was a child of the theatre to whom such things came naturally, and not just a show-off.

On another occasion, she heard me sing 'Solenne in quest'ora', the tenor-baritone duet from *La forza del destino*, on one of my television programmes, and she told me later that my musicality had made an impression on her. We began to see more of each other when we sang in the same work at the Opera Academy. *El último sueño* (*The Last Dream*) is by a Mexican composer, Vázquez, and it bears a dangerous and suspicious resemblance to Puccini's early opera *Le villi*. I played a character named Enrique, and Marta was Airam Zulamil. I told her that she sang the role so well that her name should have been Zuladiezmil! (*Mil* in Spanish means one thousand, *diez mil* means ten thousand.) That was the first of many compliments.

As Marta and I became closer, my friendship with Cristina began to cool. It was the hand of Destiny. One evening Marta and I went dancing at a popular night spot, Jacarandas, in the city's 'pink' district and near the hotel where my other friend had a singing engagement. We had to pass in front of that hotel to get from the car to Jacarandas, and at that moment Marta stumbled and fell to the ground. I do not know why, but that made a great impression on me: I could not get it out of my mind. Later that evening I asked Marta to be my girlfriend, and she accepted, while the band played Ernesto Lecuona's 'Siboney'.

The thirteen and a half months that went by between that evening – 15 June 1961, just a month after my debut as a leading tenor – and our marriage was the most wonderful period in my life. Marta and I contrived somehow or other to see each other every day, and our devices were many. In those days, Mexico was crazy about the American television series *Perry Mason*. Marta and I liked it very much, but since our families were so absorbed by it, it was the perfect time for us to talk to each other. I would phone her from a booth on the street in front of her parents' apartment, and we would chat while looking at each other from a distance. Fortunately, with a twenty-cent coin we could talk for the whole hour.

By the time Marta and I began dating, she had begun to study with a woman named Socorro Salas. I often went with her to her lessons, partly because I was interested in them but mostly in order to spend as much time as possible with Marta. I would run about a mile from my parents' home to the corner where Marta picked me up, and I got into the habit of bringing little bottles of fruit juice along for her, so that she would not have to sing on an empty stomach.

After Marta's lesson, she and I would take a walk in the park or wander around town together. We parted at lunchtime, when our parents expected us to be home, but later in the afternoon we usually met for rehearsals at the Opera Academy. There were study and practice sessions after the rehearsals, and then we would go to supper together – sometimes to her parents, sometimes to mine, and sometimes to one of our favourite haunts. I remember a sort of drive-in restaurant near the Glorieta de Insurgentes, where they made the most fabulous tortas ('sandwich' is an inadequate word for translating and describing those wonderful creations), and another drive-in restaurant called Las Chalupas. We also went to drive-in movies and generally spent a good deal of time in that Mercury!

Marta had been so outstanding as Susanna in a production of *The Marriage of Figaro* for the Opera's national season the previous year that when the work was repeated in the 1962 international season, she was invited to repeat the role as part of a company that included Cesare Siepi and Teresa Stich-Randall. Those performances caused the Mexican critics to vote her the best Mexican singer of the year. At a cocktail party she gave to thank them, we were seen together in public for the first time. Some people began to refer to me as the Prince Consort: my career still amounted to very little, while Marta's already seemed secure. I was proud of and happy for her.

During the national season that followed *El último sueño*, in which Marta and I had performed together, I sang my first Cavaradossi in *Tosca*, which Marta helped me to prepare. We used to vocalize together. I had a study habit in those days that has carried over to the present: if there is a particularly difficult passage – so difficult that I find it frightening – I practise it very little. If I were to go over and over it at home and *not* achieve what I am after, I would be absolutely petrified before the public. I do study the passage mentally and sing it softly at rehearsals, but I give it my all only at the performance. When the public is present, there is a strong psychological incentive for singing the passage well. The moment arrives, it's a matter of flying or falling flat on my face, I launch myself into the bit in question, and in the great majority of cases I succeed. Call it adrenalin, confidence, will-power, guts, or what you will, this is my method – if that is the proper word. Therefore, when I did my first Cavaradossi, there were sections that I had never really sung before – 'La vita mi costasse', for instance. I went on stage and 'La vita mi costasse' was simply there. I only relate this as a matter of interest and not to propose it as a technique that can work for everyone. It is, I suppose, part of my fatalistic outlook. That *Tosca* performance took place on 30 September 1961 and went very well, although I was undoubtedly straining a bit here and there. Since then I have sung more performances of *Tosca* than of any other opera.

During the same national season I sang my first Maurizio in Cilea's *Adriana Lecouvreur*. The public did not approve of the soprano, who was somewhat old-fashioned. There were rowdy, hysterical outbursts from the audience at times, and I had difficulty maintaining my concentration. At the end, when I was being applauded, the soprano said to the stage manager, 'What a fiasco!' 'Yes,' he replied, 'but go out and bow anyway!'

Meanwhile, Marta and her teacher had begun to interest me in singing Mozart. Marta felt that the purity of my vocal 'attacks' – the lack of swooping when going from a low note to a high one – made my voice ideal for Mozart. (Years later, when I auditioned for conductor Josef Krips, he said he wished he could pay me any amount to preserve my voice entirely for the Mozart repertoire.) When conductor Salvador Ochoa started to choose a cast for *Così fan tutte*, Marta, who was to take the role of Despina, suggested that he ask me to sing Ferrando. Ochoa hesitated. He told Marta that I was not a serious singer, that I sang too much zarzuela, and that in any case I was not right for the part. She, however, was very persistent and eventually managed to persuade him. The production was excellent. After the performances in Mexico City we took an abbreviated version of the opera to Puebla and elsewhere. (Among other numbers, the Dorabella-Guglielmo duet was cut, which of course played havoc with the story line. After a few performances, it finally dawned on the baritone that something was wrong. 'Hey,' he said indignantly, 'I'm the only cuckold in this version!') I found the production difficult not only because it was my first Mozart role, but also because the range and the coloratura passages were hard for me. The trio at the end of the first scene, the aria 'Un'aura amorosa', and the duet with Fiordiligi were particularly rough, and I still have my book of Mozart arias in which Marta made notes on my singing of certain pieces. I was even happier for Marta's sake than for my own that I managed to sing the role creditably, since it was she who had taken the initiative in getting me the engagement and who had helped me to learn my part.

Gradually, we began to think about getting married. The situation was not an easy one: like most parents, Marta's wanted the very best for their children, and my record was hardly spotless. Marta's mother was an extraordinary woman who was completely devoted to her three daughters. (One of Marta's sisters, Perla, now lives in Barcelona, and the other, Aida, lives in Washington. Perla and her husband, Agustín Rosillo, already had a daughter, Rebeca, who was three or four at the time. She would get very upset when she saw me kissing Marta goodbye as I left the Ornelases' apartment, and everyone was amused when she would attack me, shouting 'Don't strangle her!')

The problem was complicated by the fact that Mrs Ornelas was suffering from heart disease and probably realized even then that she might not have much longer to live. She was an active lady with a strong will; and when the doctors advised her to slow down, she disregarded them. Her wish was to live a full, energetic life as long as possible. I liked her very much, and I think she gradually came to see that I was not fundamentally bad, despite my credentials. Marta found it hard to convince her parents that I was trustworthy and that I loved her.

Sometimes Marta and I would be in the car, talking and dreaming about the future, and she would suddenly say, 'My God! What time is it? It must be nearly midnight!'

I would look at my watch. 'It's only quarter to eleven.'

'Good grief, let me go!'

I would tease her: 'If you thought it was midnight, why are you so upset now that you know it's only quarter to eleven?' But she wanted at all costs to avoid upsetting her mother.

I worked out a musical stratagem to win Mrs Ornelas's affection. At Plaza de Garibaldi in Mexico City the mariachis gather, hoping for engagements. These are small instrumental ensembles – violins, trumpets, guitars and guitarrones – whose name derives from the French word *mariage* (wedding), since they were originally musicians who played for weddings and other family affairs. If you are having a party and you want a band to play for it, you go to Plaza de Garibaldi and negotiate to get an ensemble of whatever size you wish. I used to go and contract a bunch of players for a certain evening, warning them, however, that I would be doing the singing. They were only surprised when they heard my operatic voice.

The Ornelas family lived on the third floor of an apartment building, and not only they but other residents as well would come to their windows to listen to the serenading. Occasionally there were complaints, and once the police were called to the scene. 'What are you protesting about?' they demanded of the complainers. 'You're getting a beautiful performance, free, by a member of the National Opera.' I serenaded not only Marta herself but also her mother, on their birthdays and at other times as well. Mrs Ornelas was a great admirer of the most famous singer of Mexican music, Jorge Negrete, and it may have been by serenading her with some of Negrete's songs that I began to wear down her resistance, although that was not easy.

At about that time, Marta and I, together with our good friend, the baritone Franco Iglesias, formed a chamber opera company and travelled around Mexico together. We performed a double bill of Wolf-Ferrari's *Il segreto di Susanna* and Menotti's *The Telephone*, both of which are scored for soprano and baritone. The set was a simple living-room, which with just a few small changes could be used for both works, and which included a piano. I sat at the piano, on the set, accompanying Marta and Franco, and at the end all three of us took turns singing various duets and arias. We also staged Menotti's *Amelia Goes to the Ball*, in which we all sang; and we performed a Viennese programme, too, in Monterrey and elsewhere, making use of excerpts from well-known operettas. Our agents, Ernesto and Conchita de Quesada, arranged our tours for us; and, strange as it may seem, we enjoyed those overnight bus trips, the arrivals at 6 a.m., the good breakfasts – usually *rancheros* (eggs with tomato and chilli – Mexican hot pepper) and fried beans – and the preparations for the performances. The tour went very well, much to my relief. I had been afraid that Marta's parents would not let her travel with me; but they trusted her, and all went well.

How I proposed to Marta is a story that requires a bit of background. Ernestina Garfias, the fine coloratura soprano who used to perform the title role in the Spanish opera *Marina* with my parents' company, was having throat problems one season, and my parents sent her to an ear, nose and throat specialist – a famous doctor, Fumagallo, who happened to be a friend of theirs and who lived in Monterrey. Fumagallo immediately liked Ernestina's tonsils, then fell madly in love with all the rest and married her. At the period I am talking about, they had a house in Cuernavaca, a beautiful town not far from Mexico City but considerably lower in altitude. (Many people with heart problems move there from the capital, which is 7,800 feet above sea level.) The drive is a short one, downhill all the way there and uphill all the way back. Marta and I often went to visit the Fumagallos at weekends, and it was in their swimming-pool on a Sunday afternoon that I finally said to Marta, 'Listen, I think we really ought to get married.' She agreed, but she was determined to have her parents' consent.

Marta's mother realized that her daughter's mind was already made up; she and her husband gave their approval, and on 1 August 1962 Marta and I were married. We went off in her own car, a pink Vauxhall, to Mexico's traditional honeymoon paradise, Acapulco, but we were only able to stay a few days: I had a performance on the 10th – my first appearance as a soloist in Beethoven's Ninth Symphony. That took place in Mexico City under the direction of Luis Herrera de la Fuente.

Marta and I had some professional photos taken of ourselves, at her prompting, and we gave them to the Quesadas. (Ernesto de Quesada, whose father was head of the Daniel Concert Agency in Spain, ran the Mexican branch of the business. His two brothers were in charge of the branches in Buenos Aires and Caracas.) Although Marta's career was much further along than mine, she was already beginning to advise me, to help me, just as she has continued to do with beneficial effect throughout the last twenty years.

Soon afterwards the Max Factor cosmetics company sponsored a series of five zarzuelas and operettas for television. I appeared with Ernestina Garfias and Franco Iglesias in *Marina*; then there was *The Count of Luxembourg* with Marta, my father and me; *Luisa Fernanda* and *Frou-Frou del Tabarin* with Ernestina, my mother, Franco and me; and finally *The Merry Widow* with Marta, Ernestina, Franco and me. I have been told that there are films of those performances, and I hope to see them some day.

After the death of a well-known Mexican music critic, José Morales Esteva, a memorial scholarship was established in his name, and some special performances were organized in order to raise money for the scholarship fund. On one of those occasions I had sung my first Cavaradossi in 1961. (I sang it again in February 1962, and in March I sang my first Rodolfo in *La Bohème*.) On 31 July 1962, the day before Marta and I were married, my friend Manuel Aguilar phoned to tell me that I had been awarded the first scholarship, and I naturally assumed that it would be a great help. Marta and I wondered what we should do with the money: should we go to Italy to study? to New York? I suppose, though, that because I had always lived in the theatre, I believed then (as I still believe) that practical experience is the best form of study. I have always enjoyed learning things by doing them rather than by mastering the theory behind them. It happened just at that time that a friend of mine, a Mexican-Jewish pianist, José Kahn, had returned from a period spent in Tel Aviv. He told me that the opera company there was looking for a soprano, a tenor and a baritone. Marta and I, along with Franco Iglesias, sent them some tapes, and we soon received what we called our 'dream contract': six months with the Hebrew National Opera in Tel Aviv. We were offered one thousand pounds a month, but we did not realize that they were Israeli pounds. What that meant was $333 for both of us per month – and we each had to sing ten performances every month! In short, our dream contract paid us each $16.50 per show.

When I got to Israel, I wrote to the scholarship committee to say that I needed the money that had been awarded to me. The committee replied by asking why I was requesting money since I was already singing as a professional. That part, in retrospect, does not bother me so much. What is worse is that they now boast that Plácido Domingo was the first winner of the scholarship. I was, indeed, the first winner, but I never enjoyed the fruits of my victory. They once gave me $300 to pay my fare from Mexico to Marseille for a production of *Butterfly*, which I could not have afforded to do otherwise, but the scholarship was supposed to have supported me for two whole years. But that, too, was for the best, because now I owe them nothing.

Once we knew what roles we would be singing in Tel Aviv, we began to have our costumes made. Marta even chose the material for them. Meanwhile, the Chamber Opera group had more engagements than ever, and there was plenty of other work as well. I sang Cassio in an international season production of *Otello* and Pinkerton in a touring production of *Butterfly* by an Italian opera ensemble. That company's Argentinian manager, Rafael Lagares, was himself a tenor who bore the nickname 'Carusino' – 'Little Caruso' – because of his incredibly striking physical resemblance to the great Neapolitan tenor. The stars of his company were a well-known Italian tenor with a great voice and great temperament, Antonio Annaloro, and his wife, the soprano Luciana Serafini. Those performances of *Butterfly*, which I sang opposite Serafini, took place in the town of Torreón.

Shortly thereafter Marta and I went to Guadalajara, where she was to sing Oscar in *Un ballo in maschera* and I Alfredo in *La traviata*. We went by train from Mexico City, and on the morning following Marta's performance we had a phone call from her sister, Aida, with the news that their mother had died. In a terrible state, Marta had to fly home by herself. I

33

could not accompany her because I had my performance two nights later; as soon as she could, she rejoined me in Guadalajara.

It was fortunate that we had so much work at the time, because it helped to distract Marta from her grief. Our Chamber Opera group performed *Amelia Goes to the Ball* and a Viennese evening in Monterrey, with a mezzo-soprano, Belen Amparan, who sang for many years at the Met, participating in the Viennese programme. That brief season finished at the end of October, only a month and a half before our departure for Tel Aviv. There were still many preparatory details to attend to, and meanwhile I had four other engagements to fulfil: a *Butterfly* in Tampa, Florida, an Arturo in *Lucia* in New Orleans, my performance opposite Lily Pons in Fort Worth, and my Cassio in Hartford with Del Monaco singing Otello.

When the time came for us to leave for Israel, we decided to go by rail from Mexico to New York, arrange there for the shipping of our large trunk, and then fly to Tel Aviv. (Franco did not come with us: he arrived in Israel some time later.) It was a terrible trip, above all for Marta because of her mother's recent death. Once aboard the train, we learned that there was going to be a dock workers' strike in New York and that the last day for shipping anything would be the day we were to arrive there. We had to change trains in St Louis, Missouri, and I had to tell the porters in my practically non-existent English to move the trunk to the other train. I screamed so hard that I lost my voice, but nobody moved the trunk. We arrived in New York without it, and since there was no telling how long the strike might last, we flew to Tel Aviv, leaving the trunk in limbo. The strike went on for months, and although the trunk did eventually reach us, we made our debuts in the company's stock costumes.

Our arrival, a few days before Christmas 1962, was very depressing. We were put in a small hotel with narrow beds until we were able to find an apartment of our own. Of course Christmas was not celebrated in Tel Aviv, which was sad for us because we were used to spending the day happily with our families. On Christmas night we went to the opera to hear *Rigoletto*, then we went home, drank some terrible orange juice and went to bed. (We were not yet even aware of the wonderful Jaffa oranges.) But if our first experience of Tel Aviv was not a happy one, the situation was soon to change. The human and artistic encounters there probably could not have been equalled anywhere else in the world. One could get as much out of Israel as one's own mental and spiritual resources allowed.

The company was directed by Mme Edis de Philippe and her husband, Evan Zohar, who was also deeply involved in politics and could probably have been elected to the Knesset (Parliament) had he not been divorced from his first wife. Mme de Philippe was American-born, a very beautiful woman even in her late fifties and extremely strong-willed. She was a remarkable stage director who took charge of all new productions herself. A Bulgarian, Ben Arroyo, served as public relations officer of the company and also had a hand in directing it. He seemed to speak every known language, which was not so uncommon in Israel.

I made my Tel Aviv debut as Rodolfo in *La Bohème* and Marta made hers as Micaela in *Carmen*. Our work was carried out under the very worst conditions. I sang most of my roles for the first time in my life without even a single orchestral rehearsal! Only new productions were rehearsed with orchestra. But Mme de Philippe made us work very hard, and we learned our craft in the best way – without a prompter and with no proper facilities to speak of. It was a trial by fire, and that, for me, was one of the most important aspects of the Tel Aviv experience.

The small opera house was right by the sea – the worst possible location for a building. On stormy days the waves actually reached the theatre, which was deteriorating from the salt. Tel Aviv is quite cold in the winter, and I recall how Franco and I had to try to stand close to a little stove while painting our half-naked bodies for our performances of Bizet's *The Pearl Fishers*. I never caught cold. The summer, on the other hand, was terribly hot, especially in the dressing-room – a single, large area with a curtain down the middle to separate the ladies from the gentlemen. The room would become so stuffy that we could hardly breathe; then we would walk onto the stage and get hit in the face by the air-conditioned atmosphere of the auditorium. That dried our throats out. Having sung under those circumstances, I knew that I could sing anywhere.

Naomi Pinchas, a mezzo-soprano with the company, ran a little café next to the theatre. I often sat around there until ten minutes before curtain time, chatting with friends or colleagues or even members of the public. Then I would rush to put on my make-up and get to the stage. In this respect, too, I learned my profession in the most rough-and-ready, unsophisticated way, and that is why I am prepared for anything and everything. Having grown up observing my parents, who had the stamina to run a rehearsal after doing three performances on a Sunday, and having then learned to anticipate any eventuality at the Tel Aviv opera, I could hardly have failed to become a professional man of the theatre. I developed the resources of energy that one must have in my field.

35

The company was extraordinary. Franco once had to cancel an appearance in *La traviata*, and the baritone who replaced him had not sung the part of Germont in Italian for a long time. He sang in Hungarian; the soprano knew the part of Violetta only in German; I did Alfredo in Italian; and the chorus performed in Hebrew. Fortunately, the conductor was directing in Esperanto. We had a United Nations' cast for *Don Giovanni*, too: the conductor, Arthur Hammond, was British; two Mexicans, Marta and Franco, sang Donna Elvira and Masetto; a Spaniard, myself, was Don Ottavio; Michiko Sunahara was our Japanese Zerlina; Donna Anna was Greek – Athena Lampropoulos; Don Giovanni, Livio Pombeni, was Italian; and William Valentine, a black bass from Mississippi, sang Leporello. Such casting was considered absolutely normal.

Ari, the prop man, was a huge, sweet and gentle Russian who loved us from the moment we arrived. He was a proud craftsman, and Madame gave him a free hand in his work. For the *Pearl Fishers* he made a panther and a tiger of papier mâché. The tiger, unfortunately, came out a bit cross-eyed; and when I, as the hunter, had to face it on stage, I could hardly keep from laughing. When he had to create a Madonna for the *Tosca* production, Ari told us that he was going to make her in Marta's image. The result was not terribly flattering to either Our Lady or my lady, but we always praised Ari's work.

After our first six months we signed a contract for a whole year, and our salary was raised to the equivalent of $550 a month for the two of us. By the time we left we were earning the enormous sum of $800 a month, or $40 each per performance. We even managed to buy our first car, a second-hand Opel, which was a great help to us since we were then living in Ramat Gan, outside Tel Aviv.

Marta had a harder time in Israel than I did because of Mme de Philippe, who, as a former soprano, made life much more uncomfortable for the ladies than for the gentlemen of the company. She was a woman of very definite opinions, and she once told Marta that it would be her (Marta's) fault if I did not have an important career, because she was encouraging me along the wrong path: I should not continue to sing, but should instead become a stage director! She never explained herself on that point. On the other hand, there were some things Mme de Philippe wanted Marta to do then that she now regrets not having done. She was singing the soprano repertoire, but Madame would have liked her to add some mezzo roles like Carmen and Amneris. At that time Marta refused, in order not to jeopardize her soprano roles, but later, when she had given up her career because of mine, she realized how much she would have enjoyed performing those parts.

I, too, had a few problems. They brought in a tenor whom I liked very much – a Sicilian, Rino Lo Cicero, who had one of the most beautiful and natural high registers I have ever heard. I once told him that Callas, in Mexico, in the *concertante* of *Aida*, had hit a high E-flat. He asked me how she had done it, and I demonstrated her way of building up to the E-flat. In our next performance of *Aida*, he hit an E-flat in that place, and with a full, tremendous sound – not with a head tone. Mme de Philippe and Ben Arroyo became very partial to Lo Cicero. They knew that I was keen to sing Cavaradossi in a new *Tosca* production, but they gave it to my colleague instead. Furthermore, when he later quarrelled with them and quit, they brought in an outsider rather than give the part to me. But I was vindicated, in a way, when I did finally sing my first *Tosca* there. Probably as a result of my dramatic involvement, I was given a spontaneous ovation after the 'Vittoria, vittoria'. That made me feel very good indeed.

The public was fantastic. Such a mixture of cultures! There were always people from Poland, Russia, Romania, Yugoslavia, Bulgaria, Germany, Czechoslovakia, Austria, Hungary and elsewhere in the audience, and all of them had a great appetite for music. One Romanian Jew, Lazer, used to tell us that he had traded the outsides of animals for the insides: in Europe he had been a furrier, but in Tel Aviv he had become a butcher. He was a tremendous opera lover and used to come to many performances, always dressed in a tuxedo. In return for our invitations to the opera, he would save us the very best meat – including pork – at the Carmel market, the Shook Carmel. Sometimes he had to give us credit until the end of the week. We also met a taxi driver who listened to classical music on the car radio. He had formerly been a cellist, and he had recognized us when we got into the taxi because he had seen us at the opera. Cases like this were very common; and they helped to explain why when we did about fifty performances of *Don Giovanni* during a single season, they were all well attended – despite the fact that the Israel Philharmonic under Carlo Maria Giulini did a number of performances of the same work during the same season, with a cast that included Renato Capecchi, Pilar Lorengar, Paolo Montarsolo and Agostino Ferrin, and again with excellent attendance. These are but a few examples of the sort of public we were accustomed to in Tel Aviv.

One season Madame put on a ballet-pantomime about an apparently shy woman who, on the night following her marriage, shows her true colours

37

and begins to treat her husband like a dog. The part of the wife was taken by a soprano, that of the husband by a dancer. At the wedding, the soprano had to hum the famous march from *Lohengrin*. When the production had ended, the conductor, George Singer (an excellent musician of Czech origin), said to Madame, 'You know, we have performed Wagner at the Opera.'

'What are you talking about? Are you crazy?'

'We have performed Wagner over fifty times!' He then explained what had happened. That wedding march has practically become folk music, so no one noticed or commented on it. Nevertheless, Wagner's music, which is unofficially banned in Israel, was indeed performed at the Hebrew National Opera.

Soon after our arrival we had rented an apartment from a Russian dentist who, like me, spoke English only in monosyllables. I must have been chosen to communicate with our Russian Benois because Marta's English was too good for him. Franco arrived before long, and we gave a little party to welcome him. As a joke, we served an incredibly smelly cheese. He ate it with great delight, we kept bringing him more of it, and in the end our apartment reeked so terribly that *we* could not stand it.

The life we led was very simple, although we changed residence six or seven times during our stay. Sometimes Franco shared a flat with us, and when his wife arrived they both lived with us for a while. Another Mexican singer, Rafael Sevilla - the tenor who had lost half a moustache in my television show - stayed with us, too, at one time, but Marta and I usually lived alone. On days when I sang, Marta cooked for me; on days when she sang, I cooked for her; and on days when we both sang, we went to a very plain and inexpensive restaurant.

The repertoire at the Opera was not very large. During my two and a half years there I sang in ten different operas: *Bohème*, *Tosca*, *Butterfly*, *Don Giovanni*, *Traviata*, *Faust*, *Carmen*, *Eugene Onegin*, *Pearl Fishers* and *Cavalleria rusticana*. Once a production opened, we did thirty, forty, or even fifty performances in order to satisfy the public. We remained so long in Tel Aviv partly because of the public's love and enthusiasm and partly because we wanted to make full use of our time. There was another reason, too, which I can only explain by relating a story.

Marta and I sang our very first performances of *Faust* together, and we had a considerable success. On the second evening, however, when I sang the line 'Je t'aime, je t'aime, je t'aime' - each time higher - my high B-

38

natural cracked into a thousand pieces, and I cracked again on the high C
in the 'Salut, demeure'. Imagine how Marta felt, having to start her aria
after the mess I had just made! But what happened afterwards amazed me.
In the first place, the press did not mention the cracks at all. Then, when
I went to Madame and said, 'I don't think I'm good enough for the theatre,'
she replied, 'No, Plácido. Here you have a chance to learn, and one mistake
means nothing. We trust you, and we want you to continue.' The other
directors backed her up, and that was the biggest boost anyone has ever
given me. They all demonstrated faith in me at a moment when I was
completely discouraged.

The results of this incident were entirely positive. Although the public
was happy with my work, I could tell from Marta's face after certain
performances that she was not. When I asked her what was wrong, she
would say, 'I cannot hear you enough, you are not projecting enough.' I
was confused, but she explained: 'I'm glad that everyone else thinks your
work is all right, but I love you and care very much about you, and I'm
telling you that something is wrong.'

Fortunately, I listened to her. We decided that my problem really lay in
my way of supporting the voice. On mornings when the theatre was not
being used for rehearsals, Marta, Franco and I would go there and they
would listen to me practice. Franco had and still has a remarkable gift for
teaching, and he is now steadily involved in voice instruction in New York.
He had many ideas that were a great help to me. Little by little, I began to
discover the secrets of supporting the voice, and as a result it grew both in
size and in security. I had always thought that one must pull back the
diaphragm in order to sing, and I had not been giving it enough space. Now
I was learning how to breathe properly, how to fill the diaphragm, and how
to maintain correct breath support. This is the technique I have used ever
since. Those early mistakes were therefore extremely important, and cor-
recting them was an absolutely determinant factor in my career.

I am also grateful to Israel for expanding my knowledge of languages.
When I arrived I spoke only Spanish and understood a bit of Italian. In
Tel Aviv, our favourite form of entertainment was the cinema. English-
language movies were shown in the original with subtitles in Hebrew and
French; if the film was in French or Italian, the subtitles were in Hebrew
and English. As a result, I established a basis for learning three languages:
English, French and Italian. And, of course, I learned Hebrew, too.
Franco's Hebrew was better than Marta's or mine, but we all spoke it with
our Israeli friends. Once, while visiting some of Jerusalem's religious

sites, we began to speak Hebrew. Some of the Orthodox Jews started throwing stones at us, because to them Hebrew is a sacred language and must not be used for secular purposes. We were also amazed by the tremendous physical energy the Orthodox used in their prayers.

Israel gave me an awareness of worlds outside the one I was familiar with. I had lived only in countries where nearly everyone was Catholic, by tradition if not in practice. Even on the flight that brought us to Tel Aviv I saw people who astonished me – ultra-Orthodox and Hassidic Jews, with their broad-brimmed hats, earlocks, and so on. And when we arrived, the mixture of cultures and languages fascinated us. All of a sudden we were living in the midst of a completely strange society. Although there were difficulties at first, we came to like it enormously.

Once every two weeks the company would go to some other town to perform – Haifa, Jerusalem (where I sang *Pearl Fishers* in the inaugural performance at the new hall), Beersheba and others. Occasionally, we travelled as tourists, too, to Jerusalem, to Caesaræa and to Nazareth. I found Nazareth disappointing. When I had read the Biblical tales as a child, the whole story of Christ and of those far-off places had seemed wonderful and fantastic to me; but when I was actually there, I could not relate the reality to my childhood fantasies. One of our excursions was to have been a drive to Tiberias on the Sea of Galilee with Mikaela, a Spanish flamenco singer then performing at the Tel Aviv Hilton, and her husband. Unfortunately, our Opel broke down before we could get there and some local Arabs used a tractor to tow it to their village. It could not be repaired until the following morning. Mikaela, however, had a performance at the hotel that evening, so she and the others took a taxi back to the city and I stayed overnight in the village. The Arabs were unbelievably hospitable. They arranged a banquet, at which I sang for them, and my host insisted that I sleep in his home. The next morning the car was fixed and I returned home.

I love the sun, so we went to the beach whenever we could, usually with other members of the opera company. On one occasion, Marta and I were in the water together only to about waist level when she suddenly said, 'I cannot feel the bottom!'

'Give me your hand,' I told her, 'because I am still standing on the bottom.' She gave me her hand. 'Don't get scared,' I said, 'but I can no longer feel the bottom either. Let's just start swimming back calmly.' But there was an undertow, and the more we swam, the farther from shore we seemed to go.

Giuseppe Bertinazzo, a tenor, was near by, and was a good enough swimmer to reach Marta and pull her out of danger. 'But Plácido?' screamed Marta. Giuseppe did not know what to do, because I was already far away and also because I am so big that he thought he and I would both drown if he tried to save me. Marta's shouts attracted the attention of a lifeguard, who jumped in and managed to pull me, already half-drowned, out of the water. I'll never forget that feeling of swallowing salty water and of being utterly helpless. We have remained in touch with Bertinazzo, who is now musical director of the Perth Opera in Australia, and when I am finally able to find the time to perform in that country, I will certainly make my debut with his company before going to Sydney or Melbourne.

For productions of *Samson et Dalila* and *Carmen*, Mme de Philippe engaged a tenor who turned out to be unsatisfactory. I was asked to take over the *Carmen* performances, and I learned the part of Don José in French in three days. Mignon Dunn sang the title role some evenings, alternating with Joann Grillo, who was represented by Gerard and Marianne Semon's agency, Eric Semon Associates, in New York. On returning to the States, Joann recommended me to the Semons. I wrote to them myself, and they were able to arrange two contracts for me for the following summer (1965): a *Samson* at Chautauqua, New York, and a *Carmen* with the Salmaggi Opera Company at an open-air theatre in Washington, DC. These unanticipated engagements helped Marta and me to decide that it was time to leave Israel, time to try our fortune elsewhere.

Our last new production in Tel Aviv was a double bill of *Cavalleria* and *Pagliacci*. I was Turiddu in *Cavalleria*, and Marta was Nedda in *Pagliacci*, with Franco singing Silvio. The first night fell on my birthday, just as *Pearl Fishers* had opened on my previous birthday. (This was by no means a special tribute to me: Mme de Philippe's birthday was on 21 May and she liked to have all new productions open on the 21st of some month. Since my birthday falls on 21 January, the coincidence of the two openings is easily explained.)

We left Tel Aviv in June. Madame gave us a party at the theatre, and I made a speech in Hebrew from the stage. Although we had had our differences with her, Marta and I were the only singers who departed on friendly terms with Madame. That was almost not the case, because she had wanted us to remain longer. I had proposed that we sign for another two years, but only for six months of each year. After all, I had no certain knowledge that we were going to be successful elsewhere when we left. I heard later that she was sorry she had not agreed to the proposal, but at the time she had been categorical: either we stayed there all year or she did not want us at all. Nevertheless, we managed to part amicably, and the reception was entirely pleasant.

On the same day that our decision to leave Israel was made, we also made up our minds that it was time to start a family. By the time we left, Marta's first pregnancy was already quite advanced. We had planned to stop in Italy, Spain and France for auditions and went first to Milan, where I sang for Alessandro Ziliani, then director of ALCI (Associazione Lirica e Concertistica Italiana). He was a tenor himself, a fine figure of a man and a good actor. As a result of that audition, I was asked to sing in *Carmen* at the Verona Arena that summer because Del Monaco had cancelled his engagement. Gastone Limarilli was singing, and another tenor was required to alternate with him. Unfortunately – or so it seemed at the time – the people in Chautauqua held me to the contract I had signed with them. I now believe that it would have been too early for me to have sung in Verona, but in any case the fact that I had had such an offer at the age of twenty-four meant that my audition had gone well.

From Italy we went to Barcelona, where Perla and Agustín Rosillo, Marta's sister and brother-in-law, were living. Being back in Spain for the first time since I was a small child was very moving for me, and as we landed in Madrid, I held Marta's hand and tried unsuccessfully to hold back my tears. There we saw all my uncles, aunts and cousins, and I revisited Calle Ibiza, staying in the same apartment I had lived in as a child. My feelings towards Spain had lain dormant in me for a long time, and that visit awakened them.

Marta tired easily because of her condition, so she stayed in Barcelona while I auditioned elsewhere. I sang for Bernard Lefort, among others, and he offered me a *Butterfly* in Marseille for later that year. That was the only immediate positive result of those auditions, but I had established some invaluable contacts.

We flew to the United States, where, with a terrible cold, I sang my first Samson ever in Chautauqua opposite Joann Grillo. It was all the more difficult for me because I was singing in English – or something vaguely resembling English. The *Carmen* in Washington was with Rosalind Elias and was very successful. Julius Rudel and John White, the directors of the New York City Opera, heard about me as a result of that performance and invited me to audition for their company. I was immediately engaged to make my New York debut that October in two performances of *Carmen*. The City

Opera also wanted me to sing a performance of *The Tales of Hoffmann* on tour in Philadelphia, and a further condition was that I agree to sing in *Don Rodrigo*, a new opera by the Argentinian composer Alberto Ginastera.

After a long absence we returned to Mexico for an emotional reunion with our families. While there I sang a performance of *Hoffmann* and a *Tosca* as well. One of the *Hoffmann* reviews was very negative. It said in effect that it was hard to figure out what Plácido Domingo was doing on a stage and that opera was definitely not his world. I was so upset that for the first and only time in my life I reacted angrily to a review. I planned to insult the critic in question and to create some sort of scandal at my next performance. But on the same day that the review appeared, Marianne Semon phoned from New York to say that I had been invited by the Boston Opera Company to sing a *Bohème* opposite Renata Tebaldi, Rameau's *Hippolyte et Aricie* opposite Beverly Sills, and Schoenberg's *Moses and Aaron*. That put matters into their proper perspective, and the idea of singing with Tebaldi, above all, revived me completely. (Sills was not then as well known as she later became.) I let the reviewer live in peace.

I had a few engagements in Puebla and elsewhere in Mexico, and before I knew it the time had come for me to go to New York to prepare for my City Opera debut in *Carmen*, scheduled for 21 October. Rudel was not to have conducted that performance, but he changed his mind when he heard me during rehearsals. I was very flattered, and I shall never forget his gesture. While I was rehearsing, the tenor appearing in the concurrently running *Butterfly* production took sick and I was asked to replace him on the 17th. Thus my New York debut took place earlier than anticipated. The conductor was Franco Patanè, an outstanding musician whom we all loved and who died prematurely a few years later. Like his son, Giuseppe, and like Nello Santi, Patanè had a most incredible musical memory. Some conductors have the ability to sit down and write out whole operas by heart, orchestra parts and all, and Patanè Senior was certainly one of them. But beyond that, his spiritual involvement with the music he conducted was very deep. We performed several works together: *La traviata*, *Butterfly*, *Tosca*, *Carmen*, *Bohème* and my first *Il tabarro*. His one defect – and he had it in common with Fausto Cleva, with whom I later worked at the Met – was that he lost his self-control when anyone made a mistake during a performance. He would become so furious that our feeling for what we were doing would quickly drain away. The rage was visible in his face, and it affected our spirits. Cleva, too, sometimes got so carried away while conducting that I feared for his health. He looked so fragile. I sang in

Adriana Lecouvreur, *Andrea Chénier*, *Cavalleria rusticana* and *Ballo* with him, and I liked him very much. He had a special affinity with the verismo composers.

The outcome of both City Opera performances was wonderful. Unfortunately, Marta was not with me: she was in Mexico awaiting the arrival of our baby. Another Plácido Domingo was in fact born, a few days prematurely, on the day that had been scheduled for my New York debut – 21 October. As Marta and I had been in Israel up to four months before Placi's birth, we call him the Asiatic member of the family. (I am the African, because my parents were on tour in Tangiers nine months before I was born.) I flew back to Mexico on the 22nd and was able to see Marta and the baby. The next day, however, I had to go to Puebla to appear in *Butterfly* opposite Montserrat Caballé – the first time I had worked with her, and a very enjoyable experience. Then I went back to New York for another *Carmen* on the 31st.

The reception I received in New York was more than satisfactory, and I also made the acquaintance then of people who have remained my friends. There were, for instance, the Cubans Norberto Sánchez, Miguel Cao and Jorge Oropeza, who had been admirers of my parents' company when it had toured in Cuba and who came to reminisce about those days when my parents would show them photos of their little Placidín and Mari Pepa. I also began to attend performances at the Metropolitan Opera. A particularly fine *Ernani* with Leontyne Price, Franco Corelli, Cornell MacNeil and Jerome Hines remains in my memory. It was a great experience: I was impressed by the size of the old theatre and by the way those voices sounded.

In November I sang a *Butterfly* in Marseille and found the public in the South of France amazing – warm, knowledgeable and quick to react positively or negatively. I did a *Carmen* there years later, and I hope to go back again some day. From France I returned to the States for a *Carmen* in English in Fort Worth. Norman Treigle, who was the Escamillo, used to tease me for the way I sang the phrase 'A kiss from my mother' in the duet with Micaela. 'Ah keeess frohm mahy moh-thair,' he would mimic.

With the New York City Opera I made my Philadelphia debut in *Hoffmann*; then I dashed to Barcelona to prepare for my Spanish debut (1 January 1966) at the Teatro Liceo in three Mexican operas: *Carlota* by Sandi, *Severino* by Salvador Moreno, and *La Mulata de Córdoba* by Moncayo. They are charming little 'local' works from different regions of Mexico. None of them was part of the standard repertoire, so the public and critics could not judge my artistic work. Nevertheless, I enjoyed the experience. My mother, too, spent Christmas in Spain, as she was under contract with a touring zarzuela company.

Back in New York I embarked on the double adventure of singing the title role in the North American première of Ginastera's *Don Rodrigo* and, with it, opening the City Opera's new home at the New York State Theater in Lincoln Center. Most of the winter I spent alone, because I thought the New York climate would be too rough for the baby. (Marta and Placi joined me about a week before the opening.) It was the first winter I had ever spent in a cold region. Seeing snow day after day, having to wear boots and gloves and ear-muffs – all this was new to me. Most days I went to the theatre in the morning and left at 11 p.m., and I learned the American custom of buying food from vending machines or quickly eating a hamburger out of a paper bag – doing whatever was necessary to avoid wasting time.

Don Rodrigo, excellently directed by Tito Capobianco, was the first opera production I had worked on very intensively, from bottom to top. The rehearsal schedule was difficult, and there were no regulations about not exceeding a certain number of hours. We rehearsed without watching the clock. When I had been offered the role, I had accepted without knowing what I was getting into. Although I am a musician as well as a singer, the intervals – the distances between the notes – in *Don Rodrigo* are hard to cope with. That the rehearsal period turned out to be wonderful was largely due to one of the greatest musicians I have ever known, the Argentinian composer Antonio Tauriello. He had come along as Ginastera's assistant, and, in fact, he always helped to rehearse all of the composer's works. He could detect false intonation in the most complicated passages; he sight-read *Wozzeck*-like scores at the piano; and he had in general an incredible grasp of whatever musical material he was dealing with. He appeared to know Ginastera's work better than the composer himself knew it.

The opening night – 22 February 1966 – was a special occasion and therefore received considerable attention. I was so accustomed to the everyday difficulties of performing in Israel that I said to myself beforehand, 'I have worked hard and I know the opera backwards and forwards. What is there to get worked up about?' But for the public it was an exciting evening: they had not seen a contemporary opera of that stature in a long time. For a young Spaniard to be able to sing, on such an occasion, the role of a Spanish king, and in Spanish, was an unforgettable experience. There was much praise for the work, for the production and, fortunately, for my

45

singing. I did not fully realize at that moment what it all meant for my future. There I was, just a month after my twenty-fifth birthday and just eight months after leaving Tel Aviv, enjoying a great success in New York. It hardly seemed possible.

The City Opera's first season in the State Theater consisted entirely of contemporary works. One of them, based on *Marat/Sade*, was not a success and had to be cancelled after a few performances. This indirectly got me into serious trouble. I had already agreed to sing my Boston debut performances after *Don Rodrigo*, but my contract with the City Opera, although it only specified three performances of *Don Rodrigo*, also stipulated that I should be at the company's disposal for a certain length of time. When the other opera flopped, two additional performances of *Don Rodrigo* were scheduled to help fill the gap. By that time, however, I was working with Sarah Caldwell in Boston. A fight between the two companies ensued; it upset me that I had unwittingly provoked it.

In those days the director of the American Guild of Musical Artists was Hy Faine. John White phoned the Semons' office and said angrily to the secretary: 'We want Plácido to sing. If the situation with Boston is not cleared up, Mr Faine will have to step in.'

'Oh,' said the secretary innocently, 'does he know the part?' White thought she was laughing at him and became even more furious. In the end, however, the situation was happily resolved. I did the two extra performances in New York, and the rehearsal schedule in Boston was altered accordingly.

My first opera in Boston was *Hippolyte et Aricie*. The role of Hippolyte contains many coloratura passages and is one of the lightest parts I have ever sung. Rameau's style, too, was new to me and very difficult. The production was done in French, and the cast included a South African singer who neither spoke nor sang the language very well. The line 'Laissez-moi respirer', for instance, he sang as if it were written 'Laissez-moi respirère'. He did, however, have a French surname, and of course one of the critics wrote that the best and most idiomatic French had come from Monsieur So-and-So. It was great fun working with Beverly Sills, and I was simultaneously introduced to the brilliant work of Sarah Caldwell.

For *La Bohème*, Caldwell wanted a truly spectacular production. Not only had she engaged Tebaldi as Mimi; she also wanted to find the best possible singers for the roles of Musetta and Marcello. All rehearsals stopped until she had flown every conceivable candidate to Boston for auditions. Perhaps she went a little too far, but I must admit that in the end she got what she wanted, and the results were outstanding. As Musetta we had Adele Leigh, a very fine English soprano, and as Marcello the excellent English baritone Peter Glossop. It was an amazing cast, but even more amazing was the fact that Caldwell managed to stage the most exciting of *Bohème* in three days! The sets were by the gifted German designer, Rudolf Heinrich, who died quite young. (He also designed a number of operas for the Met, including the 1969 *Tosca*, and a *Moses and Aaron* for Vienna.)

I was struck by the beauty of Tebaldi's voice and by her charming personality. I still treasure the pictures we have of her holding Placi, who was then only a few months old. She was always asking about him and wanting to see him. It was understandably exciting for me to be singing with her for the first time; and with her in the cast – and with the exceptionally high level of the production as a whole – our success was assured.

Meanwhile, we had begun rehearsing *Moses and Aaron*, which disturbed me very much. To this day I do not like the work and cannot understand it. Pity poor Aaron, who has to sing a terrifyingly difficult part while Moses distracts everyone's attention by reciting spoken dialogue! And Aaron's part is also cruel to the voice. Unfortunately for the company but fortunately for me, there were financial problems at the time, and as this particular production was very expensive and very risky, as far as public attendance was concerned, it was set aside for a year. I was already engaged elsewhere for the period in question during the following season, so I had a ready escape. We had quite a number of musical rehearsals, and the production was about half-way along, but I was not sorry in the least to give the whole project up.

In Mexico, before going to Tel Aviv, Marta and I had worked with conductor Anton Guadagno. In New York one evening, he and his wife, Dolores, invited us to dinner at their apartment. He was about to fly to New Orleans to conduct *Andrea Chénier* with Franco Corelli in the title role. I do not believe I have ever heard anyone else sing at as consistently high a level as Corelli. He was always in good shape when I heard him, always at the height of his powers. On the other hand, if Corelli felt for whatever reason that he was going to be less than fantastic on a certain night, he would cancel. Jokingly, Guadagno said to me, 'Plácido, be prepared!' I told him that I had never sung *Chénier*. 'Well,' he replied, 'I'm not saying anything except to be ready.' Two days later the phone rang....

I learned the whole opera in two or three days and rushed to New Orleans. As always happens in such cases, the public and critics were disappointed and angry that Corelli had not appeared. That probably worked in my favour. 'Who needs Franco Corelli?' they asked – which was unfair to Corelli, but which added to my success. For me, the most important result was to have learned this beautiful work, which I have sung many times since. I also enjoyed New Orleans, with its French and Latin atmosphere, its restaurants and its dissimilarity to the rest of the United States.

During a break in my first New York spring season I went to Mexico City, to sing in Mendelssohn's *Elijah* with Beverly Sills, Norman Treigle and conductor Luis Herrera de la Fuente. (The following year I performed the work in Lima, Peru, with the same colleagues, and had a wonderful time there. The chorus in Lima was made up of enthusiastic young people who were always singing. They even came to the airport to serenade me as I was leaving.)

I do not want to bore the reader by turning this book into a catalogue of performances and aeroplane flights. For that reason, there is an appendix at the back that lists all of my appearances and leaves me free to talk only about the more interesting details in the text itself. I recall, for example, that in the summer of 1966 I was engaged to sing *Carmen* with Mildred Miller and Norman Treigle in the annual open-air opera season at the Cincinnati Zoo, and I returned for two later seasons, once in *Chénier* and *Traviata* and once in *Hoffmann*. It is easy to imagine the sort of mishaps that can take place in such a setting. Someone would sing 'Rispondimi!' ('Answer me!'), and there would immediately be a 'quack, quack' from a nearby pond. In one of those seasons Elisabeth Schwarzkopf sang *Der Rosenkavalier*. Everyone was terrified at the idea that some animal might make a rude noise during one of her solos, but for Schwarzkopf even the beasts kept quiet. At a rehearsal of *Faust*, in which I was not singing, Guadagno was upset by a woodpecker that was carrying on particularly loudly. As he conducted, he began to shout in his accented English, 'Shot op, birrd! Shot op, birrd!' Then, reverting to Italian, he let out an incredible string of curses – all to no avail.

The Cincinnati seasons were very pleasant. Sometimes my family would join me – not only Marta and Placi, but also my parents and Pepe, my son by my first marriage. (Shortly thereafter, Pepe came to live with us at the house we had bought in Teaneck, New Jersey, near New York City.) We would meet other people from the cast around the hotel swimming-pool and have an enjoyable time together. In those days I could rest between performances – unlike today, when there are five or six interviews, a retake of some bit of a record, television appearances and countless other things to look after.

These small opera seasons – Cincinnati, New Orleans and many others – are admirable in many ways. They are often run by people who really care about music, about opera, and it is not easy to find the money to organize such seasons. The only thing about them that upsets us performers is that we are expected to attend too many parties and other social events. People try to be, and are, very nice to us, but the receptions become more exhausting than the performances themselves. Occasionally, we are even expected to attend a luncheon or a 5 p.m. cocktail party on the day of a performance; and if we accept one invitation but refuse another, all sorts of problems arise. I have made it a rule to attend receptions only after performances or on free days. When I am working and concentrating, my social life has to be kept to a minimum. This has probably offended some people, but it is a matter of survival.

That autumn (1966) I sang in an unusual production of *La traviata* with the City Opera. Patricia Brooks, one of the best singing actresses I know, sang Violetta, Franco Patanè conducted, and Frank Corsaro directed the staging. Those rehearsals were both enjoyable and useful for me – a complete theatrical experience. Corsaro had brilliant ideas, and Patricia was a very exciting Violetta. This *Traviata* was closely related to Dumas's *La Dame aux Camélias*, the play on which the opera is based, although it of course followed Verdi's ideas. In those days Marta and I were living in an apartment in Lincoln Towers on West End Avenue, having moved from the Spencer Arms at Sixty-ninth and Broadway. Corsaro used to come over for dinner or a drink, and we would discuss the theatre in general and *Traviata* in particular until 3 or 4 in the morning. That was my first serious exchange of ideas with a director about the dramatic side of opera. I think of those sessions with great warmth, and I am very sorry that Corsaro and I have not had the opportunity of working together in recent years. The *Traviata*, *Butterfly* and *Pagliacci* that we did together at the City Opera were wonderful experiences.

In the third act of *Traviata*, during the exciting music immediately preceding the 'Parigi, o cara' duet, I was supposed to carry Patricia over to the sofa, but during one rehearsal I arrived late and had to begin singing with her still in my arms. Corsaro said, 'Hold it! Could you perform it like that?' Well, I did it: I sang the duet with Patricia in my arms, and the result was very effective. We kept it in. The most difficult aspect was the breath control, but with a little practice I knew I could manage it. The production was a hit, and Harold Schonberg in *The New York Times* called me a stentorian tenor who looked as if he could pick up the Empire State Building. It was a great satisfaction for me, by the way, to have been able to open the Met's new production of *Traviata* in 1981, fifteen years after opening the City Opera's production.

Don Rodrigo was remounted that season, and Rolf Liebermann, then general director of the Hamburg Opera, heard one performance. He had Marianne and Gerard Semon schedule an audition for me, but when I came down with a dreadful cold I asked to cancel it. Liebermann wanted to hear me all the same, so I went – late, miserable and full of explanations. 'Plácido,' he said, 'I would like to hear you anyway.'

'Yes, but there isn't even a pianist – I told him not to come.'

'But I know that you play the piano, too.'

So I went to the piano and began the introduction of 'E lucevan le stelle'. I could barely sing at all, and what did come out sounded like a truck going uphill in first gear. Liebermann stopped me and said, 'I hope that you will feel better on the 8th of January.'

'Why the 8th of January?'

'Because that is when you will be singing *Tosca* in Hamburg.' Just like that. I felt so good towards that man! Liebermann was gambling on me without really knowing my voice, because although he had heard *Don Rodrigo*, he had not liked it and had felt that it was very bad for my vocal health. Without having heard me in a repertory opera, he engaged me to sing Cavaradossi in *Tosca*. I honestly do not believe that I am vain, but I knew then that I was starting an important career.

German opera houses do not devote a great deal of time to rehearsing, unless a new production is in the works. Singers are expected to arrive only one day before a performance; there is a quick run-through, without orchestra, to establish the pacing and stage movement – and that is all. But for my Hamburg debut, even one rehearsal would have seemed a luxury. Bad weather had prevented Nello Santi, the conductor, from reaching the theatre until shortly before curtain time. He came to my dressing-room to say 'in bocca al lupo' (literally, 'in the wolf's mouth' – the Italian equivalent of 'break a leg'), and he added: 'Remember, don't slow down at 'Svanì per sempre il sogno mio d'amore.' Nello, who later became one of my best friends, walked into the pit, and I walked into the wings. We were absolutely together through the whole performance.

So great was the success that Liebermann offered me a house contract, but my two and a half years in Israel had taught me to be wary of long-term commitments. As I have said, I sensed that my career was opening up, and I preferred to be free, to see what would come my way. Liebermann, who was very understanding, made an alternative proposal: would I be interested in singing *Aida* the following May, a new production of *Bohème* in December, and *Lohengrin* in January 1968? I accepted with pleasure, and that is how Hamburg became my first important European connection. With the exception of the Met, it remains the house at which I have sung more performances than anywhere else – although Covent Garden is likely to pass it soon.

Just before my Hamburg debut I had sung some auditions in various European cities. It was a lonely holiday period for me, and I recall that another auditioning tenor – Joann Grillo's husband, Richard Kness – met me for a sad New Year's Eve dinner at a big Zurich restaurant. A minute or so before midnight, we began singing 'Di quella pira' in unison, and we both hit the high C on the stroke of twelve. The first audition result was an offer, which I did not accept, to sing *Carmen* in German at the Düsseldorf Opera. In Vienna I was met at the airport by Peter Hofstoetter, a friend of Giuseppe Di Stefano's who had been tipped off about me by another Di Stefano fan, a lady who had heard me in New Orleans. I depended on Peter's help, as my German was non-existent, and I immediately realized that we were going to be great friends. The two of us and our families have indeed remained the best of friends to this day. He took me to the Staatsoper for my audition, which was rather an odd one: while I was singing 'De' miei bollenti spiriti' from *La traviata*, the auditioners told the pianist to stop but signalled to me to keep going. They were testing my ability to sing in tune without instrumental support. Afterwards, Peter and I were walking down the street when we noticed Di Stefano approaching in his Rolls-Royce. He pulled over and told us that he would probably have to cancel his performance of *Un ballo in maschera* that evening. He was not feeling well and was at that moment going to see a doctor. In the end, I was asked to replace Di Stefano. Unfortunately, I had never performed *Ballo* and did not yet know the work – otherwise I would have made my Viennese debut on the very day of my audition. I was, however, given a contract to sing *Don Carlo* there the following May.

The intervening weeks were spent performing in North and South America, and I especially remember making my debut with Erich Leinsdorf and the Boston Symphony in Haydn's *Creation* Mass. My solo aria was in three-four time, and I had prepared it in a flowing tempo. Leinsdorf, however, had decided it ought to go at a much slower pace – subdivided, in fact – which was his prerogative. I would have been quite willing to adjust to his tempo, but since we had had no piano rehearsal, I did not know what his tempo was. When we began the number at the first orchestral rehearsal, we were not together. 'Mr Domingo,' he said to me in front of my colleagues and the orchestra, 'people who have the reputation of being good musicians are supposed to know their parts.' I did not reply, but I was angry. The next morning I went to the rehearsal and sang my solo precisely at Leinsdorf's tempo, without looking at the music. Since then my relations with him have been good. My first recordings of the Beethoven Ninth Symphony, *Aida* and *Il tabarro* were made with him, and I both respect and like him. I was looking forward to singing *Otello* with Leinsdorf in Vienna in the autumn of 1982, but for some reason he had to cancel the engagement.

Appropriately enough, I 'returned victorious' to Hamburg when I made my first appearance as Radames in *Aida*. Eight days later, on 19 May 1967, I combined my Viennese debut with my first performance of the title role in *Don Carlo*, and as part of a superb cast: Gwyneth Jones, Ruth Hesse, Kostas Paskalis, Cesare Siepi and Hans Hotter. At the two following performances, Siepi was replaced by Nicolai Ghiaurov, while Hesse was succeeded first by Christa Ludwig and then by Grace Bumbry. Siepi's beautiful voice I already knew from Mexico, and hearing and working with Ghiaurov for the first time was an equally great experience. Nicolai's style provides an outstanding example of what a true legato (connected) quality can be. I never again sang with Hotter, whose personality and acting were very impressive, as were the beauty and security of Christa Ludwig's voice. Gwyneth Jones, apart from being beautiful to look at, is one of the sopranos most capable of adapting herself to the different characters she portrays. While in Vienna I heard her in *Il trovatore*, and I could hardly believe that I was seeing the same woman who had sung Elisabetta with me.

The first performance almost began with a calamity. Apart from the fact that our single rehearsal had taken place in a rehearsal room rather than on stage, no one had remembered to warn me that the stage was steeply raked for that production. I came charging out like a young bull for my first scene, 'Io l'ho perduta', and nearly launched myself into the auditorium. Fortunately, I managed to brake myself in time, and the rest of the performance went beautifully. Some years later I participated in another near-catastrophe at the Staatsoper during a performance of *Tosca* opposite Galina Vishnevskaya. The Staatsoper, like most theatres, requests that artists wear wigs belonging to the house because they are made of non-inflammable

About the age of two

With my sister, Mari Pepa, dressed in traditional Basque costume, *c.* 1947

My first piano recital, Mexico City, 1950. I am in the back row, second from right; my sister, Mari Pepa, is in the front, second from left.

With my father, 1956

The first time I accompanied my mother at the piano, Guadalajara, 1957

As Rafael the bullfighter in *El Gato Montéz*, Mexico City, 1958. Left: with Carolina Quintero as the Fortune Teller; right: with Rosa Maria Montes as Soledád.

In *The Merry Widow* with Evangelina
Elizondo, Mexico City, 1960

As Gastone in *La traviata*, Monterrey, 1960

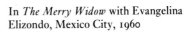

In my costume (as Normanno) for *Lucia di Lammermoor*, with Manuel Aguilar, Monterrey, 1960

In my costume (as Cassio) in *Otello*, with my parents and their friend Xtomin, Monterrey, 1960

As Remendado in *Carmen*, with another smuggler, Mexico City, 1961

As Incredibile (extreme left) in *Andrea Chénier*, Mexico City, 1961, with Giusseppe Di Stefano (fifth from left).

My first Edgardo (and Lily Pons's last Lucia) in *Lucia di Lammermoor*, Fort Worth, Texas, 1962. My mother wrote on the back of this photograph: 'Lily Pons and Little Plácido', even though I was then twenty-one and 6′ 1″.

With Marta in *The Merry Widow*, Mexico City, 1962

Smoking my hookah while Marta awaits
her turn, Israel, 1963

As Cavaradossi in *Tosca*, Mexico City,
1961. This was Marta's favourite
photograph and was used as my first
publicity picture in the United States.

materials, but Vishnevskaya wished to use her own. As she sang the words 'Questo è il bacio di Tosca' and prepared to stab Scarpia (Paskalis), she leaned back; and her wig, dipping into the flame of the candle on Scarpia's desk, caught fire. Unaware of what was happening, she was shocked when Paskalis, instead of falling to the floor, began to grab at her hair. She must have thought he had gone mad, and she tried to defend herself from him while the frightened public began to react audibly. I was already standing in the wings, waiting for the curtain calls at the end of the act; I ran onto the stage, planning to grab the 'wine' from Scarpia's table and throw it at the wig, when Paskalis managed to pull the wig off. I doused it, the fire was extinguished, and the curtain came down. When Vishnevskaya – who now realized what had happened – and the rest of us had calmed down, the last part of the scene was repeated. That was probably the only *Tosca* performance in history in which Scarpia was fatally stabbed twice, although I must say that even three deaths would have been better than the Baron deserved.

My weight tends to go up and down, and I was in one of my heavier phases at the time of my Staatsoper debut. I managed to put away a remarkable quantity of Viennese pastry at our hotel, the Ambassador, and elsewhere. But my intake of Sachertorte, Schlagsahne and other goodies was interrupted by a call from Berlin, where I was to have made my debut a few days later in *Aida*. The Amneris was ill, and an adequate replacement could not be found. Since there was an Ulrica available, it had been decided to switch to *Un ballo in maschera*. I did not tell the Berliners that I had never sung the opera. Of course I could do it, I said; and once again, as with *Carmen* in Tel Aviv and *Chénier* in New Orleans, I learned a whole work in three days. The experience was a bit terrifying, especially having to master Riccardo's tongue-twisters in the first act. In fact, the whole text of *Ballo* gave me something to think about. I barricaded myself in the Ambassador; and with the score, a piano, Marta's help and – I freely admit – Gigli's recording, I pounded the work into my head. The performance on 31 May went well, and I was quite pleased with myself for having sung – within three weeks – my first performances of three major Verdi roles, and for having made, in the same period, my debuts in Vienna and Berlin. It was a rash but successful undertaking for a young tenor whose only important Verdi part until that month had been Alfredo in *La traviata*.

From Berlin, Marta and I went to Naples, where I was to audition at the Teatro San Carlo, at the behest of Franco Patanè. We were on a turbo-prop plane between Rome and Naples, the last leg of the trip, when, just before reaching our destination, two of the four engines failed. The pilot did not feel that the airport in Naples was adequately equipped for a possible emergency, so we returned to Rome. Our plane, which had been full, could not take off again, and there were only twenty-five places available on the next flight. The commotion that went on among the Neapolitans was not to be imagined. 'You have to give me a place!' one woman shouted. 'I've come from New York and haven't seen my family in ten years!'

'Pardon me,' said a man, 'I'm getting on that flight, and that's all there is to it. My uncle is the mayor of such-and-such, and I'm getting on that flight!'

Then someone else chimed in: 'Listen, if I don't get a seat, you'll lose your job with Alitalia tomorrow. Do you have any idea who I am?'

In the end I said to Marta, 'Look, I'm so glad that we're safely on the ground again – let's take a train to Naples.' And that is exactly what we did. The audition went well, but several years passed before my schedule and that of the San Carlo coincided. While we were there, Patanè was our very kind guide, and when it was time to leave he drove us all the way to Milan – at heart-stopping speeds. Not many months later he was killed in a car accident on that same road.

Santiago, Chile, was one of the places I most enjoyed getting to know in 1967. I sang in *Andrea Chénier* with a cast that included Chilean soprano Claudia Parada and American baritone Sherrill Milnes, who was already a regular at the Met and who subsequently became one of my closest colleagues. We think alike as interpreters; and when we work together, the best of both of us emerges. I also performed in *Carmen*, which, like the *Chénier*, was staged by Tito Capobianco. Regina Resnik, a great artist, sang the title role with real temperament, while Ramón Vinay, whose outstanding interpretation of *Otello* I mentioned earlier, portrayed Escamillo. He must have been feeling nostalgic about his days as a tenor, because in the fourth act, as I sang 'Carmen, il est temps encore', I was a little disconcerted to hear him singing along with me from the wings. But Vinay, a native of Chile, was and still is a spontaneous, exuberant, warm-hearted man, always pleasant to be around. We talked a great deal about *Otello*, which he wanted me to start singing even then – much too early. 'Let's do it here next year,' he said. 'I'll give you my sword – you will inherit the role – and I'll sing Iago.' He told me that in his Otello days he had sung few other roles. 'I used to put myself in the right frame of mind while flying to my engagements,' he confided. Dark-complexioned to begin with, he would accentuate the effect by wearing a black pullover. He would scowl at and shake hands roughly with the people who had come to meet him, putting them on their guard. Vinay warned me to supervise the lighting in *Otello* in order to be certain that my facial expressions would be seen properly, because in his day individual singers were expected to have their own set ways of portraying their roles. Nowadays our characterizations are supposed to change from one production to the next, according to the stage directors' demands. He had lived so long with the role of the Moor that at social gatherings, big or small, he would invariably perform the death scene, beginning with 'Niun mi tema' and continuing through to the last gasp. Once we had a big party in the cellars where that delicious Chilean wine, Concha y Toro, is produced, and even there Vinay climbed onto some sort of platform and did his scene. It was bizarre in a way, yet at the same time very moving.

That was the year in which I made my debuts in Chicago (in *Ballo* with Martina Arroyo, who was singing the opera for the first time, and with Giuseppe Patanè conducting) and Los Angeles (with the New York City Opera in the opening season of the Dorothy Chandler Pavilion). Late in the year I returned to Hamburg for the new *Bohème* production, staged by Joachim Herz and conducted by Nello Santi. In Henri Murger's *Scènes de la vie de bohème*, the book on which the opera is based, there is a character who does not exist in Puccini's work. Euphémie, Schaunard's girlfriend, was reintroduced as a silent character in the Hamburg production: at the point where Marcello can no longer stand his painting of the Israelites crossing the Red Sea, he beckons to Euphémie who runs onto the stage stark naked – the model for his next picture. She remains shivering in the cold attic until Rodolfo has her put some clothes on, presumably to prevent her from catching pneumonia. This innovation, which had no bearing whatsoever on the musical performance, received quite a bit of attention. At the first ensemble rehearsal, the orchestral musicians suddenly developed a profound interest in operatic staging. They craned their necks in an attempt to examine the action as carefully as possible. Trumpeters were seen trying to play their instruments from their ears and double-basses were being held like violins. The rehearsal broke down until Santi had the presence of mind to ask Euphémie whether she would mind coming to the edge of the stage for a moment. 'No, not at all,' she replied. She stood over the pit for a few seconds while everyone gaped, and then the rehearsal went on.

I have sung more performances with Santi than with any other conductor except Jimmy Levine. I learned a great deal from working and talking with Nello in my early Hamburg days. He is an outstanding musician who should have had an even bigger international career than has been the case. His knowledge of the Italian operatic repertoire is encyclopedic, for he has thoroughly studied the recordings of all the singers of the past. In nearly every phrase of every repertory aria or ensemble, Nello can tell you where this or that singer breathed, what dynamics he used, what kind of tone he produced, and so on. He knows all the old traditions, good, bad and otherwise; and he has taught many singers, myself included, some fundamental truths that have served us well.

After an exciting performance, Nello and I would occasionally go to the bar at the hotel where Marta and I stayed, and he would accompany me at the bar's piano in a variety of arias. I notice, in a diary entry, that after the 600th performance of my operatic career – a *Bohème* in Hamburg early in 1969 – I felt so fantastic vocally that I sang 'Core ingrato', 'Ah Manon, mi tradisce', 'Tra voi, belle', 'Guardate, pazzo son', 'E la solita storia', 'Una furtiva lagrima', 'Amor ti vieta', the Flower Song, 'Oh Paradis', 'Sì, fui soldato', 'Come un bel dì di maggio', 'Giunto sul passo estremo', and three other arias – all at one go. Of course, I was only twenty-eight then, but what enthusiasm and energy I must have had to have sung fifteen arias after a *Bohème*!

At those bar sessions, Nello and I had a captive audience, and fortunately also a willing one, in Calvin Johnson, the black American bar-tender, who loved opera and who, over the years, had become a Hamburg institution in his own right. Calvin became a very dear friend of ours, and he loved to join our impromptu performances by adding a little nonsense phrase – 'ma-NA-ma-NA, pa-DUM-pa, pa-DA' – that he was accustomed to singing to himself while he worked. Once, in an exuberant mood, Nello and I decided that every time Calvin sang his phrase, we would smash a drinking glass. We probably broke twenty glasses that evening (of course we paid for all of them), and this strange trio was repeated on several other occasions in later years. Sadly, Calvin, who had a mild heart condition, fell asleep in the sauna one day in 1977 and never woke up. All of us who knew and loved him in Hamburg miss him very much.

My two *Lohengrin* performances in Hamburg were scheduled for 14 and 16 January 1968, immediately after the series of *Bohèmes*. This was my first venture into the Wagner repertoire, and it was also the first time I was singing a German opera. I cannot remember ever having been as nervous about a performance as I was about that first *Lohengrin*. We singers go through hell preparing the difficult parts of an opera; then, when we walk onto the stage, those problematic passages go by so quickly that we wonder what all the worry was for. Yet it is always the same for me. Those two or three days preceding a new production or some other special event fill me with apprehension, although I try not to show it.

On the evening of 14 January all went well through the Grail narrative. Then, in the middle of 'Mein lieber Schwan', I had a memory lapse and skipped quite a bit. I was very upset afterwards and did not want to take a bow. Liebermann persuaded me to go out, and I received a wonderful ovation. Nevertheless, I told Liebermann that I was withdrawing from the next performance. To my surprise, most of the reviewers, rather than taking me to task for my lapse, declared their satisfaction at hearing the part sung with a caressing sound instead of a massive Heldentenor voice. This made it easier for Liebermann to convince me to make a second attempt, and I had no further memory problems. Deutsche Grammophon taped that performance for possible release as a live opera recording. The project was eventually dropped, and I was assured that the tapes had been destroyed, but years later Uli and Leni Märkle of Deutsche Grammophon, who are close friends as well as business associates, gave them to me for my birthday – accompanied by a picture of a swan with my bearded face on it.

Despite the successful outcome of the *Lohengrin* production, the role hurt me vocally. German is much more difficult for me than either Italian or French, and I required a substantial amount of coaching in the part. Normally, I teach my new roles to myself, sitting at the piano and singing only the tough parts and only when absolutely necessary. But I was nervous about my Wagnerian debut and about trying to make my German intelligible to a German audience. Furthermore, much of the part lies in what is called the passaggio, which means too many Es, Fs and F-sharps. If a part lies basically lower in the range, it does not matter that one has to go up even as high as a B-natural now and again. What really taxes a voice is a concentration of middle-high-register singing, and that is exactly what the role of Lohengrin – which never goes higher than an A-natural – contains.

I had a heavy schedule of engagements ahead of me in the States during the following few months. In general I was singing well, but when I would come to a G-sharp it would begin well and then break, without any warning or obvious explanation. I assumed, and I still believe, that *Lohengrin* was responsible – not the Hamburg performances nor even the role itself, but all the preparation leading up to it. In New York I went to see Dr Gould, a throat specialist, although I am not a singer who makes a habit of such visits. He was very nice, showed me ways of relaxing my vocal cords, and even attended performances in order to check on me. But the problem persisted. I cancelled some engagements, fulfilled others, and worried a good deal. After all, I was only twenty-seven, and the Fates would have been cruel to me indeed had my burgeoning career been cut short so early.

At the end of three and a half horrible months, I made my Canadian debut in *Tosca* in Vancouver. To me, Vancouver is one of the most beautiful cities in the world, not only because of the incomparable panorama created by the combination of ocean and mountains, but also because during the *Tosca* staging rehearsals, my vocal problems disappeared as suddenly as they had come. My relief was indescribable. I had learned an important lesson: when I prepare *Lohengrin* for the opening of the Met season in 1984, I will allow myself enough time so I will not have to sit down at the piano and sing and sing and sing.

That summer I made my first two records – both of operatic arias. The first, for Decca/London with Nello conducting, won the Grand Prix du Disque; the second was for RCA with Edward Downes conducting. A few weeks later I appeared for the last time at a Cincinnati Zoo opera season. The management was justifiably upset with me. I had originally agreed to sing *Hoffmann* in English, but at the last minute I decided that it had to be sung in French. In the end we compromised. I sang the recitatives and some other parts in English, and the arias and other material in French. My reason for not returning, however, was simply the increasing number of engagements elsewhere in later summers.

The most important event for my career in 1968 was my debut at the Metropolitan Opera. Two years earlier I had made a sort of pre-debut debut with the company, not at the opera house but in an open-air concert performance of *Cavalleria rusticana* and *Pagliacci* at New York's Lewisohn Stadium. (My only 'performance' on the stage of the old Met had been an audition for Rudolf Bing, who was then general manager. Later, I had an offer from Risë Stevens to sing in a touring *Carmen* production with the Met's National Company, but I turned it down because of other obligations.) I was particularly pleased to sing Canio to Cornell MacNeil's Tonio in that *Pagliacci*, because when I had made my operatic debut with the Mexican Opera in the tiny role of Borsa only seven years earlier, he had been the Rigoletto. The performance was a success, but Bing did not invite me to sing during the Met's regular season. A few months later I was asked to reaudition on the stage of the new Met, which had recently opened at Lincoln Center, singing 'Cielo e mar' from *La Gioconda*. On the very day of my Viennese debut in 1967, I received a cable from Bing offering me a contract at the Met. My first Met appearance was scheduled for 2 October 1968, and I would be singing opposite Tebaldi in *Adriana Lecouvreur*. Bing also proposed that I appear in *I vespri siciliani* at the 1967 Newport Festival, but I was already engaged elsewhere. I am glad that I did not attempt the murderous role of Arrigo in *Vespri* at that early moment in my career. Everyone warns tenors about singing Otello, but no one warns them about Arrigo.

The month leading up to my debut was horrifyingly busy, because I had to continue with my City Opera repertoire as well as begin my Met rehearsals. Luckily, the New York State Theater and the Met are just across Lincoln Center Plaza from each other. I often had to rush back and forth between them. Joining the Met as a young and not entirely established tenor, I was expected not only to cover the performances of many other tenors in case of emergency, but also to take rehearsals at which the star tenors could not be present. My own rehearsals for *Adriana* were not with Tebaldi herself but with less famous sopranos, because she was already singing the work that season opposite Franco Corelli. In addition, I was performing in *Pagliacci* and *Il tabarro* at the City Opera and standing in at the Met's *Turandot* rehearsals, although I myself was not going to be singing *Turandot* until later in the season.

On Wednesday evening, 25 September, I sang *Tabarro*, and two nights later *Pagliacci*. The next afternoon, Saturday, I was called to the Met to rehearse *Turandot* with Marion Lippert, who was covering for Birgit Nilsson. Birgit was not feeling well, and as it appeared that Lippert might have to replace her, it was necessary to run an extra rehearsal. Afterwards, I returned home to Teaneck for dinner. Marta was expecting our second child, and my parents had come from Mexico both for the arrival of their grandchild and to hear my Met debut. I wanted to go back to the Met that evening for the last *Adriana* performance before my big night. While I was shaving there was a telephone call from Mr Bing. 'How do you feel?' he asked.

'Very well, thank you.'

'That's wonderful, because you are going to make your Metropolitan debut this evening.'

I was furious. 'I was not planning to arrive for the beginning of the opera,' I said. 'I got home late from the extra *Turandot* rehearsal this afternoon.'

'Just come immediately,' he replied.

It was too late for Marta to get ready to come along, and in any case it would have been too upsetting for her in her condition. My mother stayed with her while I drove to the Met with my father. As we were heading down the West Side Highway, I began to warm up, really opening up my throat. We stopped for a moment, and I noticed that some people in the next car were laughing. I rolled down my window. 'Where are you going?' I asked them.

'To the Met.'

'Well, don't laugh, because you'll be hearing me in a few minutes!'

I was very much out of sorts when I arrived – so much so that I could not help letting Mr Bing know my feelings. 'I believe that Corelli has cancelled on purpose,' I said. 'He assumes that I'll be tired from having sung three operas in the last seventy-two hours. But I'm feeling very well, so he'll be sorry!' After all, he had cancelled at 7.20 in the evening – the very last moment. It was not a case of my having been told in the morning to be ready just in case Corelli could not sing. There had been no warning whatsoever. But I do not know the true story. I like and admire Franco very much, as an artist and as a person; and later, when we were both appearing in Verona, he became very fond of my sons. But he was always a nervous performer, and it is very possible that at the last moment, for some reason, he felt he could not go on stage. It is none the less understandable that my thoughts ran the way they did that evening.

Before the performance, which began twenty minutes late, Osie Hawkins, the stage manager, went out to announce that Corelli was indisposed, and naturally there was great disappointment in the auditorium. 'But,' he added, 'a young singer is going to replace him.' The public knew who it would be even before he mentioned my name, since my debut was scheduled for four days later. The evening was a wonderful one for me. Tebaldi was very welcoming; Fausto Cleva, the conductor, was at his best in the verismo music of *Adriana*; and the general atmosphere backstage could not have been better. Everyone was helping me to do my best, to accomplish something I had been dreaming about for years. Imagine how my managers, Marianne and Gerard Semon, must have felt when I phoned them during one of the intermissions and said, 'Guess what! I'm just making my debut at the Met!'

I would probably have worked myself into quite a state had I in fact had four days of rest before my debut. As it turned out, I was hardly even aware of what was happening until it was over. Afterwards, Cleva seemed extremely moved by the whole evening, and his remarks to me were especially kind. Everything worked to my advantage, because I received attention for both an unofficial and an official debut. Most of the critics had not been present at the first one, but they all came to the second. By then I was feeling calm and relaxed.

III
ITALY, ENGLAND AND ELSEWHERE (1968-71)

On 11 October 1968, less than two weeks after my Metropolitan debut, Marta gave birth to our second son, Alvaro. Years earlier, Marta's first positive feelings towards me had been stirred when she had heard me sing the duet 'Solenne in quest'ora', from *La forza del destino* – an opera that I was now about to perform for the first time, in Hamburg. And Alvaro's middle name is Maurizio, after my role in *Adriana Lecouvreur*, in which I had just made my Met debut. Alvaro seemed a beautiful name for our new baby. The night after his birth, I sang *Pagliacci* at the City Opera. Instead of throwing candy to the children as I normally did in that production, I threw cigars to the adults. The wrappers said 'It's a boy'. A few cigars even reached the orchestra and audience.

My first Met season, which was interrupted by a lengthy spell in Hamburg and some shorter engagements elsewhere, was originally to have included only performances of *Adriana*, one *Turandot*, and a performance, as part of a Gala, of one act of *Butterfly*. At about 1 o'clock on the day of the Gala, I was in Bing's office discussing a delicate problem with him: Corelli was scheduled to sing three weeks later in a new production of *Il trovatore*, but as his father was ill, there were grave doubts about the likelihood of his participation. He had already cancelled an appearance in *Tosca* that very afternoon – Sándor Kónya was replacing him – and had missed some of the *Trovatore* rehearsals. I had just agreed to take on the *Trovatore* production when Bing's telephone rang. Kónya was not well and would not be able to sing. I was escorted from the general manager's office to my dressing-room, where I got myself ready in a few minutes to sing my first Metropolitan *Tosca*, in a nationwide radio broadcast and opposite Birgit Nilsson! I suppose that Bing was grateful to me for having stepped into the breach so many times, for while I was singing the torture scene (Act II) from the wings, he held a glass of water for me. Apparently, he did not want to leave me for a second. It was all very strange and amusing, and fortunately the performance went smoothly.

The new *Trovatore* production was conducted by Zubin Mehta. I have since worked many times with Zubin, who has a fine sense of humour and is a good friend. I find him an extremely gifted conductor and I greatly admire his fine memory and musical intuition. Apart from being charismatic, he has great facility in absorbing scores – which is both an advantage and a disadvantage. When we performed *La fanciulla del West* together in London some years later I noticed that he was not very secure at the first few rehearsals, but he mastered the work quickly and thoroughly. He is exuberant and spontaneous, and he enjoys working with singers, which contributes to the confidence we feel when we work with him.

Nathaniel Merrill staged a beautiful *Trovatore*, using Attilio Colonnello's colourful sets, and I had the luxury of singing opposite Leontyne Price as Leonora, Sherrill Milnes as the Count of Luna, and Grace Bumbry as Azucena. The power and sensuousness of Leontyne's voice were phenomenal – the most beautiful Verdi soprano I have ever heard. She is a gracious lady, and I am proud to have made many recordings with her. There was one rather gymnastic moment for me in the convent scene of the *Trovatore* production: just before Leonora's 'E deggio e posso crederlo?', I had to appear, sword drawn, on a platform about seven feet high, and then jump onto the stage à la Douglas Fairbanks. To make the jump, I had to support myself on a 'tree' and swing myself over the edge of the platform. Unfortunately, at the third performance the stagehands forgot to nail the tree to the platform and it came over with me. I landed painfully on my knees but quickly regained my composure. Stiffly, I made my way over to Martina Arroyo, who was alternating with Leontyne. Instead of singing 'Sei tu dal ciel disceso?' ('Have you descended from heaven?'), she changed the line to 'Sei tu dal ciel cascato?' ('Have you fallen out of the sky?'). Despite my physical agony, I could barely keep from laughing during the rest of the scene. Some friends told me after the performance that that scene had looked particularly dramatic, and they didn't know the half of it.

When the Met season ended, I performed in and recorded Beethoven's Ninth Symphony with Leinsdorf and the Boston Symphony. A month later, on 20 May 1969, I made my London debut at the Royal Festival Hall singing my first performance of the Verdi Requiem, with Gwyneth Jones, Josephine Veasey and Raphael Arié. The New Philharmonia Orchestra was conducted by Carlo Maria Giulini, with whom I was working for the first time. I admired his recording of the Requiem – it is still one of the very best – and so singing in it with him was a moving experience. It would be difficult to find another musician with Giulini's combination of gentleness and intensity. His music-making is extremely refined. In the 'Dies irae' he seemed to personify God the Father on the Day of Judgement. Not that he overacted or made pompous gestures: he simply *became* the music to an almost frightening degree. It was shocking to see someone who is so good and so gentle demonstrate such power, like God on the day of wrath. I had in fact made an unofficial British debut in Wales some time earlier, singing a few arias in a programme that was part of the International Eisteddfod (choral festival) at Llangollen. The engagement had been arranged by Margherita Stafford, who was then working for an artists' agency but who had such talent for her work that I convinced her to set up her own agency – which she is still running successfully. On that first occasion the airline had accidentally shipped my luggage beyond London and on to Johannesburg, and poor Margherita had had to rush me to Moss Brothers to be fitted for tails.

An engagement to sing four concert performances of *Carmen* with Mehta and the Israel Philharmonic brought me back to Tel Aviv for the first time in four years. Marta and I now had two children to show off and we spent two very pleasant weeks there, seeing old friends and revisiting familiar places. Mme de Philippe was very kind to us and invited us to attend performances of some of our old productions at the opera. I pointed out to Cuban tenor Orlando Montez, who was Nadir in *Pearl Fishers*, that he was wearing my old trousers.

I was lucky to have had that brief relaxing period in Israel, because afterwards I plunged directly into one of my most important and challenging engagements – my Italian debut at the Verona Arena, which coincided with my first performance as Calaf in *Turandot*, opposite Nilsson. (The Met *Turandot* performance had been cancelled.) To sing Italian opera in Italy is an experience I find hard to describe. 'Il tenore è arrivato,' I would hear people say. I have since become used to public curiosity, but in those days I was very impressed that even people who never set foot in the theatre would know and somehow care about the fact that 'the tenor' had arrived in town. I used to overhear people asking each other. 'Who the hell is this new tenor, this Spaniard? Does he have a voice or doesn't he?' And the intrigue! One person would come to me and say, 'Plácido, it's hopeless. I have to argue with everyone – they don't believe that you can sing.' Then someone else would come and tell me that the first person had been saying nasty things about me. I had to develop the ability to look concerned during all those conversations, while ignoring at least ninety per cent of what was said. On the other hand, I was able to meet some people whose names and voices I had always known from recordings - Piero De Palma, Franco Ricciardi - the old-time supporting tenors par excellence.

The arena is one of the best-preserved Roman amphitheatres. We had arranged to have an apartment just opposite it, in Piazza Bra. As we were going up to our room immediately after our arrival, the elevator got stuck. It was unbelievable: there we were, crammed into a tiny elevator on a hot July day! The firemen had to be called to release 'il tenore' and his family from the elevator.

I know I said earlier that I have never been more nervous than before my Hamburg *Lohengrin*, but I may have been even more anxious about my Verona debut. I remember wanting to run away, as far away as possible. When I walked onto the stage, however, I felt the warmth of the atmosphere, and everything went well. Pier Luigi Pizzi had created the lovely sets, and there was virtually a whole castle on the enormous stage. In the second act, Nilsson was sitting about a hundred steps above the stage, and every time I gave an answer to the Emperor, I would climb about twenty-five of them. I was wearing a flowing cape, and Placi, who was not yet four years old, said to Marta, 'Look, Daddy is flying!'

The vibrancy and magnitude of Birgit's voice in those performances made her sound seem a sort of thunderbolt. Through an odd effect - acoustical, psychological, or both - the farther I was positioned from her, the more monumental her voice sounded to me. There were moments when I was so overwhelmed with admiration for her vocal abilities and power that I almost forgot to continue singing. Performing *Turandot* with Nilsson was one of the high points of my life, not only as an artist but also as a worshipper of great singing. Years later, when I appeared on the BBC's programme 'Desert Island Discs', I chose a recording of her singing 'In questa reggia' from *Turandot* as one of my all-time favourites, yet it in no way approaches what I heard when she sang it in Verona. I regret that our repertoires did not coincide more often. The only works we have performed together are *Turandot* and *Tosca*, and a recording of Weber's *Oberon*.

The sheer 'spectacular' aspect of performing in the arena is overwhelming, and it was especially so that season. We were singing *Turandot* during the week of the first moon landing, so the chorus to the moon seemed particularly appropriate. I well remember the feeling of amazement, as the moon shone over us in that 1,900-year-old Roman ruin, that people were walking up there at that moment.

I also sang *Don Carlo* at Verona that summer, with a tremendous cast: Montserrat Caballé, Fiorenza Cossotto, Piero Cappuccilli and Dimiter Petkov, with Eliahu Inbal conducting and Jean Vilar directing the staging. Although it might seem an unlikely opera for the arena, *Don Carlo* was a great success. When I think about that production, I also remember Serafino. Serafino was an incredibly fat character who could only be called a professional fan. He was not part of a claque – he just enjoyed going wherever he could find some excitement and showing his support for the 'good guys', whoever they might be. When Italy's national football team was playing somewhere, he would manage to follow it and lead the cheering, and he did the same for the cycling team and others. Apparently he had been told that Verona was a good place to go in the summer: he could cheer for the singers and then come to our dressing-rooms and ask for a little donation. I remember giving him 10,000 lire (about $17 in those days) and telling him to have a bath and clean himself up.

Serafino always had the perfect line to offer at the right moment. The *Don Carlo* was a magnificent production – particularly the last scene, when Montserrat and I had our duet, 'Ma lassù ci vedremo in un mondo migliore'. We began at centre stage and then moved apart perhaps twenty yards, but we could still hear each other and blend with perfect ease. Poor Montserrat had broken a leg shortly before the season began, was on crutches and had some difficulty in moving. At the end of the first performance Serafino was ready with his one-line shouts to the singers: 'Cossotto, you're divine'; 'Cappuccilli, you're magnificent, but you're a miser' (because Piero had not given Serafino any money); 'Plácido, you're always placid'. When Caballé came out for her bow, Serafino was silent for a moment. Then he shouted, 'Montserrat – go to Lourdes!' which is the funniest thing I have ever heard a member of the public shout at a singer. Poor Serafino. He died not long ago, and I was told that he had simply eaten himself to death.

I was very happy during that period in Verona. I felt wonderful. I was a Spanish singer having a big success in the country that had given birth to opera. Placi loved Italy, too. I remember going with him from one shop or ice-cream parlour to another in Piazza Bra, and every *padrone*, every shopkeeper, would give him something. ('Why not stop at the bank one of these days?' I used to ask him.) By the time we would get to the restaurant for lunch, he had no appetite left.

After my *Don Carlo* performance I had to catch a plane from Milan to

London, and everyone warned me not to drive to Milan. It was Ferragosto
– the mid-August holiday – and I was told that traffic on the *autostrada*
would be too heavy. So I took the train, which was so crowded that I had
to sit on my luggage in the corridor. That brought me back to reality after
the triumph of *Don Carlo*.

In 1969 I participated in my first recording of a complete opera – *Il
trovatore*, conducted by Mehta and sung by Price, Cossotto and Milnes.
Decca had earlier asked me to record Donizetti's *Anna Bolena*, but when
the *Trovatore* possibility arose it seemed more interesting to me. When the
sessions began, I was shocked to have to record scenes out of sequence, to
have to express emotions out of order. The sessions took place in the
Walthamstow Town Hall, outside London, which is acoustically fine, and
I was to spend many days there during the next few years. (Three years
earlier I had given my only performance of *Anna Bolena* – a concert
performance that was not only my Carnegie Hall debut but also the New
York debut of Janet Baker and Elena Suliotis. Suliotis had one of those
extraordinary voices that one would like to pamper, to keep as it was, but
by her own choice she became a happy wife instead. Marilyn Horne was
also in the cast, Henry Lewis conducted, and Maria Callas was in the
audience.) From London I went back to the Met to sing in *La fanciulla del
West* with Tebaldi and in Franco Zeffirelli's new production of *Cavalleria
rusticana*. Unfortunately, a strike prevented the season from opening, and
I therefore had a double disappointment. I should add that that was the
only time I have been paid for performances I did not sing. Bing continued
to give a number of his singers their fees for fear of losing their services if
and when the strike was settled. In any case, I was free to relax, to do some
concerts, including participation in a London gala for the Queen Mother,
and to make my debut with the San Francisco Opera in *Bohème*.

As important as my Verona appearances had been to me, an even more
momentous event in my life was drawing near: my debut at La Scala. I was
to sing the title role in Verdi's *Ernani* at the opening of the Scala season on
7 December 1969. The original plan had been for me to make my debut in
Don Carlo the following spring. Richard Tucker had been asked to sing in
the *Ernani* production, but he told me that he had turned it down because
the tenor part was too small – a comprimario role. I disagreed, and I cabled
Luciano Chailly, who was then artistic director at La Scala, to say that
if he was still looking for an Ernani, I was interested. A contract was forthcoming. The cast originally included Raina Kabaivanska, Cappuccilli and
Ghiaurov, but Cappuccilli caught a terrible cold after the dress rehearsal

and was replaced by Carlo Meliciani. The stage director was Giorgio di Lullo.

I apologize for my lack of originality, but I must repeat what others have said about the special feeling of singing at La Scala. It is true that I had already sung at the Met, the Vienna Staatsoper and other great theatres. But when you stand on the stage of La Scala and look into that beautiful auditorium, you cannot help thinking that nearly every celebrated singer from Mozart's day to our own has performed there. I would probably have had a similar feeling in New York had I made my debut in the old rather than the new Met, which had opened only two years earlier. The new Met will of course have its own history, but that will be for future generations of performers to appreciate. There are two other factors that make La Scala special: the chorus and the orchestra. The orchestra is incredibly flexible – those players can follow the most incompetent singer to hell and back. And the chorus.... When the *Ernani* ensemble rehearsals began and I heard those tenors singing B-flats and B-naturals like *real* tenors, I was truly impressed. In the famous chorus 'Si ridesta il leon di Castiglia', at the words 'Siamo tutti una sola famiglia' ('We are all one family'), the fantastic legato of those tenors and basses gave me goose-flesh every time we rehearsed or performed.

Singing under the baton of Antonino Votto was a great opportunity for me. He had been hired as a coach and staff conductor at La Scala by Toscanini nearly fifty years earlier, and that was one of his last seasons at the house. What was wonderful about Votto was the life, the pulsation, he gave to a work when he rehearsed singers at the piano. I remember the vigour and subtlety of his playing of my cabaletta, 'O tu che l'alma adora'. When he went before the orchestra, the fire and feeling of command waned a bit, but that may have been due to his age. At my first ensemble rehearsal – my first time singing on that stage – I performed my aria and cabaletta, and Votto said to me: 'Young man, you're a bit tired.'

'Maestro,' I replied, 'maybe you're right, but don't you think that I might just be a bit moved?'

What a thrill that whole period was! Marta, the children, my parents and I all had a wonderful time in Milan. *The Barber of Seville*, conducted by Claudio Abbado, staged by Jean-Pierre Ponnelle, and sung by Teresa Berganza, Luigi Alva and Hermann Prey, was also in preparation as well as *Samson et Dalila* with Georges Prêtre conducting and Shirley Verrett and Richard Cassilly in the title roles. We all spent quite a bit of time together over Christmas and New Year. My family and I were sitting in a box during the *Barber* dress rehearsal when Placi began applauding and saying 'Brava' to Teresa, rather too loudly. An usher came and said that he had to be taken out, and my father commented, 'Unfortunately, at La Scala Placi cannot say, "They've thrown me out of better theatres than this one."'

By the time I returned to New York in February 1970, the strike at the Met had been settled, and I was able to sing three performances of *Turandot* with Nilsson. During the last of these, a broadcast, I was having terrible problems with my digestion. Because they can affect the functioning of the diaphragm, such difficulties are at least as dangerous as colds for singers. Every time I left the stage I had to make a dash for the men's room. By the middle of the second act I thought I was going to have to leave altogether, but somehow I sang the whole performance.

I was preparing to perform in Bucharest at the end of the month when I received an urgent call that changed my schedule. Leonard Bernstein asked me to replace Corelli, for the fifth time in my career, in a televised performance of the Verdi Requiem from St Paul's Cathedral, London, and to make a recording immediately afterwards. My first appearance with Bernstein was therefore also my first recording of the Requiem. I have since sung in a televised version of the Ninth Symphony and recorded the part of the Italian Singer in *Der Rosenkavalier* with Bernstein. Despite his flamboyance, he is a great musician who produces exciting musical performances. Most orchestras admire him very much, although some musicians feel that he tries to feed them every note, the way a mother bird puts food directly into the beaks of her young. It is a pity that he is doing so little conducting nowadays, because the amount of time he has devoted to composition does not seem to have produced a great deal lately. I am sorry, however, that he has not written a serious opera, and I – along with many other people – would love to have another first-rate musical like *West Side Story* from this gifted man.

One of my spring engagements was the recording, in Munich, of *Oberon*, an opera I have never performed on stage. The tenor part is terribly difficult in general, and the dramatic coloratura aria 'Von Jugend auf' is one of the most terrifying numbers I have ever sung. It was my first recording of a German opera and the first of my unfortunately rare collaborations with Rafael Kubelik, whom I found to be a wonderful and energetic conductor.

I was back at La Scala to sing *Don Carlo* in April. There are some theatres where I will not sing this great work. The tenor part is demanding but does not arouse general enthusiasm, and I sometimes feel unappreciated

68

and let down when the curtain has fallen. I consider *Don Carlo* and *Otello* to be Verdi's greatest masterpieces, but we tenors have to face the fact that after our terribly difficult aria at the very beginning of *Don Carlo*, we have no other solo numbers. I often ask myself why Verdi did not provide an aria at the most logical point – the beginning of the prison scene, when the protagonist is overwhelmed by the loss of his beloved Elisabetta, the failure of his plan for the oppressed Netherlands, the conflict with his father and the possible betrayal by his friend Rodrigo. The situation is particularly puzzling since Verdi has Carlo appear in seven of the opera's eight tableaux. If there were another aria, Don Carlo would be my favourite part. I base my characterization on Schiller's *Don Carlos*, the play that provided the story of the opera. The protagonist is not simply an unfortunate, misunderstood man, another 'good-looking tenor': he is weak, indecisive, and that is how he must be portrayed. In some cities the public is not sophisticated enough to know what to make of an unromantic Romantic tenor. My interpretation and the whole opera simply seem boring. But at La Scala the public and the critics appeared to understand what I was trying to do, and I was especially gratified by their positive reactions.

The cast in that production included Rita Orlandi Malaspina, Shirley Verrett, Cappuccilli, Ghiaurov and Martti Talvela, and the occasion gave me my first chance to work with Claudio Abbado. Although Claudio favours essentially 'clean' performances of the Verdi operas, paying careful attention to the composer's indications, he does allow singers those traditional interpolations that he believes to be valid. I admire his way of dealing with orchestras – especially the Scala orchestra – when they get out of hand. The noisier they become, the more softly he speaks to them, until he finally stops talking altogether. The musicians then realize that the rehearsal cannot proceed until there is silence and they quieten down. Although he never plays the piano for cast rehearsals, Claudio is a fantastic pianist. Once, after a concert he conducted in London with Murray Perahia as soloist, we were all at the home of some friends, Noretta and John Leech; and Claudio, Murray and I took turns playing Mozart four-hand sonatas in all the different combinations. I kept miscounting my bars of rest, which of course provoked laughter. I got back at them by conducting them in Schubert's 'Military' March, making all kinds of outrageous tempo changes that they had to follow.

At the age of twenty-nine I finally made my home-town debut, singing my very first performances of *La Gioconda* at Madrid's Teatro de la Zarzuela. It was an emotional moment for me. The ovation after my aria, 'Cielo e mar', was so great and so warm that I could not help myself – I began to cry. Some terribly difficult phrases in a rough tessitura follow soon after the aria, in the duet with Laura, and the crying was obstructing my voice. I finally managed to get hold of myself and proceed normally.

Maria Callas and EMI were at that time discussing a possible recording of *La traviata*, and I was being considered as a potential Alfredo. I made a test tape, and Callas invited me to meet her. Marta and I went from Madrid to Paris, where we had a drink at Maria's apartment and then dinner at a restaurant with her and her good friend John Coveney of EMI. Being with her was wonderful yet at the same time very difficult. In speaking of the Madrid *Gioconda* I made the mistake of mentioning that Angeles Gulin, who had sung the title role, was a fine soprano. Maria replied that she no longer wanted to sing because there were no satisfactory conductors, producers or singers around. I laughed and said, 'Thank you, Maria.' Once we stopped discussing opera, the atmosphere became more relaxed and she was very natural. We all told stories and had a pleasant time, but the *Traviata* project never materialized. I later proposed singing Giordano's *Fedora* with Callas, but that plan was another that never worked out. She could have coped well with the lead role, but she was determined to make her comeback in a part like Norma or Violetta. Unfortunately, in those roles she would have had to compete with herself. When John Tooley invited her to sing Santuzza at Covent Garden, she proposed doing Nedda as well; but those plans, too, came to nothing. I greatly regret never having worked with her.

In honour of the two hundredth anniversary of Beethoven's birth, Pope Paul VI was present at a performance of the Missa Solemnis at St Peter's in 1970, in which I was fortunate enough to participate along with Ingrid Bjoner, Christa Ludwig and Kurt Moll. Wolfgang Sawallisch conducted very beautifully, and Franco Zeffirelli was in charge of the visual aspect of the performance. I was deeply moved to be able to meet and sing for the Pope, but from what I know of the five men who have been Pope during my lifetime, John XXIII and the two John Pauls were more sympathetic personally.

Back in Verona that summer I sang in *Manon Lescaut* opposite Magda Olivero, who had made her debut eight years before I was born. Her portrayal of the young heroine was completely convincing, and the enthusiasm of the public was downright frightening. After one performance, the people sitting in the part of the amphitheatre nearest the stage rushed

towards us, cheering and shouting. We hardly knew whether to thank them
or to run away for fear of being mobbed! The sets were very realistic, and
the ship in the third act was so large that when the Captain told me to go
aboard after my 'Guardate, pazzo son', I really had to sprint.

Performers seem to be particularly responsive in Verona. One would
think that the sheer size of the amphitheatre – not to mention having the
sky as a ceiling – would make singers feel that their voices are no stronger
than a mouse's squeak. But, on the contrary, I have never felt better vocally,
in an overall way, than in Verona. Perhaps the elation comes from singing
in the open air, or from the impression the arena makes by virtue of its age,
its size and its history. 'Nessun dorma', 'E lucevan le stelle' – the atmosphere
in Verona is so right for arias of that sort that it would be impossible not to
feel good about singing them there.

Later that summer, in London, I recorded *Don Carlo* with Giulini.
People were still talking then about the famous production of the opera that
Giulini had conducted at Covent Garden a dozen years earlier with Gré
Brouwenstijn, Fedora Barbieri, Jon Vickers, Tito Gobbi and Boris Christ-
off. The London public has an incredible memory, and it is wonderful to
know that some ephemeral performances I myself have participated in may
long be remembered. Although long-range comparisons tend to be invi-
dious and are often inaccurate, I do feel that our *Don Carlo* recording (with
Caballé, Verrett, Milnes and Raimondi) is a classic. Throughout those
sessions, Giulini was never nervous, irritable, or obviously unhappy. He
always went about his task in the most constructive way, as a colleague and
co-worker.

Immediately after recording *Don Carlo*, I made my debut at the Edinburgh Festival singing the Missa Solemnis under Giulini's direction. The
tenor is the sacrificial lamb in this work. He must always be careful not to
cover the mezzo-soprano's part, since Beethoven often has him singing a
third or even a sixth above her. It is not even a matter of singing softly: the
tenor must strangle his sound and level his voice completely when the
mezzo is singing in an uncomfortable register. (This is also true of the
Ninth Symphony. If you can hear the mezzo, she has made a mistake.) But
never mind – the work is sublime, and I shall never forget Giulini's superb
handling of the Benedictus – the trombones, and the violin solo. Hearing
his rendering of the Missa also made me understand how much Verdi was
influenced by the work when he wrote not only the Requiem but also the
scene between Amneris and Ramfis in the fourth act of *Aida*.

Of my Met performances that autumn, I remember with special affection

71

a *Ballo* production with Caballé and Robert Merrill. It was my first performance with Bob, who was a legend for me from some of the opera recordings
I had heard in my early years – especially the *Traviata* with Toscanini, Jan
Peerce and Licia Albanese. His was one of the most purely beautiful voices
I have ever sung with. I also remember a *Tosca* production in November in
which I appeared with Lucine Amara and Tito Gobbi. Régine Crespin, a
wonderful artist, was originally to have sung the title role. She had not had
a separate musical rehearsal with Francesco Molinari-Pradelli, the conductor, and in the middle of one ensemble rehearsal, she took a phrase slightly
faster than he wanted it. He stopped her and said, 'Signora, that phrase
does not go that way.'

She replied very nicely: 'Maestro, if you don't mind, we can discuss these
details afterwards.'

'No, there is nothing to discuss,' he said rudely. 'It will be done as I say,
and that's that.'

'Tant pis,' was her response, and with that she walked out of the rehearsal
and the entire production.

During that same period I made my last official appearances under my
City Opera contract, singing the title role in Donizetti's *Roberto Devereux*
opposite Beverly Sills's Elizabeth – the first of the composer's three
sixteenth-century British queens whom Beverly portrayed with great success. (The other two were, of course, Mary Stuart and Anne Boleyn.) It
was always a pure joy to sing with her. Apart from being the greatest vocal
actress I have worked with, she is also a delightful, straightforward person.

Capobianco was responsible for the very effective staging of *Devereux*,
which had many similarities to the Bette Davis–Errol Flynn film, *Elizabeth
the Queen*. The fake slap that Beverly had to give me at one point looked
unconvincing at rehearsal, so it was decided that she would give me a real
one. It hurt; and, strangely enough, I think I sang the better for it in the
subsequent number. The shame, the anger – one cannot help feeling them
if one's face has just been slapped, however prearranged the gesture may
have been.

Towards the end of 1970 I flew to San Francisco to sing in some *Tosca*
and *Carmen* performances. Arriving for the first *Tosca* rehearsal, I asked
Kurt Herbert Adler, the company's director, who the conductor would be.

'Maestro James Levine,' he said.

'Never heard of him.'

Once the rehearsal got under way, I could not believe what I was
witnessing. It was clear that this twenty-seven-year-old had a grasp of all

the traditions, as well as knowledge, command and good taste. I asked him afterwards where he had studied, and he began to tell me about his background: his childhood in Cincinnati, his years at the Juilliard School in New York, and the substantial period he had spent as an assistant to George Szell in Cleveland. That was the first *Tosca* that Jimmy had conducted, and it was my forty-eighth performance of the work; yet we were together all the way through.

Within a year Jimmy became principal conductor of the Met, and he has been its music director since 1975. I have now sung more repertoire, more performances in the theatre and more recordings with him than with any other conductor, and we have often appeared together in operas that he was conducting for the first time or that I was singing for the first time. His approach to music is very direct, and those who sometimes accuse him of not going extremely deeply into the music do not realize that he is growing at an amazing pace. A conductor at forty is still at the beginning of his career, and Jimmy himself has told me that he is not now trying to give his definitive accounts of the works he conducts. Other critics have said that he conducts too many important productions himself, but I know that many other leading conductors - Kleiber, Abbado, Muti, Solti - have turned down his invitations for reasons of their own. It is far better for Jimmy to take those productions himself than to put them in the hands of *routiniers*.

What astonishes me about him is his ability to assimilate enormous quantities of music and to conduct such a vast number of styles so well. The Vienna Philharmonic musicians, who work with all the famous conductors, have told me that there is no one else as clear as Jimmy on a purely technical level - and that is of extreme importance. It is always fun, too, to make music with Jimmy, because he is so enthusiastic. I feel that I have a friend and collaborator in the pit when he is there. By this I do not mean that he merely follows the singers: I have no respect for conductors who allow themselves to be led or bullied. Rehearsals exist so that a unified production can be achieved. When there are disputes over details, they are best resolved through intelligent discussion and not simply by virtue of the fact that a particular singer, conductor or director is more famous than his colleagues. But the conductor must control the pulse of every performance, and the pulse will be feeble if he just follows a singer's request without conviction. When a performance is actually unfolding, I always feel that Jimmy is with me and not against me, and that is wonderful. He is very sensitive to what is happening on stage. If there is a difficult moment, he looks up with a smile; he is encouraging and reliable rather than panic-stricken and angry. Other conductors may be emotionally involved in a different way. With Jimmy one has the luxury of being able to feel at ease. 'Don't worry, kids,' he seems to say. 'I'm here, let's enjoy ourselves, the music is great.'

Early in 1971 my mother came to New York and gave a very successful recital of Spanish music, including zarzuela arias and Granados songs, at the Huntington Hartford Gallery. I was very pleased and proud, and also glad that our Cuban exile friends in New York were able to hear my mother twenty-two years after her last appearance in their country. Soon afterwards I went to Mexico City for a concert. Arriving a day in advance, I got so caught up in seeing family and friends, organizing appointments and attending a corrida that I had no time to rest. The city is 7,800 feet above sea level, and my unacclimatized condition coupled with my exhaustion nearly caused me to pass out during the performance. I had to stop in the middle; oxygen was given to me offstage, and I then returned to the platform to finish the concert. (That was my second minor physical calamity during that period. A few months earlier I had fallen off a bicycle while playing with my boys and broken my arm. I wonder what Serafino's comment would have been had he seen me wearing a sling while singing at the Met opposite Joan Sutherland in *Lucia*.)

Eight *Lucia* evenings in March, again with Sutherland but this time in Hamburg, were among the greatest performing experiences of my life. Joan was in incredibly good voice, and each performance was better than the last. 'Plácido,' she joked, 'if you continue to sing this so well, I won't like you so much.' But it was truly a joke, as Joan can outsing anyone!

In Vienna in April, while I was singing the part of the Italian tenor in Bernstein's recording of *Der Rosenkavalier*, an odd thing happened. The taping was proceeding at a relaxed pace, when I suddenly realized that my entrance was approaching. I heard the solo flute; then I saw Bernstein gesturing to me to get ready, which surprised me since I had not been scheduled to record so soon. He cued me in, and the aria went beautifully. When I had finished, he said, 'All right, let's record now.' Singing that impossibly difficult piece a second time was not so easy.

I made debuts in both Naples and Florence that spring (1971). At the Teatro San Carlo I sang *Manon Lescaut* opposite Elena Suliotis and with Oliviero de Fabritiis in the pit. He was a favourite in Mexico, Verona and elsewhere – a much underrated conductor who died while this book was being written. In Florence, too, I sang Puccini, this time *Turandot*, with

74

Georges Prêtre conducting and Hana Janku in the title role. There was a great deal of discussion in the Italian press at that time about the claim of some native singers that too many foreigners were taking work away from them in their own country. An Italian tenor, Nicola Martinucci, was understudying Calaf in Florence, and I decided to let him take one of my performances for me. I am pleased to say that he is now making a career for himself. The production and the company were more than satisfactory, but I have not accepted invitations to return to Florence because I do not like the Teatro Comunale. Its acoustics are dreadful and its atmosphere absolutely anti-theatrical. It would be wonderful if the old Teatro della Pergola, where Verdi's *Macbeth* and so many other operas were first performed, could be modernized and used again as an opera house. One of my dreams is to sing in that theatre and in that magnificent city the words 'Firenze è come un albero fiorito' ('Florence is like a flowering tree') in the aria from *Gianni Schicchi*. (When I recorded Puccini's opera with Maazel, my Alvaro sang the little part of Gherardino.)

A concert performance of *La traviata* at the Hollywood Bowl in August, with Sills, Milnes and Levine, provided a bit of comic relief for the participants. Sherrill had asked Jimmy to transpose the very end of the Germont-Alfredo scene in the second act from B-flat major to D-flat major so he could sing a high A-flat instead of a mere F on his last words, 'Ah! ferma!' He pointed out that the aria 'Di Provenza il mar' is in D-flat anyway. Jimmy was against the idea and said that Verdi wanted the scene to end in B-flat. But Sherrill, who loves high notes as only a baritone can, decided – without warning anyone – to go up to a high B-flat on his very last note. He duly broke the sound barrier, the audience loved it, and Jimmy, who has a wonderful sense of humour, had a good laugh over it backstage afterwards with the rest of us.

I sang a single performance of *Andrea Chénier* in Mexico City that autumn. The soprano lead, Irma González, is one of those fabulous singers who should have had a first-rate international career but, for reasons incomprehensible to me, never did. Her fine work has been almost wholly limited to Latin America. A month later I sang *Faust* at the Met – my first performances with Renata Scotto, a singer who has achieved the success she deserves. Her voice and dramatic involvement were outstanding and unforgettable.

In order to make a quick trip to Milan that autumn for two special performances of the Verdi Requiem with Abbado at La Scala, I had to ask the Met to release me from two performances of *Don Carlo*. I went to see

75

Mr Bing, who phoned Richard Tucker to request his co-operation. The telephone in Bing's office had a microphone and speaker rather than a receiver, so he could talk and listen without having to hold the apparatus. Anyone in the office could hear both parts of the conversation.

'Hello, Richard,' said Bing.

'Hello, Mr Bing.'

'Just be careful what you say now, because one of your competitors is in my office.'

'I have none,' said Tucker. But he kindly agreed to sing the performances in my place.

In mid October 1971 I gave two semi-staged performances of *Aida* in San Juan, Puerto Rico, inaugurating the island's new opera company. Alfredo Matilla, a close friend of my parents from their touring days – so close that I knew him as Uncle Alfredo – was responsible for the initiative, and I had put him in touch with various artists and helped as best I could. The first production, which was conducted by Guadagno, had a cast that included Gabriella Tucci, Grace Bumbry and Pablo Elvira. I later sang *Tosca, Carmen* and the Verdi Requiem under Alfredo's aegis in San Juan.

During that trip I met for the first time Pablo Casals and his lovely wife, Martita, who is now married to pianist Eugene Istomin. Casals was nearly ninety-five then and physically frail; but his mind was incredibly clear, and he was full of life. I remember that he was studying a score of Mendelssohn's *A Midsummer Night's Dream* the day we went to see him. It is quite a lesson to see someone studying at the age of ninety-five. One of the stories he told was about the local genus of cricket, called *coquí*. The chirping sound it makes has the musical interval of a seventh, which is the unresolved interval just short of an octave. 'In all the years I have been living here,' said Casals, 'I have been trying to find a *coquí* that can sing an octave, but I haven't had any luck so far.'

Then he said to me, 'Once, in Barcelona, when I was a boy, I was playing the cello in the opera orchestra at a performance of *Carmen*. A double-bass player was talking to me during an intermission.

' "Pau," he said, "which part of *Carmen* do you think is the most beautiful?" I thought for a moment and told him that to me the most beautiful part was the Prelude to the third act.

' "No," he said, "that is not the most beautiful part."

' "Well," I replied, "perhaps the Flower Song?"

' "No, not that either. The most beautiful part of *Carmen* is when the tenor sings, 'Vous pouvez m'arrêter. C'est moi qui l'ai tuée.' " '

76

' "It's true, that's very beautiful," I admitted.

' "Listen to me, Pau. That is *beautiful*, because when I hear that, I know that I will be going home in a few minutes."

'Do you know,' said Casals, 'after more than eighty years, I cannot forgive that man for what he said that evening.'

My Covent Garden debut, which finally took place on 8 December 1971, had been so long in coming because of my commitments elsewhere and because I had not auditioned there until 1970. Although my relations with the Royal Opera have been wonderful, the circumstances of my debut could hardly have been less auspicious. The opera was *Tosca*, and the night before the opening Marie Collier, an excellent dramatic soprano with whom I had sung the work in Hamburg, died after falling from the window of a building near Leicester Square. (By a strange coincidence, Marta and I went to a movie at a Leicester Square cinema that evening and passed next to Marie's building just moments before her tragic fall.) Gwyneth Jones, my leading lady in the Covent Garden performances, was even wearing Marie's costume from the same production.

The show must indeed go on, but there are times when one wonders why. Somehow we pulled ourselves together and even gave a good performance. I had been warned not to expect a vociferous welcome from a London audience, but that was not the case at all. The 'Recondita armonia' received such an ovation that Edward Downes had to hold up the orchestra's next attack. I am not saying this boastfully, because on some other occasions the public has not applauded me in that aria, even when I have sung it better than I did that evening. But they wanted to welcome me warmly, and I was very appreciative.

IV
THE BIG FOUR

With my Covent Garden debut behind me, I had finally sung in all of the 'Big Four' lyric theatres. I do not wish to offend any of the other great houses – the Paris Opéra, the Hamburg Opera, the Colón in Buenos Aires, the Munich Staatsoper, etc. – where I regularly have the opportunity of performing; but to me La Scala, the Vienna Staatsoper, the Metropolitan and the Royal Opera, Covent Garden, form the collective epicentre of the operatic world today. Any critical comments I may make about them in the following pages should be understood in that context.

Of these four giants, the one with the *potential* for consistently producing the best results is the Staatsoper. The theatre is a perfect size; its organization and its rehearsal facilities are more than adequate; and public support – of the institution itself, if not of everything that goes on in it – is virtually unquestioning. Between Vienna and the summer Salzburg Festival, which makes use of the transplanted Staatsoper ensemble, I have participated in five new productions – *Aida*, *Don Carlo*, *Carmen*, *Hoffmann* and *Chénier* – and have always met with enthusiasm and diligence on the part of all concerned. Everyone has worked efficiently and with great love, or at least with a great sense of responsibility.

But ... the State Opera, which until 1918 was the Hofoper, or Court Opera, has long been a breeding-ground for intrigues and cabals worthy of the Habsburg court to which it once belonged. It is common knowledge that Mahler in his day, Böhm and Karajan in theirs, and many others have all found themselves caught up in controversies that were not usually of their own making. Austria is the country in which opera personalities are talked about in the way that sports figures are discussed elsewhere, and the Viennese public is easily the most dedicated in the world. The pressure on a Staatsoper director is, therefore, enormous, and that explains why, in the sixteen years since I made my debut there, I have already sung under five different administrations. Compare that to Covent Garden, for instance, where the administration has remained the same since before my 1971 debut.

Let us look at the situation. The Staatsoper is located in one of the most gorgeous opera houses in the world and, as a result of a huge state subsidy and a consistently full house, has one of the biggest opera budgets in the world at its disposal. The Viennese usually manage to obtain most of the tickets to new productions or special performances, while the tourists fill the theatre at routine ones. Storage and mounting facilities are so wonderful that the company could, in theory, give a different opera or ballet every evening for two months without having to repeat a work – and there are seven performances a week. The Staatsoper orchestra is the finest opera orchestra in the world – the Scala orchestra under an outstanding conductor can perhaps compare with the Vienna orchestra in the Verdi repertoire, but I must stress the word 'perhaps'. Efficiency and productivity are both quantitatively high. The company performs from 1 September to 30 June each season; the orchestra and chorus then have a three-week holiday, after which they reassemble in Salzburg to begin rehearsing for the Festival, which opens on 26 July. The ensemble returns to Vienna on 31 August and the regular season begins the next day. Of course not everyone works every day. There is, for instance, a double orchestra, and this permits all players to have days off regularly. When there is a tour, only a part of the company goes on the road, while the rest keeps the ensemble functioning at home.

All of this sounds marvellous. But the Staatsoper's day-to-day programming is based on an artistically dangerous system, and thus the house does not attract the best-known singers for large blocks of each season. At the heart of the matter lie a lack of proper planning and an excess of odd internal machinations. For instance, after the success of a wonderful *Aida* production conducted by Riccardo Muti in 1973, a decision was made to mount a new *Otello* during the 1975-6 season – not long after my Hamburg debut in the title role – again with Muti, and with Sir Laurence Olivier directing. That would have been a once-in-a-lifetime experience for me! But when Olivier decided against undertaking the direction, Muti and Rudolf Gamsjaeger, who was then head of the Staatsoper, made up their minds to drop the whole *Otello* project. In my opinion the real reason for this was and continues to be a reluctance on the administration's part to touch the existing but very old Karajan production. I performed in it as

79

late as 1982, and I have now decided to sing my next *Otello* in Vienna only when a new production is mounted. The production may originally have been powerful, but it is worn and outdated. The cancellation of the new *Otello* project was merely a personal disappointment for me, but I am sure that other singers have from time to time found themselves in similar situations. These conditions can easily complicate our relationships with a theatre, and, indeed, three or four seasons went by when I did not sing much at the Staatsoper. After Egon Seefehlner became director of the house, I took part in two fine new productions, *Carmen* and *Chénier*, and it was also in his day that I made my Staatsoper conducting debut.

Another problem at the Staatsoper has been the almost impossible rehearsal system. The administration has counted on singers arriving the night before or even on the day of a performance, and winter weather can sometimes upset well-made plans. But whatever the meteorological conditions, there is often little or no proper rehearsal time. Even the great Staatsoper orchestra does not always have the conductors that it and the rest of us deserve, again as a result of complicated organizational problems. Lorin Maazel, the new director, is trying to change the system. I believe that he intends to institute conditions whereby a work being presented for the first time in a given season will receive a reasonable number of production rehearsals and a dress rehearsal, followed by a group of performances, rather than just one or two, with the same cast and conductor. If this works, singers will no longer be arriving at the last minute, throwing on costumes and simply hoping for the best. The Staatsoper has a tradition of getting rid of directors with clear, logical ideas of this sort. Perhaps Maazel will succeed where others have failed.

At the Metropolitan Opera I have already worked under four different administrations. The atmosphere of the executive offices in Rudolf Bing's time was cool and distant; I find a friendlier relationship more productive. Despite the autocratic methods of Bing and his 'cabinet', I personally had no problems with him and enjoyed our encounters. He could be very amusing. When I signed my Metropolitan contract, the photographer asked me to sit at Bing's desk. 'Just a moment,' said Bing. 'Mr Domingo is not *yet* general manager of the Metropolitan Opera.' Thinking of Edward Johnson, a singer who had managed the Met for many years, I replied, 'I would not be the first tenor-manager in the house's history!' Many good things happened during Bing's reign, but he stayed too long. Had he left a few years earlier, he would have attracted far less criticism to his regime. He was justly taken to task for not wanting to appoint a musical director, for modern operatic life requires one.

The designation of Swedish opera director Goeran Gentele as Bing's successor came as a surprise because he was so little known in America. As he began to familiarize himself with the Met, it became clear that a real revolution was about to take place. Bing had always dressed and acted formally, but Gentele came to the theatre in a pullover and got to know the stage crew and all the other personnel. His open, easy manner pointed towards a total change in attitude and atmosphere in the Met's upper echelons. When he nominated Rafael Kubelik as musical director, there was some apprehension; many thought that – though an outstanding musician – he did not have the characteristics required for looking after the problems of so monstrously large a house. In any case, we were all waiting anxiously, I think with largely positive feelings, to see what Gentele's direction would bring. Then, just a few weeks before he was to open his first season in 1972, came the tragic car accident in which he and his two daughters were killed.

Schuyler Chapin was named acting director of the company, to be assisted by Kubelik. But since Kubelik was not around a great deal, most decisions were made by Chapin along with Charles Riecker, son-in-law of Fausto Cleva, and Richard Rodzinski, son of Artur Rodzinski. Under the circumstances, which were confusing to say the least, they managed to keep the Met functioning.

In appointing Anthony Bliss as general manager, Jimmy Levine as music director and John Dexter as director of productions, the Met adopted a highly original and productive administrative system. Although the results of the last (1980) orchestra strike were widely criticized at the time, the outcome has been positive from an artistic point of view. No orchestra member has to play more than four performances a week, which means that the musicians are fresher and consequently play better. The chorus and orchestra are both improving rapidly, and at my concert with Sherrill Milnes and performances of *Don Carlo* in 1983 I found them equal to any other opera orchestra in the world. There may still be a residue of bad feeling between the management and the company, but I hope it will soon be entirely forgotten. My personal loss at the time was a new *Queen of Spades* production, which had to be cancelled. I look forward to adding the role of Ghermann to my repertoire.

Some observers say that in Bing's day to sing at the Met was an achievement and an honour, while today even singers who have not reached the top of their profession appear at the Met. There is truth in that statement, but I do not believe that the responsibility can be laid at the feet of the company's administration. The singers who are now most in demand travel even more than their counterparts of fifteen or twenty years ago, leaving gaps that have to be filled by less acclaimed artists. I am sure that Corelli and Tucker each gave the Met at least thirty or thirty-five performances a year – perhaps even forty, counting the annual tour. In 1981-2 and 1982-3, my busiest Met seasons so far, I sang nineteen and sixteen performances, respectively, and I am scheduled to sing a similar number in subsequent seasons. I had previously been singing only about twelve Metropolitan performances annually, and that has been a standard number for other singers, too. More and more theatres around the world are producing increasingly interesting seasons. And although this may sound strange to a New Yorker, many singers are not keen on spending a great deal of time in New York. For most European singers, it is not the most desirable place in the world to live in; they prefer to spend as much time in Europe as possible because their homes and hearts are there. I am readily giving more time to the Met, but there are still many cities and countries where I have not yet sung and would like to sing: Australia, Belgium, Scandinavia, and especially Italian cities such as Parma, Bari, Trieste, Catania, Palermo, Bologna and Genoa. The years pass quickly, and I would like to perform in all of these places – and many others – while I am still in my prime. Jimmy Levine therefore showed great acumen in engaging Joan Ingpen as assistant manager. She is a wonderful collaborator, responsible for organizing much of the Met's casting. Joan is so good at arm-twisting that she manages to convince many of us to give more time to the Met than we in fact wish to give. Some of us are having increasing difficulty in finding sufficient dates for engagements elsewhere, even in other major theatres – but that is Joan's job, and she does it extremely well.

The New York public seems to become more discerning as time goes by, and there are not as many subscribers as in the past who go to the Met only to be seen or to be able to say that they have been there. It is easy to say that the Metropolitan public is cold, but New York audiences have some particularly difficult logistic problems that influence their behaviour. An opera-goer in Vienna, for example, attends a performance that begins at 7 o'clock and ends, usually, at 10.30 or 11. Most people can be home quite easily within half an hour of the end of the performance. Opera-goers in New York attend a performance that begins at 8 and ends at 11.30 or midnight. They may then have to face a forty-five-minute subway ride –

which can be more hair-raising than the adventures encountered by Manrico, Siegfried and Florestan combined – or a half-hour trying to get out of Lincoln Center's underground garage followed by an hour-long drive to Connecticut. No wonder some people leave before the last act, or rush to the door at the end without applauding the artists! At the Saturday matinées, when the public is not in a hurry, the stagehands are eager to turn up the lights, end the applause and clear the stage area in order to mount the evening's opera. Yet despite these handicaps, the Met's audiences are becoming more enthusiastic and more discriminating every day.

Scheduling is carried out with great precision at the Met. This is generally to the good, but it does create a tendency to over-bureaucratize: a staging rehearsal may have to be cut off at a precise moment even if another five minutes would allow the director to finish a scene. I understand and sympathize with the exigencies of unions and their regulations, but in any artistic undertaking there must be some elasticity if the results are not to become mechanical. This danger exists in the German-speaking houses as well, and sometimes to an even greater degree. All in all, however, the atmosphere at the Met today is as good as anywhere in the world, and I find nearly as much openness and cordiality there as at Covent Garden.

Milan's Teatro alla Scala is a microcosm of Italian life. Maddening bureaucratic inanities are offset by brilliant achievements, chaotic scheduling is compensated for by the wonder and beauty of the place itself, bizarre internecine political strife alternates with warm and sincere camaraderie.

When I first sang at La Scala, Antonio Ghiringhelli was still its *sovrintendente* (general manager), as he had been since the end of the Second World War. Toscanini, De Sabata, Serafin, Callas, Tebaldi, Di Stefano, Del Monaco and many other now legendary figures had performed at the theatre under his administration. The artistic director in the late 1960s was Luciano Chailly, father of conductor Riccardo Chailly. Ghiringhelli was succeeded by Paolo Grassi in 1972 and by Carlo Maria Badini in 1977, while Chailly was followed by Massimo Bogianckino, Claudio Abbado and Francesco Siciliani. (Early in 1983, Cesare Mazzonis was appointed to replace Siciliani.) Siciliani was a dreamer: sitting with you at a desk, he could draw up the most fantastic casts imaginable; but if one of the components was unavailable, the idea of the whole production would be dropped.

Such behaviour is typical of the Scala mentality in general: everything or nothing. Not that La Scala, like every other house in the world, does not come up with a bad production once in a while ... but the fundamental idealism exists, and to a degree that would be considered insane elsewhere. Would the Scala administration think of turning over the *Otello* production conducted by Carlos Kleiber or Abbado's *Simon Boccanegra* to other conductors of international repute? I doubt it. Those productions carry the stamp of their original conductors, and putting them in other hands would seem a sort of betrayal. When the *Scaligeri* have a superb product on their hands, they try to preserve it intact. The artistic directors of La Scala are also very careful about matching conductors and stage directors. They would rather not do an opera at all than have it put in the hands of two people with conflicting ideas. Of course differences will sometimes develop as work proceeds; but the principle is a good one and explains in part the high rate of success in Milan.

Of all the major theatres, La Scala is the one where rehearsal schedules are most confused. Sometimes we rehearse from 11 a.m. to 1.30 p.m., then again from 3 to 6 and again from 9 until midnight. The German theatres' sacrosanct 1-to-5 o'clock break and the Met's rule preventing rehearsals after 6 p.m. are inconceivable in Milan. You may be told that you have a rehearsal at noon, and when you arrive at the theatre an assistant manager says, 'Sorry, it's been cancelled.' The confusion is not just attributable to lack of discipline – although that element exists, too – but is also a result of inadequate rehearsal facilities. Non-Latin singers often find the working conditions at La Scala impossible, yet it is undeniable that the endemic confusion allows for a flexibility that does not exist in any of the other top opera houses and that that flexibility in turn permits the artists involved – singers, conductors, directors – to use their imaginations, to experiment with a freedom they cannot find elsewhere. They may be in a state of exhaustion by the time the dress rehearsal rolls around, but the results sometimes have that extra measure of inspired refinement that carries them beyond the realm of first-rate professionalism into an even more exclusive category.

Many singers find the backstage noise level at La Scala very disconcerting. I, too, am somewhat disturbed by it when I am waiting to make an entrance. It is quite an experience to stand in the wings at La Scala before I go out to sing my 'Esultate!' in the first act of *Otello*. There seem to be thousands of choristers and extras rushing by or just milling about, many of them chatting with each other on any number of topics. The assistant stage directors shout at each other and at the crew, and the coaches and musical assistants give orders and counter-orders to stave off a variety of impending disasters. While I try to put myself into the proper frame of mind for declaring the Venetian republic's great victory, people smile and greet me with a 'Ciao, Plácido', as if I were about to walk to the corner for an ice-cream. Once I am out on stage, the surrounding commotion does not bother me, but I sympathize with singers who are affected by it.

The Scala chorus and orchestra – the pillars of the organization – are so good that they are able to have very powerful unions without arousing much protest on the part of the administration. Tired, apparently, of esoteric stagings that had its members virtually hanging from the chandeliers, the chorus's union obtained an agreement whereby the conductor would always have to be in the line of vision of every chorister. I remember a rehearsal of the triumphal scene from *Aida* some years ago that ended after seven minutes because three members of that huge chorus could not see Claudio Abbado from where they were standing. In any other theatre, either the difficulty would have been adjusted immediately or the three people concerned would have been told to go off and relax until there was a break in the rehearsal, when the problem could be resolved. But at La Scala, three hours of rehearsal time were lost because three members of the chorus could not see clearly. Another case: one chorus member complains that the costumes are too heavy and too hot. At the next rehearsal everyone protests by showing up in street clothes. 'All right,' says the stage manager, 'we'll run the rehearsal without costumes.'

'No,' says another chorister, 'we can't have a rehearsal that is supposed to be done in costume out of costume.'

'So put on the costumes and we'll fix them later.'

'No, we'll be too hot.' In this as in everything else, individualism is carried nearly to the point of anarchy.

Although the Scala public, or at least a certain part of it, gives Milan the reputation of being a singer's town, the newspaper critics make it a conductor's town. After a new production there may be a review that goes on forever about the ethos and melos of the work, then about the conductor's interpretation of the ethos and melos, then about the visual aspects of the production. Finally there is a paragraph about the singers: 'So-and-so was excellent, while so-and-so was miscast as such-and-such.' If a detailed review of a production is necessary, why not give all of the elements equally serious attention?

There is no doubt that London's Royal Opera is one of the friendliest houses in the world. Everyone there, from the maintenance staff and telephone operators to the top of the administration, does everything to make life as easy as possible for the performers. Their courtesy and help-fulness is amazing – and greatly appreciated. The Met, too, is a friendly house, but it is so immense that I still do not know half the people who work there. Covent Garden is small enough to maintain an almost domestic atmosphere.

By the time I made my first appearance at Covent Garden I had already sung at most of the other major theatres, and my surprise was therefore all the greater when I saw my dressing-room, with its exposed pipes and old furnishings. In 1982 the facilities were renovated and expanded, in accord-ance with the exigencies of a modern opera company. The new dressing-rooms, though by no means luxurious, are a great improvement. Much more important is the big new rehearsal room, which eliminates the ne-cessity of going to the old and distant Opera Centre, where so many rehearsals used to be held. The chorus, too, now has a proper rehearsal hall; the administrative offices are more functional; and renovations are continuing.

A year before my Covent Garden debut in 1971, the administration had passed from Sir David Webster into the hands of Sir John Tooley, a man who cares not only about the welfare of his theatre but also about that of his artists. He knows his business perfectly, gives his attention to all aspects of the running of the house, and even tries to be present at all performances – or if he cannot be there, he lets the performers know beforehand and explains why. No director of any other theatre has seen as many of my performances.

A few years ago I had a case of tracheitis that troubled me for three or four months. Although I continued to sing, I had some vocal problems as a result and even had to cancel some performances in Vienna and New York. I was still not feeling well when my scheduled performances of *Rigoletto* at Covent Garden were approaching, and I explained the situation to Sir John. He could not have been more understanding. Any other theatre manager would have recited a tragedy, trying to make me feel guilty by insisting that if I did not sing, disaster would overtake the whole production. Sir John did not even tell me to wait and see what would happen. He knew that I had never before cancelled a Covent Garden performance and that I must have had a serious reason for asking to do so. He released me from my contract without causing any difficulty. Sir John is intelligent enough to think of his singers' welfare, of their long-term relationships with his theatre, and not merely of tomorrow evening's performance. People may feel disappointed when a performer does not sing as scheduled, but no one is really indispensable. A masterpiece remains a masterpiece whether or not Mr X or Miss Y sings in it, and singers who delude themselves into thinking that certain works are their exclusive property obviously do not place much value on the music they perform.

London opera-goers do not always applaud individual arias, because they do not want to interrupt the flow of the music and the action; but they show their approval with great intensity at the end of an act or of a whole opera. The only opera in my repertoire that I would not like to sing at Covent Garden is *Il trovatore*. In most houses, if the romanza 'Ah sì, ben mio' has gone well, I can count on at least a couple of minutes of applause in which to catch my breath before attacking the short scene that ends with the killer cabaletta 'Di quella pira'. At the Royal Opera, I would not be able to count on that respite – unless, of course, I made an announcement beforehand: 'Feel free to applaud at the end of my romanza, ladies and gentlemen!'

V

OPERA HOUSES
AND AIRPORTS (1972-5)

The first half of 1972 was one of the busiest periods in my entire career. In three weeks in January, for instance, I sang single performances of five different operas, each in a city in which I had never sung before: *Lucia* in Piacenza, *Ernani* in Amsterdam, *Bohème* in Munich (I had given a concert there, but had never appeared in an opera), *Ballo* in Mantua, and *Tosca* in Turin. Less than three weeks later, I made my Yugoslavian debut with a *Tosca* in Belgrade. Meanwhile, apart from my regular engagements, I participated with Martina Arroyo in a benefit concert at the Kennedy Center in Washington and in special performances of *Aida* at La Scala to mark the one hundredth anniversary of that work's Italian première at the same theatre. In April the Met honoured Rudolf Bing with a farewell gala at which Caballé and I sang the duet from *Manon Lescaut*. Corelli, Pavarotti, Price, Siepi, Sutherland, Nilsson, Vickers, Rysanek, Tucker and many other singers also participated.

A dangerous accident occurred in Hamburg late in June, before a double-bill of *Cavalleria* and *Pagliacci*. When I got to the theatre, the make-up man had not yet arrived, and since it was a beautiful June day, I walked outside in my slippers to watch the stage crew playing soccer in the street. I could not resist joining them. I gave the ball a good kick, my left foot slipped, and I fell flat on my back. That was the second time in my life when I thought I was dying (the first was the near-drowning in Tel Aviv). I could neither breathe nor talk – I could only make faces. Everyone thought I was joking until I finally made myself say 'doctor'. An ambulance arrived quickly and, accompanied by Marianne and Gerard Semon, I was taken to the emergency room. There were all sorts of accident victims and other horrible sights everywhere, and the whole episode seemed a nightmare. I began to recover my strength enough to worry about the performance, and

I told the hospital authorities that I had to get back to the theatre. They insisted that X-rays had to be taken and other tests made, but I insisted even more vehemently that I had to leave. Finally, they made me sign a piece of paper stating that I was leaving on my own responsibility and of my own free will. I returned to the theatre and sang both operas, absolutely motionless. Fortunately, I managed to reach Marta in Barcelona before anyone else had phoned to tell her what had happened. I rested in bed and was able to sing *Carmen* three nights later.

My Argentinian debut took place in 1972. In July I went to Buenos Aires to sing *La forza del destino* with Martina Arroyo, Gianpiero Mastromei, Bonaldo Giaiotti and Renato Cesari. Fernando Previtali conducted. Buenos Aires is an exceptionally beautiful city – distinctly French in character, even though the majority of the population is of Spanish or Italian descent. The Teatro Colón is one of the loveliest and most acoustically outstanding of all opera houses, and its chorus and orchestra are correspondingly fine. It is one of the few theatres in the world that have maintained the grand nineteenth-century traditions in all their components. If a singer requires a new wig or different boots, the props department will have them ready in twenty-four hours – and they will be of high quality. And audiences everywhere else in the world are all dwarfed by the mad enthusiasm of the Argentinians. As at La Scala, the public is knowledgeable as well as warm, making an enthusiastic reception all the more gratifying. We performers feel that it is genuine. After a wonderful time in Buenos Aires I had a rather unpleasant experience in Mexico City. New people had assumed the direction of the music department of the Bellas Artes theatre. They had odd ideas about opera and spent quite a bit of money on a production of *Carmen* that was a disaster. The sets and costumes were absurd and at the same time terribly expensive, and the staging was ridiculous. It was not simply a strange, avant-garde production: it was anti-operatic. Mexico is the country where I grew up, and it would be both painful and wrong of me to name names or to go into great detail. Suffice it to say that the whole project was misconceived. So big and so shameful was the mess that I did not return there to sing for nine years.

I went to Munich with the entire Scala ensemble for guest performances at the time of the ill-fated 1972 Olympic Games. We took *Aida* and the Verdi Requiem, and we were in the Olympic Village when the Israeli athletes were massacred. It was a terrible time; everyone was tense and upset. A colleague was to have sung one performance of the Requiem and I the other Requiem and the two *Aidas*; but he became ill, and I did all four

89

performances from 4 to 8 September. Then, on the 9th, I flew to London and recorded 'Meco all' altar di Venere' from *Norma*! Those are things that one can only do when one is young. Experience is not only of no assistance, it is a drawback.

Late in the year I returned to Milan to sing at another Scala opening night, this time in *Ballo*. Abbado, who was to have conducted, had cancelled, and the veteran Gianandrea Gavazzeni took his place. Franco Zeffirelli directed the production. He kept telling me to lose weight because I was too heavy for my role, but when we got our costumes, they were in a style that made all of us look twice whatever our normal sizes may have been. Nevertheless, the production was a powerful one. A brilliant detail stands out in my mind. The stage was steeply raked in the second act, and in the Amelia-Riccardo duet Franco had the two lovers sitting at the top of the 'hill', like two helpless children, holding each other desperately in their arms. The duet is usually staged very conventionally – now I move to the left, now she moves to the right, she goes there, I go here – and whatever happens almost invariably detracts from the glorious music. Zeffirelli staged it simply and movingly. At the climactic moment of that duet, during an ensemble rehearsal, I sang my lines 'Amelia! tu m'ami?' ('Amelia! Do you love me?'); she sang her 'Sì'; and then came the fortissimo outburst – the two of us with full orchestra. Several people went up to Gavazzeni and said, 'Maestro, we can't hear the singers at all. The orchestra is too loud.'

'It doesn't matter!' he shouted. 'That's the way Verdi wanted it! This is the most sublime moment in opera, more passionate than *Tristan und Isolde*!' – and so on. I decided that since I was not going to be heard anyway, I would just mouth the words.

The soprano was an American, Lou Ann Wyckoff; Viorica Cortez was Ulrica; and Renato was sung by Piero Cappuccilli. Wyckoff sang well but was a victim of factionalism among the various Scala cliques and claques. She was poorly treated by some of them, and I was so upset by their antics that I refused to leave the theatre by the stage door afterwards, thus avoiding the autograph seekers. One day a few fans came to me and said, 'Domingo, why are you treating us so badly?'

'I am not treating you badly,' I told them. 'I am trying to make the point that if you go on behaving as you are, no singer will want to perform at La Scala. How can we concentrate on stage when we have to face that kind of hooliganism?'

At one performance, people in the gallery started to make some rude remarks. Gavazzeni stopped the proceedings and began to say, in his courtly way, 'Ladies and gentlemen, you are truly impolite because ...'

'Come off it, Gavazzeni!' came a voice from the gallery. 'Stop playing the intellectual and conduct!' As usual, these remarks were unjust. Few conductors are as familiar with the Italian repertoire as is Gavazzeni. He is a brilliant man who knows everything about the music he conducts and who has devoted a lifetime of study and thought to his work. But La Scala would not be La Scala without an occasional circus side-show.

I have fond memories of three performances of *Ballo* with Caballé in Barcelona early in 1973. Her voice was in full bloom and her style outstanding. The public at the Liceo was wild with enthusiasm, not least because two of the leading roles were being sung by Spaniards. It is no exaggeration to say that those performances, along with some *Aidas* that Montserrat and I later sang there, remain among the highlights of the Liceo's recent history.

Late in January I had my first opportunity to work with Riccardo Muti, during rehearsals for a new production of *Aida* in Vienna, with Gwyneth Jones in the title role. A piano rehearsal with Riccardo is an amazing experience, because his dramatic sense is remarkable, and he has the ability to make the singers feel the precise 'weight' of the orchestra at every moment. I especially remember the way he worked with Viorica Cortez (Amneris) on the opening of the fourth act. His explanation of her indecision ('Oh! if he could love me! ... I would like to save him.... But how? ... I shall try! ... Guards: bring Radames here') took in all the emotional factors, the timing, the changes in orchestration – and all of this was audible in his playing.

Muti is a natural conductor and a polished musician. He communicates very little verbally with an orchestra, but his gestures are extremely clear and unmistakable, and his ear for orchestral balance is wonderful. One of Riccardo's preoccupations has been to try to cleanse the Italian operatic world of what he believes to be some of its less valid practices. He concerns himself, for example, with eliminating traditionally interpolated high notes and reinstating cabalettas that are customarily cut. Yet Verdi himself often allowed interpolations and cuts, and there is no easy way of separating tolerable and sometimes even beneficial traditions from illegitimate butchery. Muti defends his opinion by pointing out that Verdi lived for half a century after having written *Rigoletto*, *Il trovatore* and *La traviata*, and that had he really been keen on the changes that were already becoming traditional in his day, he could easily have sent an approving note to Ricordi, his publisher, with whom he had frequent correspondence. I do not agree with

Riccardo one hundred per cent on this point, but I do agree with him in principle. Take the tenor part in *Trovatore*: everyone waits to hear Manrico's high C at the end of 'Di quella pira', and for many that high C is the climax of the whole evening. Tenors sweat blood over it, develop ulcers because of it. Yet the note was not written by Verdi. Verdi wrote a G – a perfect fourth lower – a note that any tenor in any glee club is expected to be able to sing. Manrico is not a high role: the highest note written by Verdi is an A, not even a B-flat. Sometimes productions of *Trovatore* are avoided altogether simply because a 'high-C tenor' cannot be found. One unwritten note has turned a middle-range part into one of the most difficult roles in the repertoire. Likewise, if a tenor tries to sing 'La donna è mobile' without the B-naturals – which Verdi did not write – woe unto him! Clearly an absurd state of affairs.

Audiences must learn to listen for the musical and dramatic qualities in an entire performance rather than for the gladiatorially effective moments. Those singers who have the ability to perform permissible interpolations easily and with good taste ought to be allowed to do them. I agree that they are exciting, but they must not become the raison d'être of an entire operatic performance.

At the time of my Viennese appearances with Muti, I made a side-trip to Budapest, where I sang *Tosca*. The city has two opera houses. One, built in the last century, resembles the Vienna Staatsoper; the other dates from the early twentieth century. The older theatre is extraordinarily beautiful, filled with fanciful architectural ornamentation in every nook and cranny. Unfortunately, it seats only 1,500, and I had to perform in the other house, which has a capacity of 2,500. It does not have as wonderful an atmosphere as the older place, but I enjoyed singing there all the same. The audience was so enthusiastic that I had to repeat 'E lucevan le stelle'. (The same happened to me twice – and with the same piece – in Vienna, where I was the first singer in the twenty-year history of the new Staatsoper to have to *bis* an aria.) I have not had an opportunity to return to Hungary since then, but I would like to be able to sing there again.

In May 1973 I at last made my debut at the Opéra in Paris, singing *Il trovatore*. My colleagues that evening included Gwyneth Jones, Mignon Dunn and Piero Cappuccilli; Julius Rudel conducted, and the production (not a new one) was by Tito Capobianco. I had heard over the years about the disorganization of the Opéra, but by the time I got there Rolf Liebermann had left Hamburg to take over in Paris on his own terms, so I never witnessed the legendary chaos. Liebermann had seen to the complete revitalization of the chorus, orchestra and staff, had engaged Solti as music director, and had galvanized the whole company. I was very happy with my first performances there and have sung frequently in Paris ever since. Because of my work there and my attention to the French operatic literature, I have been awarded the Médaille de la Ville de Paris and created a Chevalier des arts et des lettres. I am equally proud of having been made a *Kammersänger* in Hamburg, Munich and Vienna, especially since singers are usually so honoured only late in their careers.

During the same period Shirley Verrett and I took part in a memorable concert performance of *Samson et Dalila* at London's Royal Festival Hall. Georges Prêtre conducted, and this is certainly one of the works he does best. His use of rubato, sometimes excessive in Verdi, functions wonderfully in *Samson* and always to the advantage of the work itself. Rehearsals then got under way at Covent Garden for a new production of *Carmen*, which opened on 4 July with Shirley in the title role, Kiri Te Kanawa as Micaela, and José van Dam as Escamillo. Solti conducted and Michael Geliot was the producer. The opening night, a gala performance, was attended by the Queen Mother. For my taste, although the musical experience was satisfying, there was too much dialogue in that production. Of the four principal singers, only van Dam spoke French naturally, while the rest of us had to make a tremendous effort. Why have a New Zealander, an American, a Spaniard and a Belgian speaking French to a British audience?

I cannot make an either/or decision about performing *Carmen* with dialogue between the musical numbers, as Bizet conceived it, or with the sung recitatives that were substituted by the composer Ernest Guiraud and have become traditional during the past century. If the dialogue is used, it should certainly be cut. Besides, some of Guiraud's recitatives are not bad at all. In my own part, the 'Quels regards! quelle effronterie!' and 'Ne crains rien, ma mère' in the first act are stronger than Bizet's own recitatives in *The Pearl Fishers*. On the other hand, some of Guiraud's work is undeniably second-rate and falls flat next to Bizet's fresh and inventive music. Given a choice, I would keep the recitatives that are of high quality and replace the others with carefully selected dialogue.

I have also recorded *Carmen* and *Bohème* with Sir Georg Solti and I have performed *Otello* under his direction in Paris. I enjoyed the *Otello*, and have come to appreciate the *Bohème* recording much more in recent years than when it was made. (Caballé was the Mimi and my Placi sang the boy's part in the second act.) Sir Georg has invited me to perform *Tristan* with him, but I have decided to postpone that project. I do not feel that I am ready for the role. Solti is a very intelligent and serious musician who does not like to tamper with the scores he conducts. Where composers' metronome indications exist, he tries to follow them; and he will only go against printed instructions after much soul-searching and if he can see no other way. In this he is absolutely right.

While in New York to sing *Il trovatore* and *La traviata* at the Met that autumn, I made my debut as an opera conductor across Lincoln Center Plaza with the New York City Opera. The work was *La traviata*; Patricia Brooks was Violetta, and Dominic Cossa was Germont – the same people with whom I had sung the opera a few years earlier. The Alfredo was Roger Patterson. It was a big event for me, and I was pleased that it went well. A middle-period Verdi opera like *Traviata* is more difficult to conduct, from a purely technical point of view, than a later one. *Aida*, *Otello* and *Falstaff* are written essentially in long segments, each within one basic tempo, while *Rigoletto*, *Trovatore* and *Traviata* are made up of smaller units, each having its own tempo. The conductor must always be aware of making those tempi relate to each other and must concentrate on bringing off each change properly.

Strangely enough, there are still people connected with the operatic world who believe that the conductor makes little difference. It may well be true that conductors who know only how to keep things together have little influence on the proceedings, but a very fine or a very bad conductor makes all the difference in the world to a performance and to a production.

My own interest in conducting and my feeling for the orchestra were awakened by Maestro Muguerza, who conducted exciting zarzuela performances with my parents' company. When, for economic reasons, the orchestra's size had to be reduced considerably, I found the sound disappointing; but as a result I had the opportunity of filling in the missing parts on the piano. Once, when the conductor was not feeling well, I rehearsed the orchestra. By then I had observed Igor Markevitch's classes at the Conservatory and I was thrilled to be able to take the baton in hand. The idea of some day becoming a conductor took hold of me.

Other musical jobs and experiences in my early years were even more important to my interest in conducting: Pepe Esteva's 'Musical Mondays' were particularly valuable, and so were the read-throughs of Beethoven's piano trios that I used to do with two friends – brothers who played the violin and cello. Playing chamber music gave me a feeling for knowing when to lead and when to follow, the sort of give-and-take that is necessary in any kind of group music-making.

94

My parents eventually allowed me to conduct two zarzuelas, *Luisa Fernanda* and *La Chulapona*, and I also led a small ensemble in excerpts from *The Merry Widow* and other operettas my mother was performing. Other opportunities, such as conducting a small ballet orchestra and rehearsing the chorus for my parents' company, occasionally came along. When I was with the National Opera in Mexico, I was sometimes given semi-orchestral jobs like playing the offstage bells in *Tosca*. Once I played the bells when Di Stefano was appearing as Cavaradossi and another time when I myself was singing the lead role. I often seemed to have extra tasks in *Tosca*: at a performance in Toledo, Ohio, in 1966, I even played the organ, since there was no one else around to do so.

I would have liked to do some conducting in Tel Aviv, but I was singing so much and concentrating so hard on improving my vocal technique that anything else would have been distracting. I did, however, often play the piano for the singers who performed arias during the party scene in the second act of *Die Fledermaus*, which was very popular at the Hebrew National Opera.

The first time I conducted an important orchestra was in 1972, when Sherrill Milnes and I made our RCA record, 'Domingo Conducts Milnes! Milnes Conducts Domingo!', with the New Philharmonia Orchestra in London. For me it was a difficult adventure. The conductor has two main tasks: to know exactly what he wants and to know how to get it. Gestures must be clear and unmistakable, and comments should be to the point. Even Carlos Kleiber, who can visualize and verbalize music in a truly remarkable way, never lectures an orchestra. In making the record with Sherrill, the most difficult thing for me was to know what to ask of that excellent orchestra. I was fortunate to have such a fine group to work with, but I was not experienced enough to know how to get my own interpretation from the players. That recording, I now realize, was part of a sales campaign. Since then, Sherrill and I have had many offers to do concerts in which we would conduct for each other, but we have resisted them. My conducting intentions are serious and I do not want to involve myself in stunts. Sherrill, too, has been conducting, especially oratorios like *Elijah*.

Too many of the performances I have conducted so far have been spur-of-the-moment affairs with no rehearsal time. This must change if I am to refine and improve my approach to conducting. My beat is clear but not yet precise enough, as I saw in the videotape of a performance of the *Forza del destino* overture I conducted in Vienna. And because I am still very apprehensive I use too much physical energy – gestures that are too big.

95

But my conducting seems to be improving, and I was pleased when Lorin Maazel recently invited me back to the Vienna Staatsoper to conduct *Die Fledermaus*. He spontaneously assured me that he was only extending the invitation because he and the orchestra felt I was capable of coping with the task, and he added that now that he is responsible for the company, he does not intend to have the orchestra conducted by 'just anyone'.

Apart from practical experience, I have had the advantage of working with and observing the greatest conductors of my day. The test of my abilities will come when I have a chance to conduct on a regular basis. I am now looking forward with great pleasure to conducting *Die Fledermaus* at Covent Garden at the end of 1983 and *La Bohème* at the Met in 1984. Zeffirelli's *Bohème* production, which I have sung in, creates a slight difficulty by positioning the singers quite far from the conductor. In order to stay together, the singers have to anticipate the orchestra, because the sound reaches them with some delay. Although my reading of the work will naturally differ a little here and there from Jimmy Levine's, the music is well established in the orchestra's minds and fingers, and there should be no problem for me in that respect.

The only difference between conducting an opera I have sung and one I have not is that in the latter case I am not so tempted to sing along with everyone, and I am not quite as worried about all of the singers' possible difficulties. If I am lucky enough to work some day on a reasonably regular basis with a fine opera orchestra, I would try above all to refine the players' accompanying abilities. I should like them to listen to the singers, to feel that they are moving along with what is happening on stage. I am fortunate to work most of the time with the best conductors; but when that is not the case, the Maestro's presence sometimes gives the musicians an excuse for not becoming involved in the performance. I would like to eliminate that situation. From time to time, however, I have sung with bad conductors and relied on the orchestra's experience to keep the music flowing. The worst thing for a singer is to have to depend upon a mediocre conductor who leads indecisively. The performance becomes a hellish series of 'après vous', 'non, après vous'. I will want to work with singers in such a way that every phrase is properly prepared in advance, leaving as little as possible to chance. Serious conductors always adopt this method and serious singers always appreciate it.

After I have sung, I enjoy the applause, the public's appreciation; but conducting gives me an entirely different feeling. As a conductor, I honestly would not mind not taking a bow at all after a performance. Perhaps that is because the conductor does not produce the sound and is not as exposed as singers or instrumentalists, while at the same time conducting a whole work is a more fulfilling experience than singing or playing parts of it.

Symphonic music, the highest goal of most conductors, is in my opinion technically easier to conduct than opera. Much as I love symphonic music, however, I think I will feel more at home conducting opera – more in my element coping with the challenge of controlling those half-crazed horses, stage and pit, that sometimes want to pull a performance in two different directions at once. As a conductor I will tend to concentrate on the repertoire that has been closest to me as a singer – Verdi, Puccini and a few others – but I would also like to conduct Wagner, Rossini and Mozart. I would certainly love to do *Don Giovanni* – but then, what conductor would not?

A publicity agent once said to me, 'Look, you're a rare bird – a singer who can conduct. Why don't we film you conducting an orchestra in operatic arias, then project the film in Carnegie Hall while you sing to your own accompaniment?'

'That's a good idea in principle,' I replied, 'but if I make a mess of the concert, I won't be able to blame the conductor!'

I had another conducting engagement – Verdi's *Attila*, at the Teatro Liceo in Barcelona – scheduled for the Christmas 1973 holiday period. Just as I was preparing to return to Spain from New York, the Spanish prime minister, Carrero Blanco, was assassinated. There was terrible tension in the country, but we proceeded with our rehearsals and performances as scheduled. Between 26 December 1973 and 5 January 1974 I conducted *Attila* three times and sang four performances of *Aida*. Caballé was the Aida, and her singing was so gorgeous that I decided to do everything possible to record it with her. Deutsche Grammophon had already invited me to make a recording the following summer; but I wanted Muti as conductor, and he was and is under contract with EMI/Angel. I told EMI that we simply had to record *Aida* with Montserrat and Riccardo. It was arranged, and the results justified my enthusiasm. That, by the way, was Riccardo's first opera recording.

Early in 1974, in Hamburg, a terrible cold caused me to leave a performance of *La forza del destino* after the first act. That was the first of only two occasions on which I have had to walk out of a performance I had already begun. At the time, the incident seemed like the end of the world to me. Like most people who are blessed with good health, I feel angry and

97

somehow guilty on those rare occasions when my system does not behave normally. Nowadays, however, I am more realistic and simply say 'I cannot perform' when indeed I cannot. If I was in any way wrong on that evening in Hamburg, it was in having begun the performance in the first place. I am still amazed to find that when singers have colds, journalists and other well-meaning people immediately begin to speculate that they have lost their voices permanently. There is, I am afraid, a certain amount of what the Germans call *Schadenfreude* – delight in others' misfortunes – in such fantasizing. When I sang *Ballo* three days after the *Forza* incident, many people were surprised that everything was normal.

In Paris in April I sang in Verdi's *I vespri siciliani*. The tenor role, Arrigo, is probably the most arduous in the Verdi repertoire, although not as nerve-racking as Otello for the simple reason that everyone in the audience knows *Otello* and few know *Vespri*. I had already recorded *Vespri*, but this was the first time I had attempted to perform it on stage. Santi conducted, and the cast included Arroyo, Glossop and Roger Soyer. It was the best of John Dexter's productions that I have appeared in. We had a long and intensive rehearsal period, sometimes unintentionally lightened by John's comments to the chorus. When the members did not pay attention or chatted loudly among themselves, he would get upset and tell them what he thought in not very polite terms – but always in English. Then he would urge the poor young woman who was interpreting for him to 'tell them! Tell them exactly what I've said!' Embarrassed, she would come out with the equivalent of: 'Mr Dexter says he would appreciate it if you would be quieter and more attentive' – which would enrage John still more. 'I'm sure I didn't say that!' he would scream. 'Tell them what I *really* said!' In the end, his efforts paid off, and the chorus, which had many young voices in it, sounded excellent. The production was designed basically in black and white, and everyone involved was amazed by our huge public and critical success.

Very few of the front-line tenors of this century have tackled the role of Arrigo. Caruso, Pertile, Fleta, Di Stefano, Del Monaco, Bjoerling – none of them sang it, to the best of my knowledge. I do not know whether they did not attempt the role because the opera was rarely performed or whether the opera was rarely performed because they would not attempt it. Even now, *Vespri* is not done frequently. Nicolai Gedda has sung the role, and Richard Tucker was studying it at the end of his life. I saw him in Barcelona, where he was performing at the end of 1974, and he told me that he was preparing to sing Arrigo the following year – amazing for a man of sixty.

We talked about the work, and that was the last time I saw him. He died prematurely a few months later and the opera world lost a great tenor who was still at his peak.

Earlier that year I had some interesting conversations on other operatic subjects with one of the most famous tenors of the generation before Tucker's. Giacomo Lauri-Volpi was living in Valencia, where I had gone to sing *La forza del destino*. Since I was keen to meet him, I invited him to my performance, and at the end of one of the acts, I announced to the public that Lauri-Volpi was present. He was given a standing ovation and seemed very moved. I went to visit him at his home two or three times, and during our chats he even sang his famous high notes for me – not bad for an eighty-two-year-old! At that time he was making a record entitled 'The Miracle of a Voice' for RCA in Rome, and I believe that he recorded eleven arias in two or three days.

That trip to Spain was particularly enjoyable because I sang for the first time in Saragossa, my father's home town; and together with my parents, Marta and the boys I visited the restaurant that had once been my grandmother's. Placi and Alvaro, who were then eight and five, were allowed to help wait at tables. I am not sure how effective their help was; but they, at least, had a wonderful time following in their grandfather's footsteps.

I was to have gone directly from Saragossa to Moscow in order to join the Scala company for performances of *Tosca* at the Bolshoi and a concert at the Kremlin. But Princess Sofía – now Queen Sofía – of Spain asked me to appear in a special charity concert in Madrid on 5 June. I did not want to refuse her, and the Scala administration kindly allowed me to cancel my first *Tosca*. I conducted the *Vespri siciliani* overture at the Madrid concert, in addition to singing arias from seven different operas. The rehearsal took place on the morning of the performance – a very hot day – and as I had so much to sing, it was not very clever of me to have conducted as well. That evening, my rashness caused an accident during the *Pagliacci* aria: at the phrase 'sul tuo amore infranto', I lost my breath completely and could not finish. The following arias went well; but at the end, when the public enthusiastically called for an encore, I decided to challenge Fate by repeating the *Pagliacci* aria. Under the circumstances, that was psychologically difficult; and when I reached the troublesome phrases, I broke down again. The fault was entirely mine: I knew that I was tired, I had already had one bad upset, the rest of the concert had gone well, and I should have left well enough alone. But I felt grateful and generous towards an enthusiastic audience, and I learned yet another lesson the hard way.

99

My Russian debut took place on 8 June 1974. The reception given the whole Scala ensemble in Moscow was simply incredible. After that performance we were cheered and applauded for three-quarters of an hour, and the repetitions on the 10th and the 15th were similarly greeted. My parents accompanied us on that trip, and we all took a night train – or rather a 'white night' train, since there was never total darkness – to Leningrad, which is one of the most beautiful cities I have ever seen. The impression made by the lovely buildings lining the Neva River is overwhelming. I am sure that if the Soviet government relaxed its attitude towards foreigners and foreign influences, Leningrad could very easily compete with Paris as a centre of mass tourism. Visiting the Hermitage was memorable. When one sees some of the vast wealth of the Tsars exhibited in that monumental museum (I particularly remember one of their horses' bridles, studded with precious jewels), it is easy to understand why the revolution came about, however far from the ideal today's situation may be.

Like many other Western visitors, I was not positively impressed by Russian cuisine – especially the custom of serving beer warm, even in the summer. I had told our guide-interpreter that I wanted my beer cold, but I got no satisfaction. Once, at lunch, I got up from the table and carried two bottles of beer to the restaurant's refrigerator, to the amazement of all present. I managed to make it understood that I wanted them left there. When I returned in the evening, the beer was cold. A few people tried it and were surprised that it was so good. From then on a considerable amount of beer was kept in that refrigerator.

The Scala company had been to Moscow ten years earlier, so the musicians knew that the food was not the most interesting aspect of Russia. Many of them brought suitcases full of pasta, Parmesan cheese and basil.

Marta, my parents and I visited Galina Vishnevskaya at home. (Her husband, Mstislav Rostropovich, was away at the time.) She was very sad because of their impending exile from the USSR. We sang together, and I ate so many blini with black and red caviar that I had the worst indigestion of my life afterwards. The apartment was in the same building in which Shostakovich and Khachaturian had lived, and I could not help wondering how a musical evening there would have compared to our Mondays at Pepe Esteva's in Mexico.

Performing before a vast audience at the Kremlin was an extraordinary experience. At the end of the concert, the public demanded encores, and soprano Margherita Rinaldi decided to sing Oscar's aria from the third act of *Ballo*. The music was not at hand, and the pianist did not know it by heart; so I accompanied her myself. Then, as my own encore, I sang, in Russian, Lenski's aria from *Eugene Onegin*. Afterwards many people from the audience swarmed onto the stage to cheer and embrace us, and I feared some sort of stampede, with the piano rolling off the stage and crushing people below. We finally managed to leave, and no one was hurt. After the opera performances, too, I was mobbed at the stage door. The police tried to keep people away, but I wanted to shake hands and sign autographs. I put my arms around two of the most enthusiastic fans, and dozens and dozens of people accompanied me all the way back to my hotel. It may be that some of this unbelievable warmth on the part of the Russian public is because the theatre is one of the few places where they can express their feelings openly; but it is also the heartfelt appreciation of a nation with a great musical tradition.

Most sports enthusiasts know the anguish of having to work when an important game or match is being televised. When I left Moscow, I had to sing five operas in Hamburg in a twelve-day period, and that period coincided with the 1974 World Cup football championship being held there. At the end of an *Aida* performance I wanted to leave the stage as quickly as possible in order to watch the two Germanys playing each other. When I came out for what I had decided would be my final bow, I gave a little kick and pointed offstage to indicate what I had in mind, and the audience was amused and sympathetic. Still dressed as Radames, I went to the stadium to watch the game, removing my make-up en route in a Volkswagen van. On 30 June there was a *Cavalleria-Pagliacci* double-bill, of which I sang only the latter. While the audience watched *Cavalleria*, I watched the football game; and when, in *Pagliacci*, I sang 'Un grande spettacolo a ventitrè ore' ('A big show at 11 p.m.'), instead of holding up my usual '11 p.m.' sign I held up a card that read '4-3', to let anyone who might not already have heard know that Germany had beaten Sweden.

Marta and I went to Viareggio at the end of July so that I could sing in *Tosca* at nearby Torre del Lago, Puccini's home for many years. I found the swamp-like Lake Massaciuccoli rather depressing; and, whether or not there is any real connection, it made me think of some of the melancholy moments in Puccini's operas. The acoustics of Torre del Lago's outdoor theatre are not good. I suggested to Simonetta Puccini, the composer's heiress, that it be covered somehow with a glass or crystal roof, so that the view of the surroundings would not be lost, while some of the humidity would be eliminated and the sound would be improved.

In September I recorded *Madama Butterfly* with Herbert von Karajan in Vienna, not for release on record but for the soundtrack of a film directed by Jean-Pierre Ponnelle. Marta, the children and I had taken a holiday on the Costa Brava just before that, so when I got to Vienna I had not sung for seventeen days. I thought my voice would be wonderfully fresh for the recording sessions, and I did not even warm up. Luckily, the results were satisfactory, but only through the greatest effort on my part. I had unwittingly jeopardized the project by not warming up properly. Nowadays, even if only six days go by between engagements, I warm up with the greatest care.

Most important for me when I begin to warm up is not the extension of the voice – not the high and low notes – but the quality of sound in the middle. I begin by singing C-D-E-D-C-D-E-D-C-D-E-D-C with vowel sounds; then up a semitone: D flat-E flat-F-E flat-D flat-E flat-F-E flat-D flat-E flat-F-E flat-D flat; and so on. I also find singing semitones a help: C-C sharp-D-D sharp-E-E flat-D-D flat-C; then the same beginning on C sharp, etc. By doing these simple exercises, which require a smooth, legato sound that can only be produced with proper support, I make my diaphragm work. I do not go higher than about G. When the middle register is ready, I begin to sing extended arpeggios. For instance, starting on my low C, I sing upwards – C-E-G-C-E-G – and then back downwards – F-D-B-G-F-D-C. Then come scales, which I extend by one note each time: from C up to the D a ninth above it and down, then from C to E, C to F and so on, always adding notes. For all these exercises I use vowel sounds – the Continental European vowel sounds – first an *i*, then *e*, *a*, *o*, *u*. The next step is to *sing*, because adding the text adds another dimension to my work. Until very recently, I would only sing fragments of pieces during my warm-ups, but at the time of the Scala *Ernani* (December 1982) I tried a different approach. I was worried about the tessitura of my aria – which is virtually the first thing I sing, at the beginning of Act I – and I asked one of the musical assistants to come to my dressing-room and play through the whole aria, which I sang full voice. As a result, when I went on stage I felt completely ready and was able to sing my very best.

What works for one singer may not work for another and we all learn and change as the years go by. Some singers warm up very little before a performance, while others vocalize a great deal. Fiorenza Cossotto, who had the most outstanding voice I have ever heard for parts like Amneris, Azucena and Eboli, used to sing through a whole role as many as five times on the day of a performance. The idea of doing such a thing strikes terror to my heart: I would be reduced to a pulp by curtain time. But for her this method worked extremely well. Conclusion: follow your own path and don't be afraid to change it when you make new discoveries.

The period from mid November to mid December 1974 was very fruitful for me in encounters and experiences. To begin with, in Berlin I participated for the first time in the shooting of a film – the *Butterfly*, whose soundtrack I had recorded in Vienna, directed by Ponnelle, whose work in the opera house I had long admired. Next, I made my Frankfurt debut in *La forza del destino*. Finally, I gave my first performances of Puccini's *La fanciulla del West*, an opera I love, in a production by another brilliant director, Piero Faggioni, in Turin.

I had sung in many productions originally staged by Ponnelle, but the *Butterfly* film finally gave me an opportunity to work directly with him. It was very well done, and I greatly appreciated Jean-Pierre's ideas about my role. Pinkerton easily appears colourless, but not in Jean-Pierre's treatment of the part. At the very beginning, during the orchestral introduction, Pinkerton is seen in slow motion, distraught at the death of Butterfly, crashing through the wall of a fragile Japanese house and pushing Goro aside as he offers him another Japanese girl. The whole opera unfolds as Pinkerton's flashback – an old trick, but very effective here. Jean-Pierre had me play the role as a carefree, careless young sailor who has a girlfriend in every port and who wants to have a good time in Nagasaki, too – despite Sharpless's warning that Cio-Cio-San has a heart, and that he ought to be a little more serious. The scene in which Goro asks Pinkerton for money to pay family and witnesses was excellent, as was only to be expected from someone with Jean-Pierre's wonderful sense of humour.

Mirella Freni was Butterfly; she wore white make-up, and her large eyes made it difficult for the proper oriental effect to be achieved: the skin around her eyes had to be pulled so hard that she was in pain. Mirella is a natural, delightful and apparently uncomplicated person who has managed to build her career with great intelligence by moving from soubrette roles through Puccini and into the dramatic Verdi repertoire. Her vocal health is excellent, and the power of her high register is unmatchable.

I have since been able to work many times with Ponnelle, and the experience is always a pleasure. He is a work maniac who cannot relax for a minute, but his ideas are so interesting that the pressure of working with him is easier than the tedium of dealing with directors who have no ideas. I find intense labour in the theatre exhilarating rather than exhausting, whereas there is nothing more enervating than waiting for a hesitant director to decide what he wants to do next. Jean-Pierre can be capricious on occasion; and I have noticed that he, like Frank Corsaro, tends to emphasize – positively or negatively, depending on the situation – any religious elements in a plot. But Jean-Pierre is neither blind nor deaf. He will not rigidly stick to an idea if he sees that it is not working, and he listens open-mindedly to singers when they feel that certain details ought to be changed. He is not soft; but if I am not convinced by something he has asked me to do – if I do not feel, inside me, that it is right – I can talk it over seriously with him. He wants singers to understand his point of view, and he also wants to understand theirs.

The professionalism of Jean-Pierre's staff and the thoroughness of his organization are remarkable. They enable him to work on three or four projects at a time, and always at the highest level of efficiency. Like Franco Zeffirelli, he has begun the practice of creating similar productions of a single opera at various theatres – each time refining, changing details to correspond with the needs of the individual houses, but without scrapping successful ideas simply for the sake of novelty. In Jean-Pierre's case, the symmetry of his work makes this artistically possible. There is a choreographic logic to his positioning of singers that, far from being a hindrance to us, makes performing easier; and it also makes transplanting the productions from one theatre to another relatively easy. This is especially true today. When I first worked with him, he used to stage almost every bar of music. Now he trusts his instincts more, he is more relaxed, and he allows a certain amount of spontaneous expression.

Making the *Butterfly* film in Berlin and simultaneously rehearsing *Fanciulla* in Turin was something of a problem. There are no direct flights between the two cities; and Unitel, the film production company, could not fly me directly in a private plane because the international agreement on Berlin does not allow such flights to take off or land at West Berlin's airport. I had to be flown privately between Turin and Munich and then take commercial flights between Munich and Berlin.

Fanciulla is very much connected in my mind with Piero Faggioni's productions of it, first in Turin, later at Covent Garden (where I have performed it in three different seasons), and also in Buenos Aires. The second Turin performance took place on 29 November 1974, the fiftieth anniversary of Puccini's death, and there was a special commemoration at the theatre that evening. I had known Piero since 1969, when he was Jean Vilar's assistant in the staging of *Don Carlo* in Verona. A few months before the Turin *Fanciulla* I had worked with him in the new *Tosca* at La Scala –

the production that was so warmly received when we took it to Moscow. Nicola Benois's sets were beautiful, and Piero brought out some fine dramatic effects. For instance, when the soldiers brought me into Scarpia's quarters in the second act, they carried with them some things they had found in my home, including a trunk of books and a French Republican flag. When Napoleon's triumph was announced I jubilantly picked up the flag for my 'Vittoria, vittoria!' Piero's *Fanciulla*, especially in its latest and most refined incarnation at Covent Garden, is one of the most visually satisfying productions I have ever been involved in and one of the most beautiful to have been mounted in London in recent years. Although it is not among Puccini's most popular operas, it has been a huge success. Piero's study of the gold-rush period helped him to achieve great refinement of detail, even to the inclusion of the various ethnic groups that were present in the area at that time, and all of it is perfectly reflected in the music.

Piero's outstanding quality is his concentration. When he is preparing a work, he thinks of nothing else; and because he is so monomaniacal, so thorough, he cannot work on more than one project at a time. He steeps himself in the atmosphere of the opera and does extensive preliminary research. In getting himself ready for a production of *Boris Godunov* for Venice's Teatro la Fenice, he went to Russia during the winter and travelled extensively by train, photographing places and objects that were potentially important to his understanding of the setting. For the Scala *Tosca* he studied thousands of pictures of costumes and sites. He tries to get inside each character, to understand exactly why that person behaves in a certain way. I have seen him 'play' Don José, Des Grieux, Cavaradossi, Otello and others in a most illuminating way, and he is thus able to create a beautiful plasticity in his productions.

In Italy, his own country, he has not received as much recognition as he deserves, partly because of very strong competition from first-rate people such as Giorgio Strehler and Zeffirelli. But Faggioni deserves to be ranked with them, and I am certain that he will be some day. The internal politics of Italian theatres upset him, and he has been known to react violently to what he regards as injustice on the part of administrators. Piero is also an uncompromising man, which leads to difficult situations that do not help his career. He walked out of an *Otello* production in Paris because he wanted to choose his own designer and was instead given Josef Svoboda by the administration. I told him I would be very disappointed about not being able to work with him and that he should agree to work with Svoboda, but instead he threw the whole project to the winds before he had allowed himself to think the matter through. The same thing happened with a proposed *Manon Lescaut* at the Met. John Dexter offered a designer who did not meet Piero's approval, and rather than try to resolve the matter through discussion, Piero walked out. When Gian Carlo Menotti replaced him, he was allowed to choose his designer, and the same choice might well have been granted to Faggioni had he asked. I am quite certain that if Piero exercised a little more self-control, he would obtain the results he wants without compromising his work in the least. He would then have one of the top international careers in his field.

I sang *Vespri* and conducted *Doña Francisquita*, a particularly beloved zarzuela, in Barcelona during the 1974-5 holiday season. The *Francisquita* had been organized as a special tribute to my parents, who both sang. I was more nervous for them than for myself, but everything went well, and it was a very moving evening for me. I shall always be grateful to Juan Antonio Pamias, the late impresario of the Teatro Liceo, for having arranged that performance.

Katia Ricciarelli, Elizabeth Bainbridge, Reri Grist, Piero Cappuccilli and I took part in a fine new production of *Ballo*, conducted by Abbado, at Covent Garden early in 1975. The staging was by Otto Schenk, a man who likes a certain spontaneity, an improvisatory quality, in his productions. His own outstanding talents as actor and mime are probably what give him that sense of freedom. Schenk is a good, straightforward director who does not like fancy business. If there is a short ballet scene, he will let the chorus cope with it instead of bringing in the whole corps de ballet; if there is swordplay, he demonstrates the movements he wants instead of asking an expert swordsman to coach the singers. The *Ballo* was a beautiful production, although we principals were a bit put out about having been called for three days of rehearsals, only to sit around while Schenk taught the chorus to dance the minuet in the last scene. But we also had fun. Schenk likes to take the baton in hand once during the rehearsals for every production and lead the orchestra for a minute or two. Claudio agreed to let him conduct the big chords at the beginning of the second part of Act I, but plotted with the orchestra beforehand so that when Schenk gave his hefty downbeat, no one made a sound. We were rehearsing the same scene on my birthday, and as I opened my mouth to begin the aria, 'Di' tu se fedele', everyone burst into 'Happy Birthday'.

From London I went to Hamburg, where, among other activities, I conducted a performance of *Il trovatore*. Meanwhile, Giuseppe Patanè, who was scheduled to conduct *Aida* two nights later, fell ill, and the orchestra requested that I be allowed to replace him. I had to do some hard studying in a short time, and I even listened to some recordings of the opera at the home of our friends Uli and Leni Märkle. In six days, I sang four operas and conducted two others.

My heavy schedule brings up a thorny issue. Singers today are accustomed to hearing two main criticisms with boring regularity: we allow ourselves to sing too much and we sing the wrong roles. At my home in Barcelona I have a book about the famous Spanish tenor Francisco Viñas, who was in his prime at the turn of the century, and it contains a list of his performances. In one month, for example, he sang *Parsifal* twelve times; in another he sang seventeen performances of such lightweight trifles as *Lohengrin, Tannhäuser, Le Prophète, L'Africaine* and *Aida.* Doing three *Tannhäusers* in four days was not unusual for him.

Viñas was by no means exceptional in this respect. Caruso's schedule was often equally full, and many of the best-known singers, in the days before jet planes, sang a great deal more than most of us do today. 'Ah, but you travel so much further nowadays,' people say, conveniently forgetting that it is less strenuous and takes less time to go from Milan to New York in 1983 than it took to go from Milan to Rome in 1903. Perhaps we do not sing enough today!

No singers known to me want to wear out their voices or to take risks that common sense tells them will be physiologically harmful. In recent years I have been singing about seventy-five performances annually, which averages out to just above a performance every five days. Ten years ago I felt fine singing more – and I sang more. I am angered by people who say or write that I cannot resist interesting offers, because if that were the case I would be singing three times a day, 365 days of the year. I know that I sing better now, technically and artistically, than I did ten, fifteen or twenty years ago, and I must be the ultimate judge of my working system. I have no doubt that the vast majority of my colleagues would concur on this point. Critics often assume that a voice does not sound as fresh at forty-five as it did at twenty-five because it has been used too much, but I maintain that even if one stops singing at twenty-five and starts again at forty-five, the freshness will no longer be there. Instrumentalists are luckier. A Horowitz can withdraw from concert life in his forties and come back, still on top, in his sixties, but a singer cannot. Nevertheless, despite the ineluctable age factor, any competent artist will be more interesting to listen to at forty-five than at twenty-five.

As to the other question – that of singing roles that, according to self-proclaimed experts, we ought not to be singing – I have a little story to tell. When I decided to sing *Otello*, many people told me that I was crazy. Mario Del Monaco, they said, had had the proper kind of voice for the role, and my voice was nothing like his. Twenty years earlier, Del Monaco had been warned not to sing *Otello* because his voice was nothing like that of Ramón Vinay, who was then performing the opera all over the world. Vinay, of course, had heard that only a tenor with a piercing sound like Giovanni Martinelli's ought to sing the part. Some years earlier, Martinelli had had Antonin Trantoul, who had sung *Otello* at La Scala in the 1920s, held up to him as a shining example; but at La Scala, those who still remembered the very first Otello, Francesco Tamagno, had found Trantoul completely unsatisfactory. But there exists a letter from Verdi to his publisher in which the composer makes it quite clear that Tamagno left a great deal to be desired.

No singer with a reputation to defend is foolhardy enough to sing in public a role that he cannot vocally manage, or in which he feels he cannot make a beautiful impression. The myth of too much singing, the myth of singing the wrong roles, the myth that the best voices of today are not in a class with the best voices of the past – these are all old, old, old tales. It is time for the critics, official and unofficial, to find something new to talk about. If you do not like someone's voice, artistry, or interpretation of a specific role, tell him, and tell him why. But stop dredging up those time-worn reasons, groundless as they are in an overwhelming percentage of cases.

The soundtrack of the *Butterfly* film gave me my first chance to work with Herbert von Karajan. I had met him in Salzburg some time earlier, at an audition that had been arranged for me while I was singing in Vienna. He was supervising a lighting rehearsal for *Die Walküre* at the Grosse Fest-spielhaus, and I walked onto a completely dark stage. A mysterious voice called to me from the dark, in Italian, 'Good morning, what will you sing?'

'The Flower Song from *Carmen*,' I replied.

It was the only audition I ever had where I could not see the faces of the auditioners. In a way, it was like a performance.

When I arrived in Vienna for the *Butterfly* sessions, I met Karajan after dinner at the Imperial Hotel. He said simply, 'Tomorrow morning at 10 we will meet at the studio; we will rehearse; and then whenever we are ready – perhaps around 12 – we will record.' I arrived at 10 and took my place.

All of a sudden I saw the red light next to him go on. He began to conduct, and in fifty-five minutes we had finished recording the first act.

'Maestro,' I said, 'I thought we were going to rehearse.'

'Among musicians,' he replied, 'rehearsal is not necessary.'

I can confirm that we were indeed together on every note. In the afternoon we recorded the third act, and that was that. Thus my first working experience with Karajan went by so quickly that it was almost as if it had not happened. Never before had I worked with a conductor of that calibre without having a piano rehearsal - without even exchanging a word about the role. I appreciated the great compliment he was paying me.

I was then invited to sing in a new *Don Carlo* production to be conducted and staged by Karajan at Salzburg in the summer of 1975. It was a very instructive experience. In recent years, Karajan has been able to impose his will on every aspect of his Salzburg productions. He insists on having all rehearsals, from the very first one, on stage rather than in a rehearsal room, and in full costume. These are tremendously helpful techniques. The stage rehearsals make us singers think right from the beginning about projecting our characters, and the costumes make us all feel completely comfortable and natural with what we have to wear by the time we go before the public. Very often, even in a thoroughly rehearsed production, the costumes are available only for the last two rehearsals. We feel stiff in them. And when, for instance, I am supposed to be a bandit who has been living on roots and berries in the forest for ten years, I feel a bit odd in shiny clothes that appear to have just come off a department-store rack. If I am some day able to realize my goal of running a theatre, perhaps in conjunction with a school, I, too, will insist on having the singers rehearse in costume.

The one Karajan technique that I am not so enthusiastic about is that of rehearsing from a prerecorded tape of the work in preparation, instead of having the singers sing along, half-voice or otherwise, to piano accompaniment. He claims that the purpose is to rest the voice during staging rehearsals, but I feel that it creates bad habits because we hear the same timing, the same phrasing, the same breathing, every time. That gives us a feeling of false confidence, since in reality no two performances are going to be precisely alike, and it allows us to avoid singing some of the spots that we really ought to be trying out. As a result, our concept of the role is kept from growing during that all-important rehearsal period. At the *Don Carlo* rehearsals I was not even following my own recording, but an earlier one made by a different tenor. And even when your own records are being used, it is distracting to hear yourself singing all the time – the same good moments and the same discouraging bad ones.

With Karajan, we work very little at the piano, but the work done there is very intense. He uses a rehearsal pianist rather than playing himself, and he is very happy when singers follow the dynamics and other instructions as printed in the score. Of course he understands that we will have a different approach to dynamics when singing with the orchestra, and he is interested in setting up the total effect right from the beginning.

He knew that I was interested in conducting; and at one of the staging rehearsals, as I sang the phrase 'Elisabetta, tu bell'adorata', spreading my arms and pointing towards the soprano, Karajan stopped me short: 'Plácido, the arms only for conducting!' His ideas for the staging were generally very good – sometimes a bit too concentrated or too static, but always interesting.

The opening night of the production was also my Salzburg debut. It took place on 11 August, and the cast included Freni, Ludwig, Cappuccilli and Ghiaurov. All five performances were successful. During the same period I sang in an inspiring performance of the Verdi Requiem with Karajan and the Vienna Philharmonic. He wanted me to participate in the same *Don Carlo* production the following year, but I had already signed a contract to make my Japanese debut in the summer of 1976. My schedule would still have allowed me to sing four of the six *Don Carlo* performances in Salzburg, and that was in keeping with the terms of my contract. I explained the situation to Karajan, who insisted on six or none. I have always tried to honour all my commitments; and, with few exceptions, I cancel performances only when I am physically unable to sing. The situation saddened me, but I had made my career without Karajan up to that point and felt that I would simply have to accept the consequences. In 1976 José Carreras sang the *Don Carlo* and also participated in the recording. He returned for the 1977 performances, but could not schedule the première. Karajan invited me, and I returned to do that single performance. Some singers say, 'If Karajan calls me, I go to him no matter what.' I can understand them; and if they feel that way, they are right to behave as they do. But I have always allowed my career to unfold naturally, and as a result I have not always been able to adapt to his schedule. I cannot deny that I am sorry to have lost some opportunities to work with him, but first things first.

I admire the way in which Karajan has organized his life. At different times of the year he concentrates on the Salzburg Festival, recordings, or the Berlin Philharmonic in such a way that he can focus all his attention on whichever activity occupies him at any given time. As is well known,

Karajan has devoted almost all his working time in recent years to the Berlin and Vienna Philharmonics, and the musicians in those ensembles are so accustomed to his ways, to his every gesture, to his musical approach, that he can close his eyes at a performance, conduct the flow of the music and be sure that the orchestra will know what he wants. I am in complete agreement with his dictum that after 9 p.m. one cannot make music. I notice a great difference between my performances in Salzburg, where we start at 6, or in Vienna, where we start at 7, and in places where performances begin at 8 or 9 – not to speak of Barcelona, where they used to begin at 10 or even 10.30. Even if I rest and take care of myself on a performance day, by late evening I am tired of resting. In Salzburg I wake up late, have a little breakfast, vocalize and work a bit, have lunch, rest an hour, go to the theatre, get made up and dressed, and then perform with all my energy. The public, too, is more receptive. But when a performance starts between 8 and 10, people have to try to be attentive after an active day of twelve or fifteen hours. Either they must have a rushed dinner between work and the theatre, or else they must eat after the performance, at 1 or 2 a.m. The public is fresher at a 6 o'clock performance and can have a decent dinner at 9 or 10 p.m. It is more logical for all concerned, and in this as in so many respects, Karajan's ideas make sense.

VI
THE MOOR OF VENICE
(1975-81)

One of the most important dates in my career was 28 September 1975. In Hamburg that evening I performed the role of Otello for the first time. Verdi's penultimate opera, which received its première at La Scala in 1887, is among the supreme masterpieces of the lyric theatre. It is a moving and convincing setting of Shakespeare's great tragedy, and it contains the most arduous tenor part in the traditional Italian operatic repertoire. In itself, the second act of *Otello* is as exhausting for the tenor as most entire operas, and there are three other acts to be dealt with as well.

I had refused offers to sing *Otello* earlier, and even in 1975 I was thinking of further postponing the project. But my instinct told me that the right moment had come, and so it had. August Everding, who was then Intendant in Hamburg, took it upon himself to stage the production. We discussed the project at length and settled on Jimmy Levine as the best conductor for the event. It was to be Jimmy's European operatic debut. I set aside a great deal of time for rehearsals, and we were able to work on the opera in much the same way that actors work on a play. I sang out, full voice, quite a bit during the staging rehearsals in order to begin 'placing' my voice correctly. Each day we worked from 10 to 1 and from 5 to 8. During the breaks we would drink cassis with champagne, the royal drink, which we dubbed the 'Everding Special'. I was fortunate to be doing my first Otello with a man of the theatre like Everding, who helped me to approach the role first through Shakespeare, then through Boito, Verdi's librettist, and finally through the composer himself.

One of the aspects we talked most about was the time-span. Boito eliminated Shakespeare's whole first act, in Venice; and the 'crisis plot' itself, the way in which Iago gradually ensnares Otello, unfolds at a slower pace in the original drama. In the second act of the opera, only a few sentences have in fact passed between the two characters before Otello explodes with: 'Pel cielo! tu sei l'eco dei detti miei' (Shakespeare: 'By heaven, he echoes me, as if there were some monster in his thought'). We decided to soften that expression visually, as if Otello were still half amused and only beginning to become a bit worried, to pull the various threads of Iago's discourse together, until he, Otello, finally says: 'Suvvia, parla se m'ami' ('If thou dost love me, show me thy thought') in a tone that says, 'Now let's have a down-to-earth chat and get to the bottom of this.' And even after Iago's admonition to 'beware, my lord, of jealousy', Otello is still reasoning more with himself than addressing Iago when he says:

> I'll see before I doubt, when I doubt, prove,
> And on the proof, there is no more but this:
> Away at once with love or jealousy!

In short, we tried to delay the full impact as long as possible, to make the sequence of events seem at least slightly less hurried than it often appears to be. At the beginning of that act, Everding had me enter carrying a rose, a book and an apple, giving the impression that I was still thinking of the rapture of the previous night with Desdemona, feeling fresh and happy and ready to begin a day's work.

Katia Ricciarelli, whose family is from the Veneto, was as authentic a Desdemona as one is ever likely to see. Her pale complexion and blonde hair were just right for the role as was her beautiful voice. Sherrill Milnes was eager to study the part of Iago in depth, and he, too, gave special attention to that crucial second act. Once, the two of us were practising the scene where Otello says,

> Villain, be sure thou prove my love a whore,
> Be sure of it, give me the ocular proof,
> Or, by the worth of mine eternal soul,
> Thou hadst been better have been born a dog,
> Than answer my wak'd wrath.

I had to grab him by the throat, and Sherrill, who is no featherweight, was very good at helping me to throw him around the stage. At that moment, his son, who was very small at the time, wandered into the room. He burst into tears and began to shout, 'Daddy, Daddy!' We all had to reassure him that everything was all right. 'Don't worry,' I told him, 'Daddy's as strong as a mule and could easily do me in if he wanted to. Besides, he'll get back at me in the opera.'

Pier Luigi Samaritani, the designer, and Everding set the first-act Desdemona–Otello duet on the seashore. Katia and I stood on the sand, in the night, and little was visible except our white robes. The effect was beautiful. At the very end of the opera, just after I stab myself, Everding had everyone else, except the dead Desdemona, of course, leave the stage. Through the use of a transparency, our bed and ourselves, again clad in white, appeared to be transported back to that shore, so that the 'kiss' motif took place at the end in a setting similar to that of the first act. I found the idea brilliant and moving. Samaritani also created a particularly beautiful setting for the second act: the stage area was reduced, and the room in which the action took place had a sort of dome that was vocally as well as visually enhancing.

Singing *Otello* at the age of thirty-four was risky for me in the sense that I was pitting my own instincts about my vocal health and capabilities against the admonitions of the experts. My last performance before the first *Otello* was a *Bohème* in Hamburg on 14 September, which happened to be the sixty-fifth birthday of the company's former Intendant, Rolf Liebermann. He was fêted in the theatre that evening, before the performance, and he publicly made a prediction: 'Keep your ears open as you listen to Plácido, because this will probably be his last *Bohème*.' The obvious implication was that the forthcoming *Otello* would destroy my voice.

The opening night was a moment of great emotion for me. Everything went splendidly, and the public and press reacted with great enthusiasm. There were five performances in all, and I had had a *Tosca* scheduled between the second and third of them to test how my voice was reacting. During that *Tosca*, which happened to take place on Saint Plácido's day, 5 October, I gave my cry of 'Vittoria, vittoria!', made my usual dramatic fall – and landed on my nose. There was a terrible crunching sound as I hit the floor, and I soon noticed a little pool of blood under my face. Although in pain, I managed to finish the performance, but I was terribly afraid that the sonority of my voice would be permanently affected by the change in the whole nasal area. Luckily that was not the case, and my nose does not look very different today than it did earlier. (Just for the record: Saint Plácido was a martyr.) By a strange coincidence, at a performance of *Tosca* in Chicago in 1982, as I flung my head back at that same moment, I broke the nose of a supernumerary who was standing directly behind me. The poor fellow is a lawyer by profession, but he limited his suit to asking me for an autographed picture and inviting Marta and me to dinner with him and his wife. Let this serve as a warning, however, to all my future *Tosca* colleagues: do not come near me when I have to sing 'Vittoria, vittoria!'.

Far from harming me vocally or in any other way, *Otello* gradually revealed to me a new way of singing that has made the rest of my repertoire much easier for me. Perhaps I was simply maturing and would have made the same discovery in any case, but I doubt that. The vocal challenge taught me how to use my potential more fully, and the musical challenge helped me as an artist. For the first few years after I had taken the role on, every time I had a cold or made a mistake there was a critic ready to blame it on the poor old Moor of Venice. But that has nearly stopped. As of March 1983, I have performed the role eighty-two times, and clearly any damage to my voice would have been done long ago. Just a few months after the Hamburg première, Liebermann phoned to ask me to sing *Bohème* in Paris the following season.

'How is this possible?' I asked him. 'You said, "No more *Bohèmes* for Plácido."'

'I was only worried, my friend,' he replied sheepishly. Fortunately, his worry was unfounded.

The rest of 1975 proceeded normally for me. I recall that at two successive performances of *Pagliacci* in Barcelona in January 1976, I sang not only the role of Canio, but also Tonio's Prologue, as our baritone was not feeling very well. In March at the Met, together with Leontyne Price, Marilyn Horne, Cornell MacNeil and Bonaldo Giaiotti, I took part in a production of *Aida* conducted by Levine and staged by Dexter. It was a frustrating production for the singers, above all because of the heavily padded and carpeted scenery that absorbed vocal resonance. I was in Berlin at the end of that month to record the part of Walther von Stolzing in *Die Meistersinger*, an opera I have never sung on stage. I had not wanted to take on that task, but my friends Uli Märkle and Günter Breest of Deutsche Grammophon urged me to go ahead. The results were very good, but I must confess that I would have been happier had my German pronunciation been better. Sometimes, in the presence of Uli or Günter, I would practise my German on the hotel maid, using a phrase from *Meistersinger* ('Fräulein, eines zu wissen, eines zu fragen') as if it were a line from a Berlitz book. Eugen Jochum conducted the recording, and the cast included Dietrich Fischer-Dieskau, Caterina Ligendza and Christa Ludwig. Jochum's expertise in the German repertoire is well known, and I was impressed by his achievement in *Meistersinger*.

In the spring, Ileana Cotrubas, Sherrill Milnes and I began to record *La traviata* under the direction of Carlos Kleiber, with whom I was working for the first time. The sessions took place in a Munich beer parlour where a bomb had once been thrown at Hitler. Carlos can be difficult at times, and on that occasion he was not happy with the placement of the orchestra. Time was lost, and as a result the recording could only be completed the following year. At one point, Carlos was going to back out of the venture altogether, as he has been known to do in similar cases, and we had to talk him into continuing. Once we began to work seriously, he, too, wanted to bring the project to fruition, as we managed to do.

· During that period in Munich I was involved in a new production of *Tosca*, staged by Götz Friedrich. Without a doubt he is to be counted among today's major régisseurs; and despite my many, many previous encounters with the role of Cavaradossi, Götz's ideas changed my characterization. Cavaradossi is often portrayed as merely a good-looking artist who is caught up in and destroyed by the rush of historical events, while Tosca is the character with real will-power and personality. Of course Tosca has the courage to kill Scarpia and to attempt to rescue her lover, but fundamentally she is a capricious woman, a prima donna, while Cavaradossi is a very strong character who is involved in serious political matters. Götz told me that although my 'Recondita armonia' had depth to it, I ought to sing it as if with a premonition that I shall very soon be dead. The encounter with Angelotti reinforces the feeling of dread, and the subsequent scene with Tosca must not be played too lightly. There must be fear, despair and resolution in the tenor's interpretation throughout the first act. Cavaradossi's behaviour must also demonstrate that he is a great admirer of Angelotti, the Voltairian free-thinker and radical, and that he looks up to him. Although Angelotti is a comprimario role without much to sing, the tenor must remember that that small basso part is the mechanism that sets the whole plot in motion. Like Otto Schenk in his *Tosca* production at the Met some years earlier, Friedrich emphasized the authoritarian aspects of the story: Scarpia, Spoletta and the guards were all real 'heavies' – ferocious SS prototypes.

The gifted Spanish conductor Jesús López Cobos, who conducted that *Tosca*, had done a great deal of detective work in the original manuscript of the opera. Some of the differences were shocking at first but made sense when I became familiar with them. For instance, in the printed version, after Tosca says to Cavaradossi, 'O come la sai bene l'arte di farti amare' ('Oh, how well you know the art of making yourself loved'), he does not reply – which means that he lets her accuse him of misusing his charm without defending himself. But in the manuscript he answers with the

In *La Bohème* with Marta, Tel Aviv, 1963.
It was my twenty-second birthday and her
first Mimi.

As Lenski in *Eugene Onegin*, with Breda
Kalef, Tel Aviv, 1964

In *Hippolyte et Aricie* with Beverly Sills, Boston, 1966

In Ginastera's *Don Rodrigo*, 1966: the opera's North American première and the New York City Opera's first performance at the New York State Theater in Lincoln Center

In *Manon Lescaut* with Renata Tebaldi,
Hartford, Connecticut, 1968

In *Manon Lescaut* with Magda Olivero,
Verona, 1970

In *La forza del destino* (left), *Tosca* (below), *Don Carlo* (opposite above) and *Aida*, Hamburg, 1967–9

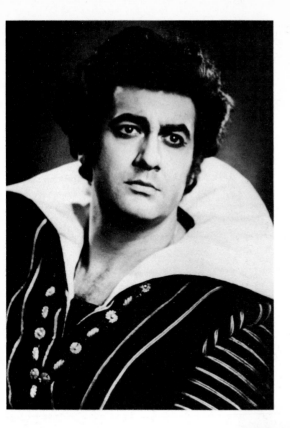

In *Roberto Devereux* with Beverly Sills ('doing our Bette Davis–Errol Flynn act'), New York, 1970

In *Don Carlo*, Milan, 1970

In *Lucia di Lammermoor* with Joan
Sutherland, Hamburg, 1971

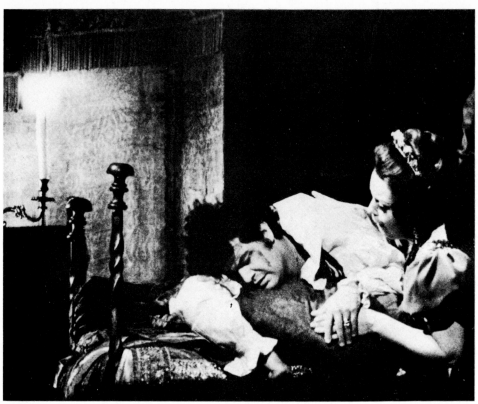

In *Tosca* with Gwyneth Jones: my Covent Garden debut, 1971

In *I vespri siciliani* with Peter Glossop (left), Paris, 1974

In *Otello*: Paris, 1976; (below) Hamburg, 1975

In *Carmen*: with Teresa Berganza, Edinburgh, 1977; (below) with Elena Obraztsova, Vienna, 1978

In *Werther* with Brigitte Fassbaender, Munich, 1977

In *Samson et Dalila*, Orange, 1978

In a German television production of *Otello* with actress Dietlinde Turban, 1978

In *Cavalleria Rusticana* with Elena Obraztsova, Milan, 1981

In *Pagliacci*: with Teresa Stratas, Munich, 1978; (below) Milan, 1981

In *Manon Lescaut* with Renata Scotto,
New York, 1980

In *La traviata* with Ileana Cotrubas,
New York, 1981

In *The Tales of Hoffmann*: with Ruth Welting, New York, 1982; (below) Salzburg, 1980

In *Manon Lescaut* with Kiri Te Kanawa, London, 1983

phrase 'Non è arte, è amore' ('It isn't art, it's love'). At the point in the second act where Tosca sings 'E avanti a lui tremava tutta Roma' ('And before him all Rome trembled'), López Cobos discovered that her note should be a D rather than a C-sharp. And there were other discrepancies, as in the chorus's first-act Te Deum.

I spent most of June in Paris rehearsing a new production of *Otello*, which Solti conducted, and in which I was partnered by Margaret Price and Gabriel Bacquier. Dexter was originally to have staged that production, but he had walked out. Piero Faggioni then accepted the task but, as I have already said, was unhappy with the choice of designer. He, too, departed. Finally, Terry Hands of Britain's Royal Shakespeare Company was invited to take over; and the results, by and large, were excellent. He was not accustomed to working with choruses, but Svoboda's stylish sets helped to eliminate any problems that might otherwise have arisen. In the first act, for instance, when the crowd watches the battle and anticipates Otello's arrival, the chorus was standing in various boxes placed at different levels on a huge wall – about four storeys in all. The impression was very strong. At the end of the big ensemble in the third act, when Otello shouts at the crowd to leave him, Hands had the soldiers surround him with their lances, ostensibly to protect him; but the visual image was that of a beast trapped in a cage, giving an extra poignancy to Otello's cry, 'Fuggirmi io sol non so!' ('I alone cannot fly from me!'). In the third-act duet, Hands wanted Desdemona and Otello to stand very close to each other – two people who love each other and cannot resist being near and touching each other, even in such a terrible situation.

There is a theory that Iago, who is Otello's *alfiere* (ensign or standard-bearer), is in love with Otello and that the whole plot he hatches stems from his jealousy of Desdemona. I do not think that this idea ought to be carried too far. On the other hand, it is true that in that period the *alfiere* was a sort of valet to his captain. He constantly attended him, dressed him and perhaps slept in the same room with him. Therefore, when Desdemona enters the picture and eliminates some of Iago's duties, it is reasonable that jealousy of her becomes an additional motive – along with frustrated ambition, contempt for mankind in general and many other venomous emotions – for his subsequent actions. At the end of the third act, when Otello has fainted after his fit, Terry Hands did not want Bacquier – a truly great Iago – to laugh and sneer at me as he sang 'Ecco il leone!'. Instead, Bacquier bent over and embraced me, almost with pity, as if to say, 'It is too bad that I have to destroy this man, but my personal ambition is stronger than my pity for him.'

The multi-level stage allowed Hands to introduce an unusually stimulating idea in the last act. Desdemona, during her Willow Song, interrupts herself to say to Emilia, 'Listen, I hear a lament', and Emilia replies, 'It is the wind.' In this production, while those lines were being sung, I appeared on one of the upper levels, weeping, out of view of the two women. It was one of the many details that made Hands's production so striking.

I had a bit too much travelling to do in September 1976: first to Tokyo, where I made my Japanese debut in a *Cavalleria-Pagliacci* double-bill, then to Spain for a single performance of *Bohème* in Elda, then to Chicago for a new production of *The Tales of Hoffmann*, and finally to Rome to make a film of *Tosca* under the direction of Gianfranco De Bosio. The conductor was Bruno Bartoletti, Tosca was sung by Raina Kabaivanska, and Scarpia by Sherrill Milnes. Placi, who had made his operatic debut at the age of nine the previous year as the Shepherd Boy in *Tosca*, played the part again in the film, which I treasure for that reason above all. I enjoyed shooting on location at the church of Sant'Andrea della Valle and the Castel Sant'Angelo. We could not, however, shoot at the Palazzo Farnese, because it is the site of the French Embassy. I still remember that filming the first-act Tosca-Cavaradossi duet took nineteen hours – from noon one day until 7 the next morning.

A few weeks later, in San Francisco, I sang in Ponnelle's brilliant production of *Pagliacci* and his not so brilliant production of *Cavalleria rusticana*. The *Pagliacci* was slightly modernized. For instance, the troupe arrived in a truck with Tonio at the wheel, rather than in a horse-drawn cart. (Zeffirelli used a truck in the 1981 Scala production, too; but in Milan I was allowed to do the driving.) One particularly fine episode in Jean-Pierre's dramatic mise-en-scène was the play within the play. Jean-Pierre had the 'public' for the comedy sitting at the back of the stage, facing the real public. The artists were therefore performing with their backs partially towards the auditorium, which meant that the real public was able to see what was happening backstage. It was very difficult for all of us, because we had to create the illusion that we were performing for the on-stage public while in fact projecting to the real audience. While Nedda (Noelle Rogers) and Beppe (Joseph Frank) sang their duet, Tonio (Ingvar Wixell) was seen passing the props to them, and Beppe passed the props to Nedda and Tonio during their duet. This was complicated and difficult for them, but the effect of seeing the backstage movement and the communication by innuendo among the members of the troupe was very powerful. It was hard, too, for me to sing my aria to both the real and the stage public, but the results were well worth the effort.

Jean-Pierre based his *Cavalleria* production on Greek tragedy, but he exaggerated certain details. Santuzza (Tatiana Troyanos) appeared to be in an advanced state of pregnancy and was kept on stage through the whole opera, while Alfio was portrayed as a mafioso with dark glasses. The religious parade was a procession of fanatics: people flagellated themselves and used broken bottles to inflict wounds on their own bodies. Jean-Pierre did not ask me to do anything particularly eccentric; but I found, for instance, having to sing 'Resta abbandonata' and other parts that refer to Santuzza disturbing, since she was standing on stage the whole time. The setting was bleak, all the costumes very dark. I felt the production was a bit extreme.

Opening La Scala's 1976-7 season with *Otello* was a great occasion for me for a number of reasons. *Otello* had had its world première at La Scala nearly ninety years earlier, and although there may be no tangible reason for feeling a special responsibility towards the work in that theatre, the feeling is nevertheless real. It was also my first collaboration outside the recording studio with Carlos Kleiber, the first joint Kleiber - Zeffirelli venture, and the first live television broadcast from La Scala of an entire opera. Mirella Freni was the Desdemona and Piero Cappuccilli the Iago. (Piero is renowned among his colleagues for his extraordinary breath control, which enables him to achieve a long, even vocal line.)

I freely admit that much of my present characterization of Otello was learned from Franco Zeffirelli - or perhaps I should say from Sir Laurence Olivier, since Franco was greatly influenced by Olivier's interpretation of the role. In Hamburg and Paris I had emphasized the Moorish, North African aspect of the character, but in Milan I began to think of Otello as a black man, alienated from the white society in which he moved.

At one staging rehearsal of the second act, Franco took the part of Iago to my Otello. Everyone present was amazed by the simplicity and depth of his characterization. He played Iago as a good, trustworthy man, and that is absolutely essential for a convincing portrayal. If Iago is obviously a villain, who can possibly find him credible?

Zeffirelli keeps both Otello and Iago fairly busy doing mundane things on stage during that act, and I believe that his instinct there is right. The less Otello looks Iago in the eye - the less attentive he is to Iago's way of manipulating the situation - the easier it is for him to fall into the trap.

Otello *must* miss the sub-text in this scene; and if the two men talk directly to each other, Otello's failure to see through Iago becomes less credible. Everding had had similar ideas about this spot; but Karajan, in his Vienna Staatsoper production, had only a fountain at centre stage. I found it very difficult to bring off the dialogue convincingly under those conditions and was finally allowed to pore over a book during the scene, to distract my attention from Iago's obvious insinuations. For Otello's third-act monologue, Franco had me kneel, slowly rotating my head and torso in pain and supplication – a movement that had in it something of a man in prayer and something of a wounded beast. The approach rang true. He also wanted my reactions to some of Iago's suggestions to be very naive. For instance, when Iago says, 'Do it not with poison. Strangle her in her bed, even the bed she hath contaminated', Otello replies, 'Good, good! The justice of it pleases! Very good', and this reply usually comes as a strong exclamation. Franco suggested that I sing it not with rage, but rather like a child accepting the first suggestion presented to him – as if to say, 'Yes, you are right, why not do it like that, after all?' Otello, the once great commander, has so completely lost his sense of direction that he clutches at everything Iago suggests to him as if it were revealed truth. He is at his most pathetic here.

Marta, the children and I became very close to Franco at the time of the *Otello* rehearsals. We often went to eat with him, and sometimes he would cook for us. He is a fabulous cook! We were very touched, too, when he gave us a private preview showing, in his home, of his film *Jesus of Nazareth*.

Carlos Kleiber, who conducted the *Otello*, is one of my favourite topics of conversation. His gifts – musical and dramatic insights, analytical abilities, technique, methods of explaining himself – make him the greatest conductor of our day. When I work with him, I feel that he knows somehow why the composer wrote every note, treated every phrase, conceived of every bit of orchestral colour in a particular way. He is meticulous about every detail of his work, but the meticulousness stems from conviction, not pedantry. When he indicates a certain bowing for the string instruments, it is not necessarily to resolve a technical problem, but more likely to achieve a specifically musical goal.

His extraordinary seriousness towards his work makes Kleiber's career a difficult one. He will only conduct in certain places, with certain people, and under certain conditions; and although I do not believe that he himself is bothered by the restrictions thus imposed upon his professional life, the result is that the public sees very little of him. There are still professional musicians - especially in America, where he has worked hardly at all - who respond to a mention of his name with 'Who is he?' Some artists suffer from over-exposure, but Carlos is a case of under-exposure. The public is the loser.

Because I am a musician as well as a singer, I love to work with Carlos; but there are singers - those whose musicianship is weak - who are either frightened to death of or simply put off by him. If, when you begin to rehearse with him, you have not already read deeply into your role, you must at least be quick to understand and accept his own illuminating revelations. If you are both unprepared and incapable of assimilating his ideas, the results may be disastrous. Not that Carlos is cruel or nasty. On the contrary, he has a marvellous sense of humour, and he is a decent and compassionate man. But his pursuit of his musical goals makes him seem almost hysterical at times. When he does not achieve something that at least approaches what he is seeking, he becomes very frustrated, and the frustration shows itself plainly to his co-workers.

He suffers when people do not understand him; and, strange as it may seem, I believe that this is partly because he does not realize just how extraordinarily gifted he is. He becomes not so much angry as despondent when things do not go as he had hoped; and although he may ask the orchestra why they can't do this or that, off stage he will mutter, 'I should stop conducting; I can't explain myself properly.' Full of self-doubts, he cannot allow himself to believe that his way of interpreting music is a superior one. The outward results of his complex make-up are his rough relationships with certain artists, his walking out of rehearsals, his cancellation of contracts - not out of capriciousness, but as a manifestation of his overall dissatisfaction. The inward result of this complexity is the greatness of his musical vision.

Sometimes he is so caught up in what he is doing that he is ungrateful, unable to understand when we really are trying to give our best, to do everything to satisfy him; and this can generate tension. Because the specifically musical standard of the operatic world, although higher than it used to be, is not as high as that of the symphonic world, he might have a more productive existence if he devoted more of his time to symphonic music. If he were to become the permanent conductor of a major orchestra, he could turn it into the greatest ensemble in history. He would probably drive the musicians crazy in the process, but they would learn so much that they would come to accept him. On the other hand, I personally hope to work much more with him in the theatre in coming years.

He is a very pleasant person to be with. When Marta and I have dinner with him, we can sit at the table for hours, talking about a thousand different things. We even discovered that we have a favourite song in common from childhood (mine in Spain and his in Argentina), an impressive work that begins: 'Tengo una vaca lechera, no es una vaca cualquiera' ('I have a milk cow, it's not just any old cow'). (The tune is even better than the text.) And like Claudio Abbado, Carlos is a great eater. Claudio loves to try different cuisines, while Carlos, although thin as a rake, is capable of eating everything in sight. He leads a very private life and prefers to be left alone. Most of all, he hates long-range commitments. If the manager of an important opera house were to ask him now, in 1983, to conduct a particular work in 1986, he would moan, 'No, I can't think that far in advance.' But if the same manager were to say to him, 'Come tonight and take over the performance of such-and-such', he might be in just the right mood and bring off a splendid performance.

His active repertoire may not be large, but I can imagine him conducting anything he puts his mind to and conducting it superbly. In 1981, shortly after Karl Böhm died, there was a concert in his memory in Munich; and Kleiber, as one of the participants, conducted the second movement of Schubert's 'Unfinished' Symphony. The sonority and the intensity of the playing very much moved all who were present.

Even physically, Carlos is just right for a conductor – tall and slender, with long, endless arms. And what technique he has: the independence of his right and left arms, the subtlety of his subdividing, his way of anticipating beats that he knows tend to drag and of delaying others that tend to come too soon. He once told me that in some three-four time or slow waltz-like passages, where the orchestra may become a bit careless, he purposely conducts the third beat unclearly in order to increase the players' attentiveness. He feels, understands, knows everything about conducting and about making music. I have now sung twenty-five performances of *Otello* with him, and every time Carlos Kleiber conducts that opera, a transfiguration takes place in the pit. It is as if he were playing every instrument. He creates the entire atmosphere with his body; he lives every role; he is an impressionist who is somehow able to indicate every touch of colour.

The Scala *Otello* opened in an embattled atmosphere. There was a violent demonstration outside the theatre by young people protesting against the use of public money to support an elitist form of entertainment. I thought it strange that this protest came precisely when the then general director of

La Scala, Paolo Grassi, a brilliant man with forty years' theatrical experience, was doing everything in his power to open the theatre to everyone, when La Scala was registering 100,000 special attendances annually, at very low prices, of young people, students and trades union members, and when television was finally beginning to bring some important productions into millions of homes throughout the country. But the disturbance did occur all the same. The centre of Milan was closed to traffic, and we performers had to be taken to the theatre by police escort. Nevertheless, the evening was a great success, and later performances went off without incident. Grassi left La Scala the following year to become president of R A I, Italy's national radio and television corporation. He died prematurely in 1981.

Zeffirelli directed the television broadcast of the opening performance and received some criticism for occasionally showing Kleiber in the pit. To us on stage, Carlos was part of the drama, and I think that making him part of the video document was a good idea. Far from being offended by having him on screen during part of my monologue, I found, when I saw the tape, that his visual presence was an asset to the whole presentation. How could Franco have deprived future viewers of seeing what was happening in the orchestra at that moment? In the big opera houses nowadays there are monitors in the wings that show the conductor via closed-circuit television. Since the sound from the pit is also broadcast backstage, I would like, some day, to make my own videotape of Carlos conducting *Otello*. It would be a priceless document.

Of the many productions I participated in in 1977, two stand out in my mind. The first was *Carmen* at the Edinburgh Festival. Claudio Abbado conducted the London Symphony Orchestra; Piero Faggioni directed the staging; the sets were by Ezio Frigerio; and the cast included Teresa Berganza in the title role, Mirella Freni as Micaela, and Tom Krause as Escamillo. Although Claudio's reputation as an opera conductor is based above all on his Verdi interpretations, *Carmen* is the opera in which I have most enjoyed performing with him. He captured all the elements of Bizet's score – its lightness, its temperament, its sensuality – and managed to produce, with that wonderfully flexible orchestra and with us singers, a truly remarkable version of this classic. I am glad that a recording exists of essentially the same production.

Teresa's success as Carmen was a source of great pleasure to me. It is wise not to sing dramatic roles too early in a career, but things can be put off too long. The years pass quickly; and for a mezzo who wants to sing

Carmen some day, singing only Mozart and Rossini is dangerous, because the voice will not necessarily develop in the desired direction. I had always asked myself why Teresa had not sung Carmen, especially since her singing of Spanish music in concert was always so outstanding. As anticipated, her performance of the role was magnificent.

It was I who had proposed Faggioni's name to Peter Diamand, who was then director of the Edinburgh Festival, when Peter had invited me to sing in the production. Teresa, who did not know Piero's work, at first wondered why he had been selected; but she, too, came to admire him very much. Working closely with Frigerio, Piero created a Goya-like setting. He also went back to the original *Carmen* story by Prosper Mérimée, which begins with Don José in prison. During the preludes to each act, José was shown in his cell, thinking back upon the events that had landed him there.

Almost as important as the *Carmen* performances themselves – the second of which was my hundredth appearance in the role of Don José – was the London Symphony vs. *Carmen* cast football game. Abbado, who is an enthusiastic sportsman, Faggioni, Krause, my Pepe and I were in the latter team, and we won four to three. My Placi was also ready for action and played for a few minutes. There was a second game – the London Symphony against the Scottish Orchestra – but given the Scots' reputation for bad behaviour at such events, I joked that I did not want to participate: I thought there would be trouble. I did, however, serve as a linesman, while Claudio actually played for the Londoners. He is so youthful that no one would ever guess that he is turning fifty in 1983. He looks younger than any of us. Marta, the boys and I are very close to him and his wife, Gabriella, and we always have a good time when we are together.

The other particularly memorable production that year was my debut in Massenet's *Werther*, an opera I love, in Munich in December. The sets were stark and extremely effective, and the production, by Kurt Horres, was outstanding, as was the conducting of López Cobos. Brigitte Fassbaender sang and acted magnificently as Charlotte, and our performances were very well received. A little over a year later I recorded the work with a different company at studios in Bayer-Leverkusen, just outside Cologne. Bayer aspirin is produced there, and it occurred to me during those sessions that poor Werther would have done much better to resolve his problems with aspirin than through the more drastic means he eventually resorted to.

In respect of my work, then, 1977 was a fine and active year for me. It was also the first year in which I donated two prizes, now annual, in the Francisco Viñas singing competition in Barcelona. One is awarded to the best tenor, whatever his country of origin, and the other to the best Spanish singer. My schedule that year allowed me to award the prizes myself on the stage of the Teatro Liceo. But 1977 was a sad year for me personally because of the premature deaths of three friends. The first was Calvin Johnson, whom I spoke of earlier. Then there was Alfredo Matilla of the San Juan opera company in Puerto Rico. Alfredo had had heart by-pass surgery and seemed to be doing well, but I noticed when he came backstage to greet me after a concert in Madrid in June that he looked ill. It had been very hot in Madrid that day, and later that same evening Alfredo had to be taken to hospital. He died in July. Fortunately, his work in San Juan has been carried on by Guillermo Martínez, who has become my best friend. (Under his administration I have performed in *Chénier* - originally programmed by Matilla - and then in *Pagliacci* and *Carmen*, as well as a concert with Renata Scotto.) Four months after Alfredo's death, Manuel Aguilar, who had insisted that I audition for the Mexican Opera back in 1959 and whose encouragement had been crucial at the outset of my career, died while still in the prime of life. One of my dearest links with Mexico was broken.

I was in Milan early in 1978 for a single televised performance of *Don Carlo* at La Scala, with Margaret Price, Elena Obraztsova, Renato Bruson and Yevgeny Nesterenko. Abbado conducted, and the staging was by Luca Ronconi. The engagement had come about as the result of a dispute with La Scala and RAI on one side and Unitel and Karajan on the other. The production had opened a month earlier with Freni, Carreras, Cappuccilli and Ghiaurov in the lead roles, but they were already under contract to film the work for television with Karajan. He and Unitel would not give them a release to appear in another televised production. The ins and outs of the story were bizarre, but in the end the cast had to be replaced for the one performance that was to be televised.

Shortly thereafter I was in Paris to record Berlioz's *The Damnation of Faust* - an opera I have never performed in the theatre - with Daniel Barenboim. One day he and I had lunch with Artur Rubinstein at his Paris home, just a week or so before his ninetieth birthday. We talked mainly about music, women and cigars. Danny and Rubinstein were smoking Monte Cristo cigars, which, to be properly enjoyed, must last three hours. (I do not smoke, but I appreciated their enjoyment.)

Some weeks later Renata Scotto and I recorded an album of duets under Kurt Herbert Adler's direction. Too many unnecessary repetitions during those sessions and a nasty cold brought me into the worst period of vocal problems I had had since my post-*Lohengrin* woes ten years earlier. At first

I honoured all my commitments, including five performances of *Otello* in Munich with Freni, Cappuccilli and Kleiber. They were a nightmare. I should have cancelled but did not, and my problems increased. In April, while singing *Manon Lescaut* in Madrid, I received an SOS from Karajan. He was conducting *Il trovatore* in Vienna, and one of the performances was to be televised world-wide. Some difficulties had developed with the tenor, and the people from Unitel came to take me away from Madrid and have me step into the breach. I refused to break my Madrid commitment, so the Vienna dates were changed. Because of my vocal problems, what would normally have been a valuable opportunity could not have come at a worse time. Most of the performance went very well, but I was quite tense, especially in 'Di quella pira'. Karajan had staged that production, and I noticed that he was very interested in the visual aspect for the television cameras as well as for the auditorium. When he spotted singers in positions that would not look good on camera, he shifted them. There was a second performance of *Trovatore*, and then I had to go to La Scala for four *Manon Lescaut*s. The role of Des Grieux is a tricky one, and I was not at my best. I finally had the sense to cancel a recording of *Pagliacci* that I was to have made with Muti in June. For a time the people at EMI and even Riccardo himself thought that my real reason for cancelling might have been an objection on my part to his intention to record the opera as written, without the traditionally interpolated B-natural and B-flats, and with the line 'La commedia è finita' taken away from Canio and given back to Tonio, as Leoncavallo intended. That was absolutely not the case, and I was very sorry when I learned of the misunderstanding. I was delighted, however, when I gave my next performances – *Otello* in Paris – for my vocal problems had disappeared.

I did not entirely like Ponnelle's staging of *Otello* in San Francisco that September; but as the production was not a new one, I was not working directly with Jean-Pierre. I had no objection to the staging of my own part, but I found that the general scale was too small. The castle in the first act looked like a fairy-tale set, and the ambassadors in the third act were little dancers, contrasting poorly with the scale and power of the music in those scenes. Such moments require pomp. Instead of children surrounding Desdemona in the second act, during that lovely, evanescent ensemble scene, Jean-Pierre had beggars and maimed people approaching her. I quite understand that he was trying to demonstrate Desdemona's kindness and pity, but the freak show did not mesh with what happens musically at that moment in the score. I will say this, however: Jean-Pierre never does these things as gimmicks. He is a man with a strong sense of irony, and he is not afraid to show the ugly side of life in the midst of great beauty.

In October I sang five performances of *Werther* at the Met with Obraztsova, Rudel conducting. The production, by Paul-Emile Deiber, was too sugary for my taste. That quality is already present in the music, and a good, strong mise-en-scène is required to mitigate it.

In complete contrast to that experience was the Kleiber-Zeffirelli collaboration on *Carmen* in Vienna a few weeks later (December 1978). Carmen was sung by Obraztsova and Escamillo by Yuri Mazurok. It was a very busy time for me. As is often the case in Vienna, the new production had been decided upon at the last moment. Since I had performances of *L'Africaine* in London during the period that was now being set aside for *Carmen* rehearsals in Vienna, I had to commute between the two cities. Obraztsova was ill at the time of the rehearsals, Mazurok could not be on hand for some reason or other, and the Micaela had not yet been chosen (Isobel Buchanan was eventually engaged); so despite my long-distance travels, I was the only one of the principals who managed to be at all the sessions.

Carlos permitted numerous cuts in the score, especially of repetitive passages. At one point Zeffirelli said, 'Why don't we cut the Habanera? I've never been able to stand it.' We all had a good laugh about that, although the Habanera had been tacked on by Bizet only when the mezzo complained about not having a solo number at that moment. The music was taken from an old Spanish folksong, 'Si tu me quieres, paloma mía'. Carlos was greatly amused by the idea of saying casually to a mezzo, 'Oh, by the way, we're cutting the Habanera', and seeing what her reaction would be – although of course it was left in. We used some of the spoken dialogue and a few of the sung recitatives, but only enough of each to make the action intelligible.

There were many outstanding details in Franco's production. The fight in the first act, for instance, was so well done that it did not look staged. It was chaotic, anarchic, not just one group of choristers running one way and a second running another way. In the fourth act, at the corrida, he was again able to create a sense of disorder – one of the most difficult achievements in the staging of a massed scene, since people tend to move in blocks. Some observers said that there was too much movement and congestion in the scene, but to me it was absolutely true to life. Since both Micaela and Don José are supposed to be from Navarra, in the Basque country, where many people, including my mother, are fair-complexioned, Franco made us both blond. This underlined the contrast between the two of them on the one side, and the Andalusians and gypsies on the other – and especially between Don José and Carmen.

Zeffirelli gives a great deal of leeway to the actors and singers he trusts. He has a wonderful eye, and in constructing his sets he puts things around his players that stimulate them, make them think about what they are doing. The frame and ornamentation of every scene are perfectly planned, so if the action is even reasonably well done, it will look magnificent. Franco did very little to alter my characterization of Don José. Since, like José, my mother is from the Basque country, I spent much time there as a child; and I have based my approach to the role on my understanding of the Navarrese temperament In any case, I had already sung the part many, many times before the Vienna production. My third-act costume was based on a drawing from the original production of 1875. I wore a *calañés* (a hat with upturned brim, typically Andalusian) and a *traje corto* (riding outfit), and I arrived on stage on a beautiful, big white horse.

The 'Chanson bohème', as Kleiber conducted it, was one of the most exciting performances of anything I have ever heard. It must begin very slowly in order to be effective. The laziness, the lethargy of a hot evening must be felt, and the atmosphere must gradually become more and more charged, the accelerando and crescendo must increase almost impercep- tibly, until the whole piece explodes in a Dionysian frenzy. The colours that Franco put on the stage for that scene provided the perfect background. Carlos received an ovation afterwards such as I had never witnessed. It was a grandiose *Carmen*, as befitted both the Staatsoper and Carlos's approach to the score. *Carmen* can also be done successfully in a more reduced, intimate production, but Franco profited from the resources at hand, with spectacular results. The first performance was telecast live, and I had a hard time remaining motionless for more than three minutes during the applause that followed the Flower Song.

I associate two weeks early in 1979 with three productions of *Il trovatore*. On 17 February, in that opera, I gave my only performance to date at the Zurich Opera House. I found the acoustics so unsatisfactory that I have never sung there again. The theatre is now being redone – obviously I was not alone in my opinion – and I look forward to singing there in the future. In Frankfurt four nights later I sang the best *Trovatore* of my life, and on 3 March I conducted *Trovatore* in Vienna in a performance noteworthy for Eva Marton's portrayal of Leonora. In my opinion, Eva has the best Verdi voice among singers of the new generation.

Although I had already made a significant number of recordings with

Lorin Maazel, especially of Puccini operas, my first chance to work with him in the theatre took place at Covent Garden that year, in *Luisa Miller*. Maazel's musical knowledge is profound and thorough. He is a highly sophisticated conductor but he is sometime leery of showing much involvement. There are conductors who believe that dominating the music and the musicians is sufficient and that it is cheap to communicate the music's intensity. Ideally, a balance between passion and control is desirable. Maazel is not a cold human being, so I assume there must be a deliberate decision on his part to stay in a cool frame of mind and to govern everything from the outside. His new job as director of the Vienna Staatsoper entails much bureaucratic work as well as artistic responsibilities, and my hope is that when he actually walks into the pit to conduct a performance, he will want to enjoy himself. His already outstanding music-making would benefit if he let himself go once in a while. In fact, when I recently recorded the soundtrack of a *Carmen* film with him, I found him much more involved.

I had been looking forward to recording *Bohème* in Milan with Kleiber and the Scala ensemble in June 1979, but Carlos became upset in the middle of the first act and refused to go on. I understand that he later listened to what had been done, found it wonderful and could not imagine what had angered him. But that's Carlos. In the time available we recorded the Verdi Requiem, Abbado conducting, with Ricciarelli, Verrett and Ghiaurov, and gave a benefit concert for Milan's Casa di Riposo, the rest home for musicians founded by Verdi, at which I sang 'Quando le sere al placido' from *Luisa Miller* and 'O terra, addio' from *Aida*, with Freni, and conducted an excerpt from *Rigoletto* with Cotrubas and Leo Nucci.

In July I sang *Tosca* at Macerata, Italy, and went to nearby Recanati, the home town of Beniamino Gigli, to visit his tomb. I was then to have made a recording of *La Gioconda* that suddenly had to be cancelled, and I thought I would have a few days' rest. Piero Faggioni put an end to that notion when he phoned me from Buenos Aires: he was staging a *Fanciulla* at the Teatro Colón, and the tenor was ill. Well ... I made a little jump over to Argentina, sang the opening performance, flew back across the Atlantic for a benefit concert with Cotrubas in Monte Carlo (I had promised Princess Grace that I would participate), flew back to Buenos Aires for two more *Fanciulla*s, and returned to Europe for a brief holiday, which I dare say was particularly well-earned!

Two projects were to have occupied me in Vienna in the first half of September: a UNICEF benefit gala and a *Rigoletto* recording conducted by Giulini, with Cotrubas and Cappuccilli. But while I was there I was asked to come to the rescue in another emergency. A concert performance of Mercadante's rarely heard *Il giuramento* was scheduled for the 9th, but on the 7th the tenor became ill. Although I had never heard the work or even seen a score of it, I accepted the challenge, studied hard, and did the performance. The music is very beautiful, very much in a bel canto, pre-Verdian style, and the nicest compliment I received afterwards was that it appeared to have been one of the staples of my repertoire. With the emergency over I returned to the *Rigoletto* recording.

There have been complaints that some of Giulini's tempi in *Rigoletto*, as in the earlier *Don Carlo* recording, are excessively slow. I can only say that when a conductor is heavy-handed, or if he takes slow tempi because he is tired, the tempo does indeed become a lead weight. But when a conductor like Giulini takes a slow tempo out of conviction and pursues it with great energy, it is every bit as exciting as a fast one. Tempo is in any case relative. Think of Riccardo's barcarolle in *Ballo* and of 'Questa o quella' in *Rigoletto*. They are similar in meter, rhythm and structure, yet the barcarolle is usually taken much more slowly than 'Questa o quella'. These tempi are fine, but a convincing case could be made for taking the former faster or the latter slower. To a great extent, the tempo of an individual number in an opera depends in the first place on the text and then on the general tempo of a scene or even of a whole act.

At the very beginning of *Rigoletto*, Giulini did not want the Duke's recitative, which is sung over the off-stage band's accompaniment, to be sung with metronomic precision. He wanted me to sing 'Della mia bella incognita borghese', and the words that follow, with the naturalness of speech, but without distorting the tempo. The words had to press forward, without . laying stress on the beginning and on the middle of every bar. He was absolutely correct in this. The band automatically emphasizes those beats, and if the tenor makes the same accentuation, the text will not be heard.

I observed with fascination Giulini's extraordinary way of working with the strings when he was preparing the first Rigoletto-Gilda scene. His way of obtaining beautiful sound quality, little accents and so many other refined touches was amazing. The ex-viola player in him really came to the fore. There are thousands of such details to be learned in the operatic repertoire, and they can indeed be learned from the special people I am fortunate enough to work with. Ten or twelve musician-conductors stand at the top of their world, and it is no accident that they are there.

Towards the end of 1979 I went to Washington to take part in a programme given on President Carter's initiative to honour five great Americans: Aaron Copland, Ella Fitzgerald, Henry Fonda, Martha Graham and Tennessee Williams. The President was unable to attend, however, because of the Iranian hostage crisis.

In March 1980 the Met mounted a new production of *Manon Lescaut* in which I sang opposite Scotto. I was very pleased when I was told afterwards that our dramatic involvement was such that the performance could have stood as a theatre piece, even without the singing. That was the Met's first live telecast to Europe, and it was wonderful to have participated in it with one of the greatest singing actresses of our time. Levine conducted, and Menotti directed the staging. Menotti's talents as a director are often obscured by his fame as a composer and as organizer of the Spoleto Festival. I had already worked with him in *La bohème* in Paris, and I found his ideas to be refined and refreshing. I also admire his compositions more than is fashionable. He is often criticized for being too Puccini-like, but Menotti was already studying music in Milan at the time of Puccini's death, when that composer's influence was very strong. There are so few composers writing singable music these days that it seems a shame to criticize Menotti's works for their easy-to-grasp vocal qualities.

Now that I have begun a digression, I may as well finish it. I do not believe that in fifty years the average human ear will have developed the ability to become familiar with the sort of music that most composers have been creating during the past generation or two. It is music for specialists. If that is what they want to produce, well and good, but they are fooling themselves if they believe that the public that wants to hear Bach, Schubert, Verdi and Stravinsky will ever be able to cope with today's academic music. Even a truly theatrical work like Berg's *Lulu*, great though it is, has not entered and cannot enter the popular repertoire – I use the word 'popular' in its finest sense – and *Lulu* is already half a century old. I think it is a pity that people like Menotti are discouraged from proceeding with their work, which is why I have asked him to write an opera for me based on the life of Goya.

On 1 April 1980, my parents' fortieth wedding anniversary, Marta, the boys and I went to Mexico to be with them. The evening before the anniversary we announced that we were taking them out to dinner, stopping first at church. There, to my parents' surprise, we had arranged a big Mass with over two hundred friends and relatives in attendance. I sang during the service, although I was so moved that I could hardly manage to finish. The 'dinner' was a big banquet for everyone.

At the age of eighty-nine, Federico Moreno Torroba, our old family friend, completed an opera for me, *El Poeta*, and I was able to sing the lead role at its première in Madrid on 19 June. *El Poeta* has some truly beautiful pages, but the story is not strong enough. The orchestra, under Luis Antonio García Navarro, played marvellously; and Angeles Gulin's singing was wonderful. I was enormously pleased to be able to give my dear friend the thrill of having his new work performed. Two years later, when I gave an outdoor concert in Madrid for 250,000 people, I called Moreno Torroba onto the stage and invited him to conduct one of his own pieces. The man's energy was still incredible, and he had an enormous success. Unfortunately, only a month or so later he became ill, and he died in September 1982 at the age of ninety-one, after a full, beautiful life dedicated to music.

Another strike at the Metropolitan in the autumn of 1980 allowed me to take part in an improvised project with Giulini and his Los Angeles Philharmonic. They were to have performed and recorded *Das Lied von der Erde*, but one of the soloists became ill, and the plan had to be scrapped. Since I was already scheduled to do a benefit concert with the Philharmonic, Deutsche Grammophon's Günter Breest had the idea of using the planned taping sessions to record part of our programme. Conductors of Giulini's stature rarely participate in records of arias, and I felt very honoured. His warm praise when we were preparing the pieces also meant a great deal to me. I only wish that he would add Puccini to his repertoire. I understand that everyone has his personal likes and dislikes, but I know that Giulini would perform that music marvellously.

One of the great regrets of my life is that I was able to work so very little with Karl Böhm. I recorded the Beethoven Ninth with him, and that was all. We had planned a new production of *Otello* in Vienna, but the scheduling did not work out; and I considered taking part in his *Ariadne auf Naxos* production in Salzburg in 1979 but decided against it. Strauss, generous as he is with female singers, is rather stingy with tenors, and Bacchus would have been both an ungrateful and a vocally dangerous part for me. I am terribly sorry, however, not to have had the experience of singing Strauss with Böhm, who had known the composer so well.

For me, Böhm was the music itself. When we recorded the Ninth in Vienna in 1980, he was eighty-seven; he arrived at the session looking frail and barely able to walk. But when he launched into the music, all his greatness was evident. Energy and strength seemed to emanate from every finger. On the interpretative level, I was impressed by the natural tempo he chose for the 'Alla marcia' section, the tenor's solo. Conductors tend either to rush frenetically through it or to kill you with a tempo so slow that you run out of breath. His tempo was just right. And he was absolutely in control of the proceedings, feeding the words to the soloists and chorus, cueing the orchestra, and throwing himself unstintingly into his work. Before the recording session we had had a piano rehearsal with a co-*répétiteur*, supervised by Böhm. He worked particularly hard on the difficult quartet passages in the last section.

I had many opportunities to see him conduct some of the staple works of his repertoire - always an emotional experience for me. I would go to see him after performances, and he was very kind. He telephoned me during an interval in the opening performance of the new *Manon Lescaut* production in New York, to find out how it was going and to wish me well, and I cherish several telegrams he sent me at important moments in my career. He even made me a present of his own piano score of the Beethoven Ninth - the copy he had used throughout his career.

In May 1981 I went to see him in a Viennese hospital. He was hoping to be able to attend one of my performances of *Andrea Chénier* there during that period, but he could not do so. On 10 August, four days before he died, I again visited him at his home in Salzburg, but by then he was unconscious. On the day of his death, I had a *Hoffmann* performance in Salzburg, and I went early to the Festspielhaus to vocalize. Since I was preparing for my television special about operas set in Seville, I began to sing Florestan's aria from *Fidelio*, which I had never sung before. For the very first time in my life I sang the moving opening phrase: 'Gott, welch Dunkel hier!' ('God, what darkness here!'). I had no sooner sung those four words than Uli Märkle opened my dressing-room door to tell me, in tears, that Böhm had just died.

Karl Böhm served music in a humble way. He was one of the great conductors of our time.

VII
SINGING 'HOFFMANN'

The centenary of Jacques Offenbach's death fell in 1980 and that of the posthumous première of his uncompleted opera, *The Tales of Hoffmann*, occurred in 1981. In connection with those anniversaries, I sang the title role in four new *Hoffmann* productions – a total of thirty-nine performances between August 1980 and August 1982. Had I not turned down other offers, I would have been singing nothing but *Hoffmann* during that period.

I had lived through other important anniversaries during my career, but none had created such interest as these. I suspect that this was because *Hoffmann* was never a front-runner in the operatic repertoire, and the centenaries provided an excuse for re-examining a great work beset with textual problems. I once asked Callas why she had never sung the soprano parts in *Hoffmann*; she said that no one had ever invited her to do so. There are indeed works that suffer periods of neglect and that then, for one reason or another, seem to be reborn. Look at Verdi's *Simon Boccanegra*, a rarity for decades and now so often revived – probably as a direct result of the extraordinary Abbado–Strehler production at La Scala. The same is true of Mozart's *La clemenza di Tito*, which was given a great boost recently through the Levine-Ponnelle Salzburg production, which was later filmed. That the role of Hoffmann has not appealed to more tenors is a great mystery. The part would have been ideal for Gigli and perhaps even for Caruso, Pertile and Fleta. Later, too, Bjoerling could have sung it wonderfully. Tucker did sing it, and so did Campora. In fact, when I was first going to tackle the role, people warned me against it, saying that it had harmed other tenors vocally; and it is true that *Hoffmann* could be a ruinous work if sung too much too early in a career, without enough technical preparation.

My first encounter with *Hoffmann* took place in Mexico in 1965, just after I had left Tel Aviv. It came about not because I had any special interest in the role, but simply through the offer of a contract. I was only twenty-four, and although I was not really careless in undertaking it then, I was somewhat rash. Still, at twenty-four one can afford to be, and perhaps even ought to be, rash sometimes. I mentioned earlier that *Lohengrin* is a difficult role because so much of the writing is concentrated in the passaggio, the middle-high register, which puts a strain on the voice. The same is true of *Hoffmann*. And there is another problem in *Hoffmann* that I can only describe as the unnaturalness of the French style. Certainly *Hoffmann* can be very dangerous for a young tenor. Early in a singer's career, the easiest composer to sing is Puccini. In a sense, we can sing Puccini as we can sing a song, because those magnificent melodies have a natural ebb and flow, an inevitable up-and-down quality. Puccini was a Tuscan, and his aria writing followed the natural pattern of the Tuscan *stornello*, making it possible for young tenors at the outset of their careers to sing *Bohème* and *Tosca*. I would rather not comment on *how* they sing them, but they *do* sing them – whereas they could never begin to sing *Aida* or *Boccanegra*, which require tenacious concentration on the terse, muscular Verdi 'line'.

I am often amazed that people understand so little about such problems – not casual listeners, but so-called experts. Someone will make an all-embracing statement to the effect that Domingo's voice used to be more lyrical than it is today; yet even a few years ago I could not sing a supremely lyrical role like Hoffmann as well as I know I sing it now. My technique and voice have changed so much that I can now cope with this high-lying part much more easily than before. 'Domingo is singing dramatic roles,' people say with alarm, but they do not seem to notice how much easier the *Bohème*s and *Hoffmann*s are for me after having sung those dramatic roles. When I performed *Hoffmann* in Mexico, I was unable to sing the duet with Giulietta in the right key: I had to have it transposed down a semitone. Now it poses no problem, although according to the experts' theories the opposite should be true. These days I may pick and choose among both the lyric and the dramatic roles. It is fantastic to be on stage for a *Hoffmann*, on an ideal day when I am in perfect health and psychologically relaxed, and to *sing*, just sing, just make music and concentrate on interpretation, without having to think about technical problems – because in certain roles those problems have become very minor over the years. I do not have to prove to the public or to myself that I can do it. I just sing and feel good about it.

But in Mexico in 1965 I was offered *Hoffmann* or nothing, and I accepted the task without being entirely aware of its proportions. Tito Capobianco directed, and at the time I liked the production very much. Thinking back on it, I realize that it was not very convincing, centring as it did on the four baritone roles. Norman Treigle, who sang those roles magnificently, had a big personality, and it is understandable that Capobianco wanted to focus attention on the diabolical aspect of the work. The focus was so strong that the Epilogue was omitted altogether. The show concluded with Treigle as Dr Miracle, a part he did fantastically well. He was dressed all in black; and at the end, through a lighting effect, the public saw only the white skeleton that was painted onto his costume. When I cried out 'Un médecin! un médecin!', he appeared in the orchestra pit, next to the conductor, for his last words – 'Présent! Morte!' – and the opera ended. I had three Mexican leading ladies: Olympia was our friend Ernestina Garfias, who had a very pretty coloratura voice; Giulietta was Belen Amparan; and Antonia was Rosa Rimoch. I was really just taking a stab at my role, as I certainly was not ready for it vocally. The success was great, but that may have been because it was my return home, my ¡bienvenido! As I mentioned earlier, there was one critic who was not so keen.

Three months later I sang another *Hoffmann* at the Academy of Music in Philadelphia as part of a New York City Opera tour. The governing concept was essentially the same as in the Mexican production because Capobianco had directed it and Treigle was singing the baritone parts. Beverly Sills performed all the soprano roles. I was called upon to sing *Hoffmann* from time to time during the next few years, and in 1971 I recorded it with Joan Sutherland and Gabriel Bacquier under Richard Bonynge's direction. Two years later I performed *Hoffmann* at the Met with Sutherland, Thomas Stewart and Bonynge. Richard, who knows and loves the French repertoire, had done a great deal of research on *Hoffmann* with fine results. He prefers the version in which Stella comes at the end. The septet is not sung in Giulietta's scene, but instead is transformed into a quartet during the Epilogue – with different words, of course. Richard even managed to find an exciting E-flat for Joan to sing there. Although singing the quartet at the end, after all that had gone before, was murderous, the production definitely appealed to me more than earlier ones and began to make me realize the greatness of my role. I had been aware of its beauty from the start, but without the Epilogue it had always been an incomplete artistic experience. Now I began to think seriously about what the part should be.

I see a great deal of Beethoven in the character of Hoffmann. We know that E.T.A. Hoffmann was one of Beethoven's greatest admirers among the composer's contemporaries, but that is not the point. Hoffmann, as he appears in Offenbach's opera, is a man who suffers at the hands of humanity. He is too idealistic, too passionate, to be able to find 'normal' ways of life tolerable; and besides, he has taken it upon himself to use his own troubles as the raw material with which he creates a higher way of communicating with people. That in itself is a sad task, because art is usually misunderstood – thought of simply as entertainment, nothing more, and so on. Even a Rigoletto is less tragic than a Hoffmann: people may laugh at his physical deformities, but he strikes back with a spiteful, vindictive humour that they hate but understand. A Beethoven, a Hoffmann, is laughed at for his personal tragedy; he reacts with and through love, and even the products of that love are misunderstood and taken as cause for amusement. The moments of inspiration, of enlightenment, have to be their own reward.

The reader who is not fully aware of *Hoffmann*'s textual difficulties will more completely understand their peculiarities through a brief extract from Jean-Louis Martinoty's notes for the Salzburg programme book:

> Offenbach died before he could complete the opera, and at its première it was very severely edited (for instance, an entire act was omitted). There is no authentic manuscript of the work as completed by Guiraud and the scores of the first performances, which might have helped to clear up one or two problems, were destroyed in the fires that occurred in the Ringtheater in Vienna in 1881 ... and in 1887 in the Opéra-Comique in Paris. The first printed version of *The Tales of Hoffmann* did not reinstate the arbitrary cuts made at the première. A few years later, second, third and fourth editions [by Choudens] published the 'Venice' act, which had originally been cut, but it was included before the 'Antonia' act. . . .
>
> At last, in 1978, an absolutely spectacular 'critical revised edition' by Fritz Oeser appeared ... and this included for the first time hitherto unknown parts of the work and allowed a re-evaluation of certain aspects of the opera. . . . As far as *The Tales of Hoffmann* is concerned, only one thing is certain: that it is impossible to arrive at any kind of certainty. The decision rests with the realization on stage.

The curious thing about *Hoffmann* is that it is both very difficult and very easy for the stage director – difficult because there is so much to be done, easy because there is so much leeway. In large portions of the work we have only a vague idea of what Offenbach intended, and in some of it we have no idea at all. Directors may all say that they are being faithful to the composer's spirit without having to be faithful to the letter. Although I have strong convictions about Hoffmann, as about my other roles, I like to renew myself completely, to refresh and recharge from time to time.

My next *Hoffmann* after the Bonynge production was scheduled for Chicago in 1976. By then I had begun to think that it was too light a role for my voice. I decided not to do it but changed my mind again. The production made use of the Choudens edition, but included the Epilogue. Bruno Bartoletti conducted; Virginio Puecher directed the staging; the ladies were sung by Ruth Welting, Viorica Cortez and Christiane Eda-Pierre; and Norman Mittleman was the villain throughout. My taste for the opera was further stimulated by this version. It occurred to me that the Offenbach-*Hoffmann* centenaries were only a few years off, and I began to plan accordingly. Jimmy Levine and I discussed the idea of doing the work at Salzburg. Although the festival is dedicated to Mozart, many other composers' works are also performed there; I had made my Salzburg debut in Verdi's *Don Carlo*, and performing Offenbach there did not appear to me in any way sacrilegious. I was not optimistic about our plans coming to fruition. Jimmy, however, aroused Ponnelle's enthusiasm, and since the Levine-Ponnelle team had already been so successful at Salzburg with *La clemenza di Tito* and *The Magic Flute*, the festival administration decided to proceed with *Hoffmann*. Gradually, other enticing *Hoffmann* proposals began to accumulate on my desk, and before long I had agreed to take part in productions at the Cologne Opera, Covent Garden and the Met once the Salzburg project was launched.

The Salzburg production opened in August 1980. The stage of the Grosses Festspielhaus is so special, both in size and in mechanical possibilities, that it has to be handled with great care and only by people who are thoroughly familiar with it. Jean-Pierre is truly a master in that theatre and, not surprisingly, he created a masterly version of the opera – one of his finest achievements. As Salzburg productions go, this was not expensive, but it was done with such elegant taste that it looked phenomenally costly. Everything was well planned, and a subtle use of mirrors and of the highly polished floor gave a high-class and expensive appearance. I sang in the production in three successive summers, and I found it as magical in 1982 as in previous years. Only the strange (in my opinion) substitution of a ballet prevented *Hoffmann* from returning to Salzburg in 1983.

There was a great deal of discussion about which version of the work to use, and in the end we opted for the new Oeser edition wherever it seemed to make the most sense, returning to the traditional Choudens edition, despite its faults, where Oeser appeared to have gone out on a limb. For instance, we used the Nicklausse-Hoffmann-Coppélius trio that Oeser included in his edition; but the 'Scintille, diamant' aria, eliminated by Oeser, was allowed to remain. Material that had become popular over the decades was not removed, even if in some instances there was no case for its authenticity. I think that the judgements made were largely excellent ones, and the 'new' material was often exciting, although there is some second-rate music in the Epilogue – especially the re-entry of Stella, which always made me think of the villain's motif in the Mighty Mouse cartoons. The most positive change was the return in the Epilogue of Hoffmann's 'Kleinzach' motif from the Prologue. When I sang my last 'Voilà, voilà Kleinzach!', Ponnelle had me point to myself as if to say, '*I* am Kleinzach.' How much stronger this was than Hoffmann's usual repetition of 'O Dieu! de quelle ivresse'!

One of Jean-Pierre's interesting ideas was to present the servant as the devil's ally. In the 'Antonia' act, Ponnelle had Frantz siding clearly with Dr Miracle rather than showing respect towards Crespel and affection towards Hoffmann, as is usually the case. Jean-Pierre made the servant a sour, meddlesome character throughout, and by the end it was difficult to know whether the man was deaf or feigning deafness. Ponnelle saw Antonia herself not as simply a naive, romantic girl who loves to sing but as a somewhat neurotic and at times almost crazy character, reduced to despair, brought to the verge of madness, by her wild desire to sing. (Jean-Pierre has worked with so many singers over the years that he must have drawn the character from experience.)

I found his approach to my character confused in the Prologue. In the later, very realistic New York and London productions, I had to appear already drunk when I made my entrance, and the atmosphere of the wine cellar in both versions added to that impression. But in Salzburg the table was set up in the square, in front of the theatre where Stella was performing. Since the atmosphere was surreal, the idea of Hoffmann arriving drunk would not have fitted in, and in fact Jean-Pierre wanted me to do the whole Prologue as a sober man. But why was I lying asleep at the side of the stage, after being given drink by the spirits of wine and beer, if I was not supposed to be drunk? Ponnelle's interpretation did, however, give me a chance to do the Prologue in a more dashing and even in a more natural way, since my actions did not have to be limited to those of a drunken man. A sober Hoffmann could be a more interesting one. What really disturbed me was my long wait on stage after my ambiguous entrance – a wait that extended right up to my first words. It detracted from the subsequent action because the public had already seen too much of Hoffmann. Furthermore, in this work, where there are so many different editions with so many textual variants, spectators easily became confused at the very beginning: 'Why is Hoffmann already on stage? What is he doing? What is happening?'

I had always done 'Giulietta' as the second tale and 'Antonia' as the third, but in Salzburg they were reversed. This is the better approach. The three loves recounted in the three tales are focal points, syntheses of all the loves in Hoffmann's life. Olympia, the first, is the symbol of naive, idealized love, unreal to the point of illusion. She is a doll, a symbol of superficiality. Then comes the very real, passionate love for Antonia – perhaps a bit on the platonic side, but still very intense. For Hoffmann, Antonia is not just a woman – she is Woman; and when she dies, his ability to love dies, too. Finally, there is Giulietta, a whore, to whom Hoffmann comes with a cynical attitude. 'Friends!' says Hoffmann, 'Gentle, dreamy love is a mistake! Love amid revelry and wine is divine!' It is true that all Hoffmann's love affairs are unbalanced: he never manages to combine the ideal, the passionate and the carnal aspects of love; and in that sense the order of the tales does not matter. But I think that psychologically and dramatically, Olympia-Antonia-Giulietta is the most effective sequence. It is not enough that this man has suffered disappointment and disaster: in the end he is also deceived, and by a whore. How *could* he proceed to Antonia after that destructive resolution? It would not make sense.

From the vocal angle, too, when I go directly from 'Giulietta' to the Epilogue, I am charged up in a way that I am not when I go from 'Antonia' to the Epilogue. Although Hoffmann's part in 'Antonia' is very difficult, very high, it is of minor importance compared with the power of Antonia's own music and the Antonia-Mother-Miracle trio. Hoffmann returns at the end and sings eleven words, and that's it for him. To make the physical and emotional transition from that to the Epilogue is very unnatural. But after the 'Giulietta' scene I feel exhausted, finished – which is exactly what the Epilogue requires. 'Giulietta' was left in the least complete state of any of the acts; yet, in addition to having the tenor's most difficult music, it has four of his most magnificent vocal moments: the couplets, the aria, the duet and the septet. It is true that the music of the 'Antonia' act is of a generally higher quality than that of the 'Giulietta' act. Nevertheless, I feel that I, as Hoffmann, can pull the whole work together in a more logical and satisfactory way by putting 'Giulietta' before the Epilogue.

Jean-Pierre's 'Giulietta' suffered a little from the brilliance of the basic idea behind it. The act is, of course, set in Venice, and his invention of the 'gondolas' – pieces of material being pulled around the stage with people sitting on them – was so beautiful that I think he missed some opportunities later in the scene. It would have been like Jean-Pierre to have had, say, a bishop with a young girl in a gondola, but instead he left the scene alone – which was perfectly legitimate.

Though he has conducted far less French repertoire than Italian or German, Jimmy Levine had a wonderful feeling for *Hoffmann* – open, sincere, happy and, in the 'Antonia' scene, very dramatic. The Staatsoper orchestra, despite a tendency to overplay, sounded magnificent.

Immediately after the Salzburg production came one in Cologne, in October 1980. Of all the *Hoffmanns* I have done, that one had the strongest Opéra-Comique flavour. It was very cleverly staged by Michael Hampe, the Cologne Intendant. He is a cellist, a serious musician, who thinks deeply about his work. A tendency to over-intellectualize, to go a bit deeper than the material calls for, occasionally betrays itself; but he is very thorough and, like Piero Faggioni and Zeffirelli, very good at showing singers how he wants them to act. Hampe had us include some spoken dialogue. 'Giulietta' was again the last act; and at the end of this version, as in Bonynge's, the poor lady died of poisoning. The conductor was John Pritchard, an assured and refined musician, who did a good job, although I had the impression that he did not greatly enjoy working on *Hoffmann*. The only other time I worked with him was on the 1977 recording of *L'elisir d'amore*, and there I found him superb – much happier and more at ease than with *Hoffmann*.

It was a great pleasure for me to work with John Schlesinger on Covent Garden's *Hoffmann* because of his fine feeling for the music. He confessed to me beforehand that he was scared to death of the project, but I never had any doubts about his ability. Schlesinger's sensitivity is such that he could not have gone wrong. He decided to follow the Choudens version, and in that he may have been influenced by Carlos Kleiber, who was originally scheduled to conduct. Carlos's cancellation was a big disappointment. I can hear in my mind's ear what he would do with that work. I would like to convince him to conduct *Hoffmann* at La Scala, and perhaps he will try it some day. In any case, we were lucky to have had Georges Prêtre to replace him at Covent Garden. There were some ensemble problems when he tried to achieve tricky rubati with the chorus – a virtually impossible feat in such a big space as the Royal Opera House. But he was completely at home in *Hoffmann*, and the performances were very fine and highly successful.

Schlesinger had three different leading ladies: Luciana Serra as Olympia,

Ileana Cotrubas as Antonia, and Agnes Baltsa as Giulietta. I do not think that one soprano ought to sing all the roles, and I say this despite having performed the work that way with such magnificent artists as Joan Sutherland, Catherine Malfitano, Edda Moser and Christiane Eda-Pierre. The constant in the opera is the contrast between the guileless Hoffmann and Lindorf, who is the spirit of evil – the evil that surrounds Hoffmann everywhere. Each of the women must, on the contrary, present a completely different personality, a different female prototype; and that is nearly impossible for one singer to achieve in the course of a single evening. Also, the vocal difficulties for the soprano vary so widely in type from one act to another that a soprano who sings a fantastic Antonia will not necessarily be equally effective as Olympia or Giulietta. Schlesinger also had four different bad guys: Robert Lloyd as Lindorf, Geraint Evans as Coppélius, Nicola Ghiuselev as Dr Miracle, and Siegmund Nimsgern as Dapertutto. The innovation worked quite well because Lindorf reappeared at the end of each act, controlling the proceedings. In a way, the symbol was even more effective when presented in this way. Schlesinger made Hoffmann drunk and disorderly not only in the Prologue but also in the Epilogue, giving the work a greater dramatic unity than in any of the other productions. The Venice scene was also excellent in Schlesinger's version – a real orgy where anything could happen. Fortunately, there exists a videodisc of this production. It was nominated for a Grammy award, but lost to Olivia Newton John's 'Physical', and I am puzzled as to how both productions came to be considered in the same category.

The Met's *Hoffmann* was staged by Otto Schenk, and I confess that in the beginning I had my doubts. It seemed to me that the 'Olympia' act was too funny, too incredible even for the credulous Hoffmann. I overcame the problem by playing the scene as if I thought that Olympia was a real girl imitating a doll. Ruth Welting was perfect as the doll – so completely believable that it was almost frightening. When she would sing her high F, Cochenille would touch her and react as if he had had an electric shock. Schenk had the chorus respond exaggeratedly to everything that took place on stage, and the whole scene went beautifully. He and Riccardo Chailly, the conductor, decided to use the Choudens edition. *Hoffmann* marked Chailly's debut at the Met, and his reading of the score was very good. Since he had also shown fine feeling for *Werther* in the recording we made of that work, we may now have an Italian conductor who can deal beautifully with the French operatic repertoire. His *Hoffmann* improved from performance to performance, as he became more accustomed to the theatre's acoustics and to the Met orchestra, and as his feeling for the work deepened. The production was an amazing success, the triumph of the Met's season. Hundreds and hundreds of people tried unsuccessfully to get tickets.

Although I am lucky to have been able to alternate productions, I wish I had also sung in the version directed by Patrice Chéreau at the Paris Opéra. He came up with a very amusing idea for the 'Olympia' act: he used a robot and had the voice coming from the wings. Some sort of radio hook-up was used, and I have been told that during one of Olympia's coloratura passages, her voice was transmitted into a passing police car en route to a bank robbery, while the sound of the police siren was broadcast into the Opéra. I would have liked to have heard that!

VIII
INTO MY FIFTH DECADE

On 21 January 1981 I celebrated my fortieth birthday in Milan, where I was rehearsing a new production of *Cavalleria* and *Pagliacci*, by giving a big party. In addition to my family and my Scala colleagues, the guests included Renata Tebaldi, Mafalda Favero, Giulietta Simionato and Franco Zeffirelli.

The new production, conducted by Prêtre and staged by Zeffirelli, was quite special in that it was being simultaneously produced as a film. (The *Cavalleria* co-starred Obraztsova and Matteo Manuguerra; the *Pagliacci*, Elena Mauti-Nunziata and Juan Pons.) Franco made the film in three different ways. First, we had two entire shooting days at La Scala, one for each opera, with the orchestra present, repeating passages as required; then we did some filming in the studio. All of this went quite well. But when Franco sees something good, he wants to make it better. He decided that we needed some exterior footage, and therefore we all went to Sicily – to Vizzini, the village where the story behind Verga's 'Cavalleria rusticana' is supposed to have taken place. There I did the Brindisi, the Siciliana, and some of the scenes with Santuzza. The whole project was an experiment, and I hope it will prove to have been a successful one. The film is now (1983) ready for showing, but it is being held back until our later film, *La traviata*, has had a chance to circulate. The reason is that the *Traviata* is in every respect fully cinematic, and Franco feels that it is better to release it before the less orthodox *Cavalleria–Pagliacci* film.

In *Cavalleria* Franco and I disagreed for the first time about the basic characterization of a role. He believed that Turiddu is a superficial fellow who plays with Lola and Santuzza and does not take either of them seriously – someone who combs his hair, counts on his good looks to win him new conquests, and enjoys the dispute between the two women. To me, how-

144

ever, Turiddu is as much a victim as Santuzza. He was in love with Lola, and then, while he was off doing his military service, she married Alfio, the local rich boy. Turiddu, on returning, feels that he has been deceived, and he is both angered and saddened. Out of spite, he begins to see Santuzza, to lead her on. But Santuzza is a possessive woman, given to complaining, and he soon tires of her. I am not trying to say that Turiddu is a noble or honourable character, but I do see him as a three-dimensional figure who is capable of a variety of emotions. Usually, when I sing this role, I even like to show a certain compassion for Santuzza. The problem is that I, Turiddu, find her tiresome and certainly cannot see her as my future wife. Besides, I am still fascinated by Lola. The sorrow of having lost her and the predicament of Santuzza's pregnancy overwhelm Turiddu, and his behaviour at the tavern shows him in an almost suicidal light.

It is a beautiful film indeed, and I am very pleased to have a document of myself performing both operas in one evening – especially since the wig I wear as Canio makes me look a generation older than my Turiddu. Again, the authentic flavour that Franco achieves in both operas and the thoroughness of detail in the costumes, sets and surroundings are amazing, and unparalleled in the work of any other director.

A new production of *La traviata* at the Met in March gave me another opportunity to work with Ileana Cotrubas, a great musician and cultivated artist with marvellous temperament and a beautiful voice. She and her husband Manfred Ramin, a gifted conductor, are wonderful company, too.

For the Domingos 1981 was hospital year. My father had a completely successful operation in Mexico in March; Marta underwent gall bladder surgery, also successful, in Barcelona in July; and Alvaro had to be hospitalized and operated on a week later when he hurt his shoulder badly. Fortunately they all mended quickly. In other respects it was a normal year for me – a great deal of performing and much travelling, too. I recall, for instance, that in June, after singing four *Lucia*s in Madrid and a *Tosca* in New York's Central Park (with Scotto, Milnes and Levine), I went to Buenos Aires for five *Otello*s, and that immediately after each of the last three of those performances had ended I spent the rest of the night in the recording studio, making my album of tangos – just to keep busy. I chose that method because my voice is much less fatigued by continuing to sing immediately after a performance than by 'opening up' again two days later – and two days before the next performance. During that entire period a Spanish television crew followed me around, shooting a special feature for the series 'The 300 Million'.

Shortly before that I had recorded *Turandot* with Herbert von Karajan. It is not an opera that he has conducted a great deal, yet it was a great experience to have participated in the project with him. The sound of the Vienna Philharmonic at those sessions was simply fabulous. The way the chords seemed to sink downwards, the way Karajan delayed the upbeats so that when the downbeats came, one would hear full, rich chords, from the double-basses right up to the flutes: it was unbelievable. For some his tempi may be on the slow side, but one hears things that have rarely been heard before in the orchestral texture. The invocation to the moon, as Karajan does it, is an example of extreme discipline perfectly balanced with intensity of feeling. My European agent Michel Glotz, who is a great producer as well as a manager, was in charge of that recording. Karajan respects Michel's judgement and responds to his sense of humour. He once convinced the reluctant conductor to retake one section of the work by offering him a reward of two deutschmarks (fifty pence).

At the Bregenz Festival that summer I sang three performances of *Otello* with Anna Tomowa-Sintow and Silvano Carroli; Santi conducted and Faggioni directed. In principle, I liked Piero's adoption of a rotating stage, but in actual fact he used it too much. Some people in the audience complained to me that the rotation made them dizzy. At my first entrance for the 'Esultate!', I wore a turban; and when I entered the bedchamber in the last act, again wearing the turban, I unwound it slowly, ceremonially, as if unravelling my whole life. That innovation seemed very beautiful. Another of Piero's ideas was to have me go about barefoot when I was 'at home' in the second act. Otello is himself there, the master of his situation, not a fake Venetian. (This, I believe, owed something to Olivier's Othello.) And in the same act there was a real fountain for me to drink from at moments when the course of events was beginning to overwhelm me. Of course I had to be careful about my make-up – otherwise I might have become the first striped Otello in the history of the opera. Owing to Marta's and Alvaro's operations during that period, I had little time to rehearse with Piero. I hope to work on another *Otello* with him some time.

From mid December 1981 to early January 1982 I was in Seville with my family, combining a Christmas holiday with the shooting of a film about that city's place in operatic history. The idea for the film was mine: since so many opera plots take place there, why not film a programme on location? I suggested it to Ponnelle, who proposed it to Unitel, who in turn approved the idea with the proviso that we find a great conductor for the task. Jimmy Levine was asked, and he accepted. I very much liked Jean-Pierre's ideas.

Filming Florestan's aria from *Fidelio* in the ruins of the Roman amphitheatre in Itálica, outside the city; using Goya's drawings of *The Horrors of
War* during the introduction to that aria; showing Don Giovanni, that great
sinner for whom nothing was sacred, singing of his conquests from the top
of the Giralda, the great tower of Seville's cathedral; setting the final
Carmen-Don José duet in, rather than outside, the bullring, because she,
like the bull, cannot escape her destiny; the humorous back-and-forth
cutting between Figaro and Almaviva (both sung by me) in their duet from
The Barber of Seville – all of these details helped to make the programme
valuable and beautiful. I could never have realized my idea without the
cooperation of a genius like Ponnelle.

We all had a good time during the shooting. One day Jean-Pierre and I
and three or four others were having lunch in a tavern across from Itálica,
when an old man, obviously an habitué of the tavern, pulled up a chair and,
in a thick Andalusian accent, began telling Jean-Pierre about a Spanish
actress who had once made a film on the site and who had eaten in the same
tavern. Jean-Pierre speaks French, English, Italian and German, but not
Spanish. After smiling at the old man and shrugging his shoulders for quite
a while, he said to me in Italian, 'Plácido, I think I'm going to have to stop
smiling now, otherwise we could spend a month here and this old-timer
wouldn't know or care that I don't understand a word he's saying.' Another
time, during a terrible downpour, Soledad Becerril, who was then Spain's
Minister of Culture, the Domecq brothers, of sherry-producing fame, their
families and several other friends turned up to see how the shooting was
going, only to find us taking shelter in the tavern. A first-class restaurant
would probably have collapsed under the circumstances, but not that little
tavern! They managed to extend the table and to prepare good food for
everyone.

Early in 1982 I sang two performances of *Luisa Miller* in Hamburg with
Giuseppe Sinopoli, a young Italian conductor who has a very fine feeling
for the old traditions, as well as temperament and a wonderful sense of
timing. The freedom he allows his singers is anything but laxity or care-
lessness. It is carefully planned, and it is always permitted for a specific
reason. He and I share a theory about upbeats: the upbeat, in slow arias
with light orchestral accompaniment, should be slightly – extremely slightly
– delayed in order that each phrase may have its proper weight. At the
beginning of 'Quando le sere al placido' in *Luisa Miller*, for instance, the
tenor has a quarter-rest at the end of each phrase. If the orchestral accompaniment is pushed along during the tenor's rests, which fall on upbeats,

the feeling of absolute calm is destroyed. A cliché worth repeating is that the orchestra, in such passages, must in effect breathe with the singer; and the conductor must have a 'long arm' to help the players feel the phrase and to keep the pit and stage harnessed together. In such a situation, when things go right, I feel no agitation; I feel free to be unexaggeratedly expressive and to sing softly without fear of being swamped by the orchestra, because the still quality extends to the volume as well as the movement.

On 16 January I was in New York to perform in a 'Live from Studio 8-H' televised tribute to Caruso, with Mehta and the New York Philharmonic. By chance that telecast took place on the twenty-fifth anniversary of Toscanini's death, and in the same studio where he had conducted his NBC Symphony Orchestra for many years. In New York during February and March, in addition to rehearsing and performing in the new *Hoffmann* production, I also sang in *Norma*, *Bohème*, the Verdi Requiem and a concert with Tatiana Troyanos. In the benefit gala, 'Night of the Hundred Stars', I added a new partner to my list of leading ladies: Miss Piggy of *The Muppet Show*.

Above all, 1982 was *Traviata* year for me. My participation in Franco Zeffirelli's filmed version of the opera – with Teresa Stratas as Violetta and Cornell MacNeil as Germont, and with the outstanding support of Jimmy Levine and the Metropolitan orchestra and chorus – came about in a strange way. I had originally been approached by Franco and Sir John Tooley to take part in a film that was to have been based on a new Covent Garden *Traviata* production. That production never took place, and I could not have appeared in it even if it had, since it was to have been produced during one of my Met engagements. The idea was then transformed into a straight cinematic project, and prior bookings again made me unavailable, much to my disappointment. José Carreras was contracted to sing Alfredo, but he, too, had scheduling problems. He had asked to be released from some performances at the Paris Opéra in order to make the film, but the administration would not let him go. A difficult situation developed, and in the end José had to give up the film. Franco turned to me again, and by a strange coincidence I was able to help. It may be recalled that three years earlier I had saved the Teatro Colón in Buenos Aires from a difficult situation by flying in for three performances of *La fanciulla del West* when another tenor was ill. In May 1982 I was scheduled to sing seven performances of *Tosca* in Buenos Aires, and I felt justified in requesting the favour of being

 c. 1972

At home (in Teaneck, New Jersey) with Marta, Placi and Alvaro, 1969

Holding Alvaro, with Pepe, Placi and Marta, New York, 1971

Signing my Metropolitan Opera contract, with
Rudolf Bing, 1968

A concert at the Kremlin, 1974

With Sherrill Milnes and Leontyne Price at a party given to launch our recording of *La
forza del destino*

Rehearsing *Carmen* in Vienna, 1978, with Franco Zeffirelli, Carlos Kleiber and Elena Obraztsova

With Pope John Paul II, The Vatican, 1982

Listening to a playback of a recording of opera arias, with Carlo Maria Giulini (right) and technician Hans Weber, Los Angeles, 1980

Karl Böhm presenting me with Böhm's own vocal score of Beethoven's 9th Symphony while recording the work in Vienna, 1980

With John Denver, Los Angeles, 1980

With Milton Okun, Los Angeles, 1980

With footballer Kevin Keegan, near London, 1980

Los Angeles, 1980

With Richard Baker, Sir John Tooley, Kiri Te Kanawa and Bernard Levin, near London, 1980

In front of the Paris Opéra, *c.* 1975

With Federico Moreno Torroba, *c.* 1980

With Anthony Bliss, Marta, and James Levine at the Met after the opening of *The Tales of Hoffmann*, 1982

The Maestro: rehearsing *Attila* in Barcelona, 1975

released from some of them in order to participate in the unique *Traviata* project. The administration kindly acquiesced.

The filming took place at Cinecittà in Rome and stretched over a longer period than originally anticipated. Thus, I found myself commuting to Rome from such places as Buenos Aires, Vienna, Barcelona and Madrid, where I had long-standing commitments. I worked harder than I had ever worked before, but the results were worth the effort. Filming is demanding and exhausting; but, since the sound track is prerecorded, it does not involve using the voice. Therefore, it need not jeopardize the quality of concurrently running live performances.

At first there was great pressure to keep to the pre-established shooting schedule, and I was constantly being asked to give up my other commitments. The producers pointed out that I had a ready-made excuse for not going to Argentina when the war in the Malvinas/Falklands broke out. Everyone told me that the working situation there would be impossible and that since so much of my work takes place in England and the United States, the repercussions might be damaging to me. But I had already asked for and been granted a reduction in the number of performances I was to sing in Buenos Aires, and I was not about to renege altogether on my contract, just as I would not have reneged on a Covent Garden contract had I been scheduled to perform there at that time. As my own country was not involved, I felt that I had to be impartial. The film production people then said that if I should somehow be trapped in Argentina – if, that is, the airport should be closed or some other disaster should occur – the company insuring the film would not pay. But I promised to book on a different plane every day of my stay; and there was the additional possibility of getting out through Montevideo, Uruguay, if the worst should come to the worst.

In the event, it was only Buenos Aires's morale, and not its physical situation, that was affected by the war. To me, a territorial war is the ultimate in nationalistic childishness, especially in our day, and to see the demonstrations of inflated patriotism in Argentina, and to read of the same happening in Britain, made me very sad. But whereas military service is voluntary in Britain, and the flow of information free, the Argentinian boys were draftees who had little idea of what was awaiting them. Every evening there were wild demonstrations of patriotic fervour in the theatre, with anthem-singing and flag-waving. The enthusiasm began to wane, however, as the days went by and as the news, official and unofficial, became worse. One man at the Teatro Colón was feeling particularly euphoric towards the beginning, and I asked him whether he had a son of draft age. 'Oh, no,' he replied, 'my son is twenty and is unlikely to be called up.' A few days later, the boy was conscripted, and his father was no longer so enthusiastic about the war. That, of course, is the tragedy of wartime patriotism: it is fine in the abstract, but more difficult to rationalize when it touches home.

Although I do believe in the seriousness and importance of art, I also feel that it is a performer's responsibility to distract people from their daily problems and at the same time to make them feel better about their own existence. Performers and their art, therefore, are most important during times of crisis. I was able to sing my four performances and to return to Europe under normal travel conditions, but with my heart broken because two countries I dearly love were involved in senseless acts of destruction against each other. I very much agree with an article I read in the *International Herald Tribune* a few days after the 1982 World Cup soccer games had ended. It suggested that territorial disputes be settled by athletic or other matches. Yes: either Mrs Thatcher and General Galtieri could have faced each other in a chess tournament, or the English and Argentine football teams could have tried to win the islands by scoring three brilliant goals in ten minutes. Four years later, there could be a return match. That sounds and is ridiculous, but it is certainly far less ridiculous than war. In either case, nothing is achieved.

When I returned to Rome, Teresa Stratas, who had been working extremely hard every day, non-stop, left the set for three or four days in order to rest. I worked on the other scenes during her absence, and then things returned to normal – if one can call normal flying back and forth to and from Rome between performances of *Otello*, *Chénier* and *Carmen* in Vienna, *Bohème* in Barcelona, and *Samson et Dalila* in Madrid. Franco soon recognized the possibility that this could become a truly major film, and he decided that the worst thing would be to rush. We proceeded with great care, the shooting schedule was extended, and all those involved were able to breathe at least a little bit more easily.

The World Cup games were being held in Spain, and in the early stages my Italian colleagues and I commiserated about the weakness of both our national teams. When Spain was eliminated, my friends in Rome began to tease me, despite which I immediately switched my allegiance to Italy, which is like another homeland to me. I even managed to see the final game and to greet King Juan Carlos of Spain and President Sandro Pertini of Italy in their box. In the euphoria that followed Italy's victory, Pertini invited me to fly back to Rome with him and the team the next morning, but I had to catch a much earlier plane in order to be at Cinecittà on schedule for another day of shooting.

The scheduling problems, even excluding my own, were massive, because the film had been decided upon relatively late. The Flora was flying back and forth, the Baron was flying back and forth, and so on. Singers live in a computerized world: our lives are programmed day by day and even hour by hour. In the movie world, on the other hand, a film scheduled to be shot in June, say, may be entirely postponed until September. Fine: everyone adjusts his schedule. So the most difficult aspect of this film was to iron out, as far as possible, the conflict between the operatic and cinematic worlds.

Franco wanted me to be fair-haired for the film, mainly because my black hair looks almost bluish under the movie lights, and I had to have a beard as well. My hair had to be dyed every ten days and my beard every three days during the shooting period, and that was torture. Still, my admiration for Zeffirelli increased even more during the filming of *La traviata*. To see him at work on the two art forms he loves most, opera and cinema, is an amazing experience. Again I must emphasize his eye for detail; his way of filling space beautifully – of moving a plant, a table, a chandelier, just so far in order to create the loveliest effect; the plasticity of his effects; his attention to lighting. Gianni Quaranta created the wonderful sets, Piero Tosi designed the costumes, and Ennio Guarnieri was responsible for the magical lighting and camera effects. Tosi is a man of tremendous sensitivity, taste and knowledge. Franco has indeed surrounded himself with a superb team of experts in all fields relating to his work, from technical crew to secretaries to domestic staff. He also pays more attention than anyone else in the profession to what others tell him. If he is busy staging a scene and a member of the chorus or a supernumerary approaches him to enquire about something, he will ask him to wait a moment. When he has finished doing what he is doing, instead of letting the matter drop, he will find that person and say, 'Sorry, what did you want to tell me?' He listens to and weighs everyone's comments and ideas. That does not mean that he will necessarily accept others' judgements, but he listens seriously.

I do not know what would happen if Franco really had to act a part in a play or film, but his way of demonstrating the acting of a role to singers or actors is perfect. Whoever it may be – Iago, Santuzza, Carmen, Don José, Alfredo, Violetta – he takes on the personality in the most extraordinary way.

My family and I became friendlier than ever with Franco, staying at his home and spending much time with him. At night we would sit down to eat and Franco would serve enormous portions of pasta. 'Now, Franco,' I would say, 'you want me to look trim, and then you give me enough pasta to sink a ship!'

'Well,' he would reply, 'you've worked hard today, you skipped lunch, and you can afford to eat heartily.' It is true that I rarely ate lunch when we were shooting. I usually feel very sluggish after eating, and at Cinecittà I had to be alert all day long. Once, Franco was preparing a fantastic spaghetti sauce with mushrooms and other delicious ingredients, but Alvaro said he just wanted tomato sauce. 'Alvaro, you're a real pest,' Franco teased him, 'and I hope you realize it.' He made a special sauce for Alvaro. Naturally, when Alvaro tasted the more elaborate sauce, he wanted it instead of his own. 'I told you you were a fool, Alvaro!' Franco said to him.

I was scheduled to sing six performances of *La Gioconda* with Marton and MacNeil at the Met at the beginning of the 1982–3 season, but a terrible cold caused me to withdraw from the last of them after singing the first act. The mayhem that ensued during the rest of that performance was worthy of an opera audience in a Latin country, and I am sure that 20,000 people now claim to have been present that night. But as I was not present for the rest of the evening, and as, furthermore, I do not want to embroil myself in polemics with some of the people who were directly involved (and I am not referring to any of the other singers), I shall not say anything more about what happened after my departure. My own part in the story is that I did indeed have a bad cold and had informed the management earlier in the day that I did not want to perform. They urged me to sing, and I agreed to try. As the first act proceeded, I could feel that I was hurting my voice, even though there was no noticeable alteration in my sound. I decided to withdraw, and at that point no one was going to make me change my mind. I can only add that Eva Marton was a great Gioconda.

At the end of October, while rehearsing at Covent Garden, I made a quick trip to Rome in order to sing in a benefit concert, attended by 8,000 people, at the Vatican. While there, Marta, the boys and I had an audience with Pope John Paul II, and President Pertini made me a Commendatore of the Republic.

With Muti, Freni, Bruson and Ghiaurov, I opened a Scala season for the fourth time in a new production of *Ernani*, staged in a controversial manner by Ronconi. After spending as much of the holiday period as possible with my family in Barcelona, I returned to Milan to begin 1983 by recording

Don Carlos with Abbado, the Scala ensemble, and a cast that included Katia Ricciarelli, Leo Nucci, Lucia Valentini Terrani and Ruggero Raimondi. We did the opera in French – Verdi originally wrote it for the Paris Opera – and the album will include the material that the composer cut at the time of the première. I was the one who proposed doing a French version. Giulini's 1970 *Don Carlo* recording, in which I had had the honour of participating, is so fine that a new attempt seemed to require an extra raison d'être.

On 21 January 1983, while in Miami performing *Chénier*, I celebrated my forty-second birthday, and I decided that if I did not get busy and finish this book, I would have to think of a new title for it....

IX
ELECTRIC PERFORMING EXPERIENCES

In the 1980s singers are spending more and more of their time in front of microphones and cameras – television and movie cameras; and the public ought to know something about the special sort of preparation that is required for these specialized tasks. Many people, for instance, have incorrect ideas about the modern recording process, at least as far as opera is concerned. They seem to think that it is possible to do anything today – to make a bad performance sound great and to doctor all the flaws. I am sorry to report that recordings are often made in a frantic race against the clock, and that the results are not always what they might be.

The best opera recordings today are those made from concurrently running productions. When the orchestra, chorus, conductor and soloists have thoroughly rehearsed a work together and then given a series of performances, the whole ensemble can make a recording that sounds naturally cohesive and requires a minimum of patching. Very often, however, recordings are hybrid affairs, and although the results may still be exciting, we performers feel an additional and unwelcome pressure in making them. In recent decades, a high percentage of operatic recordings has been made in London, not only for economic and contractual reasons but also because British orchestral musicians are outstanding sight-readers. In a work that is not part of the standard repertoire, such as Montemezzi's *L'amore dei tre re* or Verdi's *Giovanna d'Arco*, both of which I have recorded, a typical three-hour session will begin with an orchestral reading of a segment of the opera. They will rehearse alone for a while and then with the singers. An hour after that bit of music has been played by the orchestra for the first time in the musicians' lives, it is recorded for posterity. This is a frightening way of working because of the pressure, and a frustrating one because it does not allow the work to ripen naturally.

When conditions are different, when the players already know the work, when the singers are used to performing it together, when we are not starting every little excerpt from scratch, then we can allow ourselves what is often the luxury of bringing a refined interpretation to a work. We are, of course, professionals, and we are supposed to be able to work the other way as well; but no matter how thoroughly professional we may be, we cannot completely command a role or give it true depth under negative circumstances. It has happened that after recording a role I know well with a company that is familiar with the work, I have been told by this or that critic that I sang my part superficially, while on the other hand I have been complimented for a penetrating interpretation of a role recorded by the rough-and-ready method. Nevertheless, what is important to me is that *I* be convinced of my own ability to put a role across properly – and I have now been in the profession long enough to know when that is the case and when it is not.

Sometimes, in a situation where the orchestra is sight-reading an unfamiliar work, it would be ideal for the conductor to have two or three orchestral rehearsals to prepare the entire piece before we approach the recording sessions together. That is already a great improvement over the piecemeal system, which drives me and many of my colleagues to despair. But many times scheduling problems make the better method unpractical.

There is also a myth in circulation that being able to repeat a passage or a whole section is entirely advantageous. Well, sometimes it is a help; but if a singer is having vocal problems on the day of a session, that option is useless. And although I may not be satisfied with the way I have sung something on a certain take, with every repetition my voice becomes more tired and the chances of improving the passage in question are reduced. A singer would be foolish to believe that if he cannot sing something properly the first time, he will succeed the tenth time. In my early days of recording, I would fanatically repeat arias as many times as I dared, in order to convince myself that I had really done my best. That method confused me. I would find a phrase that was better in one take, another bit in another, and in the end I would simply lose the continuity of the performance. Nowadays I tend to record whole arias or other segments straight through, and I find that first takes are best about eighty per cent of the time. If there are major defects, I correct them in succeeding takes; but if I am satisfied with a take as a whole, I will even allow certain vocal flaws to remain in order to preserve the continuity.

I am sorry that I never made any monaural recordings. Monaural sound in opera favoured the voice, while stereophonic techniques are not flattering to singers. Conductors and orchestras were the great beneficiaries of the developments in stereophonic sound. I know that I am far from being the only singer who would be delighted to have a considerable number of his recordings remastered with a finer balance between voice and orchestra. I do not mean that the singers should overwhelm the orchestra, but simply that everyone should be heard in proper proportion to everyone else. This is mainly controlled by the technicians responsible for the mixing process, during which odd things sometimes happen. When I leave the studio after approving a take, I am at least reasonably satisfied with what I have done – otherwise I would not have given my okay. But weeks or months later, when I receive the acetate proofs, I find them changed and no longer satisfactory. I am not talking here about not liking my interpretation or even the way I sound, but rather about technical problems that have crept in between the recording sessions and the preparation of the master. For example, when I recorded *Otello*, I sang the 'Esultate!' three times. It went very well – not just in my opinion, but also according to Jimmy Levine, the chorus, my colleagues and everyone else present. I listened to the playbacks and approved them. When I received the acetates, the E-sharp – the third syllable of the word 'esultate' – was inaudible, so what you hear on the record is not what I heard in the recording studio's playback.

Digital sound is a tremendous development. The equipment for listening to it properly is not yet widely available; but despite that, it is already a great advance. Voices can now be recorded in correct balance with the orchestra, and there is even a system whereby each voice can be recorded on a completely independent track: the singers stand in separate, soundproof booths, while what is happening outside is piped into each booth. The sound of an individual voice can then be mixed in precisely the right proportion to the rest of the sound. One interesting by-product of this new technique is that the great singers of the future will be able to sing duets with the famous singers of today. If Mr X in the year 2025 would like to sing with Montserrat Caballé, a technician will have merely to remove my track and let Mr X take my place. Now that I think of it, we had better start immediately to look into the contractual problems that could develop out of this new possibility!

The most reasonable way to record an opera is for the conductor to rehearse the orchestra and chorus thoroughly beforehand, and then to have the whole cast on hand to 'perform' the work straight through two or three times. The tension and excitement of a live performance would then be preserved, yet enough material would be available to make an ideal performance, given the limitations of the people involved. Today we would record, say, *Tosca*; in two days we would rerecord it; and two days later we would record it yet again. Everyone's concentration would be at its maximum, and the sort of scheduling problems that arise when the soprano flies in one day to record her aria and ensemble scenes and the tenor the next day to record his would be completely eliminated. Everyone – offstage band, cowbells, contrabassoon and so on – would have to be present on those three days; and then the whole project would be done.

One advantage of the imperfect recording techniques that have been used up to now has been that when people have heard me live for the first time, they have told me that I sound better than on record. Perhaps in the future that will not be so.

Regarding my own singing and interpretation on record, I can only say that I am usually happy when I hear the playback, very unhappy when I hear the finished product, and more reconciled to the results when I listen to the record five or ten years later. I do feel that in cases where I have recorded the same work two or three times, there has been steady improvement, and I have made up my mind that in the future I will not rerecord a work unless I have something fresh and different to offer.

The most important development in the operatic field in recent years has been the growth of televised opera. I wholeheartedly support not only opera on television but opera on television with subtitles in the language of the country where it is being shown. This silent, simultaneous translation helps the public to follow the action closely, thus breaking down the barrier of incomprehension that has often been cited as one of opera's negative qualities. Singing opera in translation is usually not a solution to the problem, because often the words are still unintelligible. In the high registers, especially where women's voices are concerned, the diction is not usually clear even if a highly competent soprano is singing in her native language. On British television in 1982 I saw Wagner's complete *Ring* in the Boulez-Chéreau version from Bayreuth, and I enjoyed it very much. The subtitles were a great help, since my German is not good enough to allow me to follow the ins and outs of the story as it unfolds. Both as a performer and as a spectator, I am glad to be around at a time when television is coming of age.

I am a man of the theatre, and I do not believe that opera or any other performing art form on television will ever replace the experience of a live performance. Being there, seeing and hearing the real thing, creates a psychological situation that cannot be recreated on television. I shall go even further and say that the most positive aspect of televised opera is that it brings more people to the theatre for a more powerful form of what they have experienced electronically at home. Of course there are other advantages as well to televised opera: it reaches people who, for reasons of ill health, age or isolation, cannot go to the theatre; and it permits those who live in cities with major opera companies to see the productions that are being done elsewhere.

The four theatres in which I have done the most television work have been the Metropolitan, Covent Garden, La Scala and the Vienna Staatsoper; but I have also participated in telecasts from Paris, Barcelona, Madrid, San Francisco, Tokyo, Mexico City, Guadalajara, Monterrey, and elsewhere. Each theatre has its own procedures, which depend upon the size of the house and other questions as well.

When one of the Met's new productions is about to be telecast, the television director works closely with the stage director from the outset. Nowadays many productions are born with the camera's exigencies in mind, to avoid time-consuming alterations and adaptations later on. That was the case with both *Manon Lescaut* and *La traviata*, which were directed for television by Kirk Browning and Brian Large, respectively. (Both productions were telecast live to Europe.) The cameras were brought in for some of the rehearsals, and two performances were used as practice sessions by the cameramen before a performance was actually broadcast. Sometimes it is possible to see a complete tape of one of the non-televised performances; if it is good, you cannot help saying to yourself, 'Damn it! I wish they would broadcast this one. Who knows if the next performance will be as good?' But union rules forbid that, and the night originally agreed upon is the one that must be televised.

It would be ideal if the unions would allow several performances to be taped, so that an edited version with the best parts of the whole series could be shown. The unforeseeable element in a live performance can indeed make it more exciting, but if you are watching a delayed relay anyway, what difference does it make to the level of excitement whether it is edited or unedited? If the quality can be improved through editing, I say edit!

At the Met, a modern theatre, there are wide aisles where the cameras can be left in place without disturbing the view of anyone in the audience. London's Royal Opera House is older and smaller and therefore not as suited to accommodating television crews and their equipment. The cameras block the view from a considerable number of seats, which means that those places cannot be sold when the cameras are set up and, therefore, that the house cannot afford to have the cameras set up during more than the single performance that is being broadcast. Thus, for Covent Garden telecasts, we have to face many extra rehearsals to enable the crews to prepare themselves properly. They will, for instance, run rehearsals on Friday and Saturday mornings, removing the cameras after each session, then again on Sunday morning, afternoon and evening, since there are no Sunday performances. There will be another rehearsal on Monday morning and finally the televised performance on Monday evening. In short, the Covent Garden system is the exact opposite of that used at the Metropolitan.

I have already participated in two televised opening productions at La Scala (1976 and 1982). While preparing for an opening night – always on 7 December, the feast-day of Milan's patron saint, Ambrose – the whole theatre is given over almost single-mindedly to that production. For the *Ernani* that opened the 1982-3 season, the cameras were in the theatre during virtually the entire rehearsal period, although they were removed for the first performance itself. Ticket prices for that show were so exorbitantly high that the administration would have had a hard time excusing itself if anyone's view had been even partially blocked. Two performances of *Ernani* were taped, and besides having been broadcast in Italy on Christmas Day and elsewhere thereafter, the edited final version is intended for eventual use as a commercial videodisc.

In Vienna the unions are very tough, and when I sang *Carmen* and *Chénier* there on two different opening nights, the television crews were allowed to shoot only the dress rehearsal before broadcasting the first performance live. As a result of other rules and regulations, Vienna is also the most expensive of theatres for the television companies.

Editing performances is very difficult, partly because of the lighting, which is rarely precisely the same from one night to the next. Or, if a singer's costume looks slightly different from one performance to another, only one of the two versions can be used. The result of all this is that vocal and musical qualities count for very little when the final selection of material is made. Major blunders are avoided, but if a singer or conductor feels that a certain passage came off much more effectively on Evening A than on Evening B, his or her opinion will count very little against the visual argument. The situation will improve when the musicians' and other unions realize that it is to their advantage as well as ours and the television companies' to allow a group of performances, rather than just one or two, to be taped, and a selection to be made from the whole series. So far, the unions have been insisting that orchestra, chorus, technical staffs, and so on be paid extra for every performance that is taped, even if in the end only one composite tape is going to be made for broadcast. If, say, six performances were taped and the best material from each chosen, a final version that would be nearly ideal, both musically and visually, could be produced.

Still, the television director must be the person to make the final decisions. Imagine what would happen if, in a duet, the tenor insisted on one version and the soprano on another, or if the baritone wanted to use the ensemble scene from a certain performance because he sounded good in it, while the rest of the company was a mess. Some of those violent opera plots might well come true. But I would like to see closer co-operation between whomever has staged the opera in the theatre and the director responsible for the television broadcast. Television people are sometimes very experienced in their own field but not so expert theatrically or musically. For example, in some of the *Otello* telecasts, when Iago sings his 'È un'idra fosca, livida, cieca' (Shakespeare: 'It [jealousy] is the green-eyed monster'), the camera focuses entirely on him rather than switching sometimes to Otello – and the important thing at that moment is the reaction that must be visible in Otello's face as the poison begins to work on him. Likewise, when Otello sings 'Una possente maga' ('She was a charmer'), the camera not only must focus on him but must also show Desdemona's terror and confusion. Ideally the co-ordination between dramatic text and the demands of television should be arranged in the best possible way.

In almost all opera houses the stage lighting has to be substantially altered to accommodate the television cameras (a noteworthy exception is the Paris Opéra, which uses an advanced system that requires only minor changes). Adjusting to more brightly lit sets, after rehearsing and performing in lighting that creates the right atmosphere for each scene, is very disturbing. The tension of singing to thousands in a theatre is already great, and it becomes greater still when millions are watching on television. I find my concentration noticeably reduced by strong television lights, and I hope that other houses will adopt Paris's system.

Cable television is the empire of the future, against which the networks will have to struggle. There will come a time when an opera lover will be able to say, 'Tonight I am going to watch the broadcast from La Scala' – or from the Met or wherever. It is wonderful that performers will be able to leave a substantial visual as well as aural document of their work. Some day we will be accustomed to having our performances televised regularly, and there will be no special nervousness connected with the experience. As the videodisc begins to come into its own, the digital recording process related to it is also creating a revolution. More and more opera houses are going to want to record and market their performances by this means, which is fine in itself. For us artists, however, it also raises a new problem: exclusivity. If I make a videotape of *La bohème* at one house, should I have to sign a contract stipulating that I will not do the same opera on television with another company for a certain number of years? We singers clearly prefer not to put our names to such agreements, partly for our own reasons and partly because the big opera companies are beginning to look at television as an important source of much-needed income – a source that would be partially impeded if the singers most in demand did not have the right to participate freely in a variety of telecasts. My own feeling is that the *Bohème* I tape for one theatre can then be exploited as best suits that company's needs, but in return no one has the right to stop me from singing in another *Bohème* televised from a different house. The potential help to Theatre No. 2 is much greater than any possible harm to Theatre No. 1. As televised opera proliferates, this problem becomes more pressing, and it is clear that opera houses and video companies will have to come to terms with it by working out a sensible agreement. Some observers have said that by appearing in more than one televised version of the same opera we risk over-exposure. I do not agree. If you like a movie, you may go to see it two or three times – and a movie does not change. Here we are talking about entirely different productions of the same work; and, in any case, no singer sounds exactly the same even from one performance to another.

Most televisions have inferior speakers, which means that concerts and operas are not heard as well as they are seen. Now, however, the videodisc system is changing all that. It has the advantages of digital sound plus outstanding visual reproduction, and there will even be the possibility of turning off the video track and just listening to the music. By the late 1980s, at the latest, these systems will be coming out at prices that will not be hopelessly high for most music lovers. The one disadvantage is that the recording companies will want to rerecord the basic repertoire using the new techniques available to them, which will cut down on the exploration of lesser-known works.

The continued growth of televised opera is going to mean that singers will have to look their best in order to be credible. A few singers will always be in demand for their extraordinary voices, no matter what their appearance, but people with good but unexceptional voices are going to be in trouble if they do not stay in decent physical condition. It is one thing to be a sixty-year-old, 300-pound Carmen or Don José when you are fifty or 100 feet away from the spectactors in the theatre, and quite another when you are being shown close up on television screens in people's living-rooms.

Learning how to act on camera should now be a normal part of a singer's training, because it is certain to be a major factor in the careers of most of today's and tomorrow's singers. We must learn to make smaller and subtler gestures, for instance, and to bear in mind camera angles so as not to block our colleagues at key moments. Similarly, when a singer is working at, say, the Metropolitan, there is such a distance between him and even the nearest member of the public that eye movement is of negligible importance. As a result it is very difficult for us to learn to 'discipline' our eyes, as a cinema actor must do, when we are singing on television. An instant's loss of concentration can destroy the theatrical illusion for the viewer. This is all very taxing, but in the end it will help us to be better performers. When I see the videotapes of the Met's *Manon Lescaut* or Covent Garden's *Fanciulla*, I have the impression that I am really acting, and that makes me feel very good. The moment the viewer says to himself, 'That guy is singing,' the production has failed as theatre, no matter how well it may be succeeding musically.

Filming opera for the cinema is different from performing for television. First the sound track is recorded and edited; then the film is shot as we mouth the words to playback. I find this difficult, because if I try to sing along with myself – really singing out, that is – I cannot hear myself, and I end up out of synchronization with the recorded sound. On the other hand, if I barely sing at all, in order to hear the soundtrack better, the visual element loses credibility: it is ridiculous to hear powerful sounds emerging from a voice while not seeing any signs of strain in the singer's mouth and throat muscles. I do not normally have an angelic little smile on my face when singing a high B-flat.

But the most trying aspect of making a film is the amount of repetition that has to be done. In the course of a day's shooting, perhaps four minutes of the final product will be realized. After half a dozen attempts, you may finally be satisfied with the way you have acted a sequence, only to find that the lighting was not good or that the flowers in the vase behind you were not arranged properly. It is particularly hard to maintain the right frame of mind for a sad scene that has to be shot over and over again, because there are hundreds of people milling around all the time and, just before a take, loud warnings not to interrupt the proceedings are broadcast. I always try to be alone, concentrating until the last possible moment on what I have to do. I was supposed to cry during one of the scenes in Zeffirelli's *La traviata*, and after a number of takes I had to tell Franco, 'Sorry, I've dried up. I can't produce another tear.'

The discipline of the cinema is very different from that of the opera house. In the theatre one must put oneself in the right frame of mind for a performance; and even twenty-four hours before the show begins, the performance-state starts to take hold. A performance day is totally devoted to preparing for the evening, one way or another. Then it all takes place, for better or for worse, in a period of three or four hours. For the cinema, one needs first of all to be in good physical condition. There may be a make-up call for 6.30 a.m.; and for a stage performer who is used to going to bed between 1 and 2 a.m. and getting up at mid morning, this is quite a shock. One tries to adapt, but it is not always easy – especially when there are live performance days interspersed among the shooting days. There were times during the shooting of *La traviata* when I would leave a theatre at 1 in the morning, have something to eat, catch a bit of sleep, head for the airport, fly to Rome, and go directly to Cinecittà. But I got used to the situation, and fortunately my nerves are very steady.

You rehearse a scene, and then you have to wait while the lighting is being set up. The technicians say they will need forty minutes, which means an hour and a half. Then you rehearse again before the cameras, and finally the shooting begins. After a few takes the director decides to change the lighting, or to use a close-up instead of a long shot, and after another pause the shooting begins again. In the end, a thirty-second sequence may take five or six hours to film. The important thing is to know how to rest. I used to go to my dressing-room, when there was an hour's lighting break, and have a wonderful little nap. Sometimes I even fell asleep right on the set, on one of Violetta's divans, which were as big as queen-size beds.

Performing for the cinema means doing a great deal of work for a distant and almost vicarious reward, because by the time the film is released and you learn how people are reacting to what you have done, you have forgotten your state of being at the time of the performance. In that respect the work can be frustrating, especially for someone who is accustomed to working in the theatre, which offers the performer an immediate reaction or even conflicting reactions on the spot, and which makes him see a connection between what he thinks he has done and the impression he has made on the public. But although a film does not provide the immediate satisfaction that a good performance does, it is a document that can last a long time. And if, during the shooting of a film, a singer feels himself to be little more than a simple foot-soldier, caught up in the midst of a mammoth battle, when the film is finally shown he is seen in close-up – every expression, every gesture – in a way that is not possible in the opera house.

Still, spectators, including myself, tend to remember specific live opera performances with a special emotion. The reason is not always that this or that singer has performed exceptionally well on a certain occasion, but often simply that the individual member of the audience happened to be particularly susceptible to certain feelings on that occasion and was thus able to involve himself to an unusual degree in what was occurring on stage. When we remember a performance with warmth after the passage of years, we are really re-experiencing something of the emotion we felt that evening.

X
PARTING THOUGHTS

The Don Juan of Tenors?

Back in my Tel Aviv days, I sang forty-two performances of Mozart's great masterpiece, *Don Giovanni*. Though nominally the good guy, Don Ottavio, the tenor – Donna Anna's fiancé – is a lily-livered fop, who appears uninteresting not only next to the towering figure of the protagonist but also in comparison with every other character in the opera. Mozart intentionally gave Ottavio two lovely but absolutely conventional arias, setting them, by way of contrast, in the midst of some of the most extraordinary music ever created.

The role of Don Giovanni is quite a different matter. Here is a personality bursting with life and vigour, alternately repellent and attractive – the sort of complex, energetic character that any singing actor would love to explore. Unfortunately for tenors, Mozart wrote the role for a high bass or baritone. A few nineteenth-century tenors, including the celebrated Manuel García, successfully attempted to cope with the role, but no tenor in our day has done it. In 1980, in the course of an intermission interview during the Metropolitan's *Manon Lescaut* telecast, I opened my big mouth and said that I would like to try to sing Don Giovanni some day – that it would be a great challenge and, if met, a great accomplishment. The next day I received a telegram from Herbert von Karajan, who told me that if I was serious, he wanted to do *Don Giovanni* with me. In fact, the prospect so excited him that he suggested scheduling a production for Salzburg in 1983. I answered that I was indeed serious, but that I wanted to wait, and I have since explained to him that I cannot contemplate taking it on before 1986.

The decision is an extremely hard one for me. Karajan would stage and conduct the production, and we would have to be in complete agreement on dramatic as well as musical questions. Don Giovanni is usually portrayed as either a very aggressive, macho character or as a cold, calculating seducer. Both of these views seem shallow to me. This is a man who must be capable of showing great tenderness to women. Perhaps after so many adventures he no longer feels that tenderness, but he must demonstrate it convincingly – otherwise he could not be so successful. There must be something of the sweetness and correctness of the *hidalgo*, the Spanish gentleman, in his behaviour. At times he exaggerates and becomes theatrical, when he feels that that is necessary in order to reach his goal, but those moments must be temporary departures from his normal behaviour.

From a purely technical point of view, the role poses no problems for me. I know that I could achieve the sort of musical line I would want without excessive difficulty, and I can sing all of Don Giovanni's notes. The thorny matter is that what sounds brilliant for a baritone does not sound brilliant for a tenor. For example, I sang the Don's aria, 'Fin ch'han dal vino', in the original key for the Seville film. The lower parts were not difficult, but they bothered me all the same because I could not achieve the kind of sound I was seeking. There are two moments – the two Don Giovanni-Leporello-Commendatore scenes – that would indeed be vocally dangerous for me. The first takes place at the beginning of the opera and ends in the Commendatore's death, and the second occurs at the end of the opera, when the dead man returns as the Stone Guest and drags Don Giovanni down to hell. In both of these, I would run the risk of being swamped by the two deeper, heavier voices. The scenes between Don Giovanni and Leporello would not be perilous if Leporello were cast properly – and in any case, I think a heavy Leporello goes against the character of the role. Numbers like 'Là ci darem la mano' and 'Deh vieni alla finestra' are in no way problematic for me.

This is a very tempting project, but I must give it much more attention before committing myself to it.

The Reality of Singing Verismo

Performing the so-called *Cav-Pag* double-bill often makes me think about that hectic but fascinating period in Italian operatic history when the verismo composers – all born in the 1850s and 1860s – were becoming popular. The theatrical environment in Italy is difficult enough today, when the emphasis is on performances of traditional repertoire. In those days, when composers were struggling for the approval of an immense public, the atmosphere must have been absolutely hellish. To have their works performed, they had to compete with each other for the support of major publishers. It was an out-and-out fight for survival.

I love *Cavalleria rusticana* and *Pagliacci*; and, although Gigli in his day used to perform them both on the same evening, I believe that I am the only tenor active in the big houses today who undertakes that task. What makes it frightening is not so much having to do two very different characters in quick succession, or even the amount of singing that has to be done – and if you start counting, you have the Siciliana, the duet with Santuzza, the Brindisi, 'Compar Alfio' and the goodbye to Mamma Lucia in *Cavalleria*, followed by 'Un grande spettacolo', 'Un tal gioco', the little duet with Nedda, 'Vesti la giubba', and the 'No, Pagliaccio non son!' in *Pagliacci* – widely varying, but all emphatic. What is most difficult, however, is simply having to start and finish one character, one life, and then having to begin again with another. By the time I have lived through Turiddu's tragedy, I feel emotionally drained; but I must then live through Canio's, which is another full circle.

Vocally, Canio is a more immediately satisfying role than Turiddu, but Turiddu provides the greater overall challenge. Canio's character is obvious and unchanging: he simply becomes more upset and violent as the work progresses. Turiddu, on the other hand, has to experience a whole range of feelings, some of which he must hide. He loves, lies and betrays, and he is always conscious of what he is doing. I have now sung the roles together in Hamburg, Vienna, Barcelona, San Francisco, Munich, Verona, at the Met, La Scala, Covent Garden and elsewhere, and in the future I shall save this exhausting feat for special occasions. (An aside to the critics: after I have sung my heart and lungs out in these two roles, I am discouraged to read reviews that say, 'As usual, the parts of Turiddu and Canio were sung by the same tenor.' The statement is incorrect to begin with, and I think that the humblest person in the world would find it deflating under the circumstances.)

It is strange that *Cavalleria* is always done before *Pagliacci*. Once, at a Scala dress rehearsal, I tried doing them the other way round, and the arrangement worked beautifully. I had feared vocal problems, but they never came. The other order may be preferred because of the more atmospheric opening of *Cavalleria* and for the closing words of *Pagliacci*, 'La commedia è finita.'

Mascagni's music for *Cavalleria* is greater than Leoncavallo's for *Pagliacci*; nevertheless, I am always grateful to Mascagni for not having made his masterpiece into a three- or four-act work. Singers could not have lasted through it. I have never sung any of Mascagni's other operas, although I was to have done *Il piccolo Marat* at the Met during the 1982–3 season. The cancellation was disappointing, but I must admit all the same that I find the work, like some of the composer's other operas – *Iris* and *Guglielmo Ratcliff*, for example – unhealthy for the voice. The dramatic element is so underlined that it causes strain. Some of Leoncavallo's other operas, however, are very powerful. I am thinking especially of his *Bohème*, which did not withstand the competition from Puccini's opera of the same name. I have recorded the arias 'Io non ho che una povera stanzetta' and 'Musetta, o gioia della mia dimora', and I would love to perform the whole opera some day.

Of Umberto Giordano's operas, I have sung *Andrea Chénier* and *Fedora*. *Chénier* has been vastly underrated in recent years, partly because verismo opera has often been misrepresented through vulgar, exaggerated performances and partly because of the disapproval of many musical intellectuals, real and otherwise. Nevertheless, it is a highly original work with a wealth of beautiful melodies in it. I must grant, however, that the baritone role of Gérard is more interesting than that of Chénier himself. Gérard's human development in the course of the opera is gigantic. At the beginning of the first act, he is an embittered servant, a lackey; and by the end of it, inspired by Chénier's words, he has thrown off his bondage and escaped. Then he comes to power in revolutionary France, where he can take revenge on the class that was responsible for his servitude. His abuse of power leads him through a whole range of experiences and eventually to self-contempt. By the time the work ends, Gérard has transformed himself into a noble, feeling human being. Chénier, on the other hand, is purely an idealist whose head is always in the clouds. Certainly he is the 'better' character of the two, but he is less interesting dramatically. His arias, his scene with Roucher in the second act, and his duets with Maddalena make this one of the most taxing roles in the lirico-spinto tenor's repertoire. The music is wonderful, with some exceptions here and there, and *Chénier* is one of the operas I most enjoy singing. It would be perfect if the role were of a higher dramatic quality. *Fedora* is much weaker. Giordano adopts a narrative approach to the first act, and it takes him a long time to make his point. Apart from a few silly moments, the second act is masterly, but the third is less strong. It is a minor work, especially in comparison with *Chénier*. Some day I would like to do Giordano's later work, *La cena delle beffe*.

Adriana Lecouvreur is the only opera by Francesco Cilea that I have sung. Not only did I make my Metropolitan debut with this work in 1968:

it had also been the opera with which I made my first important success in Mexico City six years earlier. The day after that performance there was a newspaper article that stated, in Latin, 'Habemus Tenor' – we have a tenor – just as the College of Cardinals announces 'Habemus Papa' after the election of a Pope. *Adriana* has many brilliant moments along with a considerable portion of inferior music. Some of the repetitions in the first act, for example, are trite. But the tenor's part, with the exception of the inane, difficult and pointless aria in the third act, is wonderful. I have also sung Federico's beautiful lament from Cilea's *L'arlesiana*, but I do not know the rest of that opera or any of the composer's other works.

What Price Opera?

Changes ought to be made in the ticket pricing systems of the major opera houses. I agree with those who say that the public should go to the opera in order to see and hear a fine overall production, even if the singers are not the best in the world. Nevertheless, one of the functions of the most important lyric theatres is to present the best-known singers. If and when they do not, they ought not to demand that the public pay top admission prices. When most or all of the lead roles are taken by people who have not yet established their international reputations, the audiences at the Met, Covent Garden, La Scala and other front-ranking houses have every right to complain. People do not pay Series A prices to see a Series C sports event, and the same principle ought to apply in the theatre. Let me stress that a Series C event can be very exciting and worthwhile, but the hard fact is that it remains Series C.

Top Billing

I dislike arguments over whether the singers, conductor, stage director or designer is or should be the key element in an operatic production. Opera, when well done, is the most wonderful thing in the world; and in order to bring off an outstanding performance, all of the components must be excellent. On the other hand, opera cannot exist without singers. People can, if necessary, imagine a set when the stage is bare; they can make themselves believe that a production that has all the performers standing around like so many hunks of sausage is really a representation of a dramatic situation; and they can, if there is no alternative, hear a work accompanied by a piano rather than by a whole orchestra with conductor. But, I repeat, opera cannot exist without singers. Still, I must admit that I do not perform at my best when the orchestra is not good. I find my concentration diminished; and if the orchestra's intonation is bad, mine is affected as well. There is no point in engaging an expensive, first-rate cast for a production that is third-rate in other respects.

Learning to Hate Opera

Intelligent, musical people who do not like opera have usually been introduced to it through less than top-level productions. And who can blame them for hating it? There is nothing worse, nothing more farcical, than a bad opera performance. Confirmed opera lovers can be very forgiving of defects; and I therefore recommend that when they take a friend or relative – especially a young person – to the opera for the first time, they should be very careful in choosing the event. When I see an opera performance in which a number of elements leave much to be desired, I feel not only embarrassed but also ashamed, because people will get the wrong idea of what opera is, or at least of what it can be.

Advice to Directors

I have noticed in working with Ponnelle and Zeffirelli that they have a great advantage in being the designers of their own productions. The action and the background to the action have a unity that is difficult, although not impossible, to achieve when staging and sets are the work of two different people. Faggioni is now beginning to design at least parts of his own productions, and this is probably because he is fascinated by the idea of being able to integrate his ideas so completely.

I also believe that stage directors would do well to avoid interpretations that are so intellectualized and abstruse that members of the audience need a book if they are to understand what is happening. The art of interpretation in the theatre is the art of clarification; and if any detail of a production has confused rather than elucidated the substance of a work for a reasonably intelligent person, it has failed in its function. Take, for example, Patrice Chéreau's staging of Wagner's *Ring* at Bayreuth. Many people complained, the first year, that it was too complicated. Then Chéreau wrote a book about the production, and suddenly everyone was saying how wonderful it was; until then, it had been greatly criticized. That, to me, is snobbery in the first place, and in the second place it negates the immediate, human values of the theatre.

Hispanic Music in the United States; Why I Sing Popular Music
One project close to my heart concerns the Hispanic community in the
United States. It is my impression that this group's cultural roots are being
ignored or forgotten in a shameful way. The Spanish-speaking population
in the United States now numbers about nineteen million, and many of
these people feel justifiably offended by what is presented to them and to
the outside world as their cultural heritage: long-running television soap
operas; brash, rhythmical music from the Caribbean; and not much else.
This is hardly an adequate representation of such a rich multi-national
culture. Plenty of people may well be content with soap operas and uninteresting music, but I am certain that at least some of them would come to
appreciate and love other things if given the opportunity. I know that if I
have been working all day in a language other than Spanish, I like to relax
by speaking my language or hearing it spoken. If the only entertainment
available to Spanish-speaking people in the States is the sort of thing I have
described, they may watch or listen to it for lack of anything better. René
Anselmo, director of the Spanish International Network, is trying to improve the situation.

I now spend about one-third of my time in the States, and I would like
to be able to carry the musical flag for these people. First of all, there is the
zarzuela. I am already planning fully staged performances in Los Angeles
to coincide with the 1984 Olympic Games, and I hope that they will attract
attention to the situation. But apart from the zarzuela, which is an art form
that originated in Spain itself, I am trying to interest Hispanic Americans
living in the States in the music of their own countries of origin – and there
are some glorious treasures to be found. This music, too, deserves to be
done properly. As a young man I was fascinated by Jorge Negrete, the ne
plus ultra of Mexican song, and Carlos Gardel, who occupied a similar
position in Argentinian music. The songs they sang were loved not just in
their own countries but throughout Latin America.

At about the time that I was beginning my career in Mexico, Jorge
Negrete and Pedro Infante, another famous Mexican singer, died, and there
was a good deal of discussion at the time about my following their path and
making popular Mexican films in which I would sing native music, as they
had done. By then, however, my romance with opera had begun, and there
was no turning back. If, however, my capacities as an opera singer had not
been sufficient, I would most likely have gone into the other field. My love
for this music also explains why in recent years I have recorded some of the
songs of Mexico and Argentina.

The recording I made of American popular songs with John Denver came about in a very different way. Milton Okun, an independent record producer, and his wife, Rosemary, happened to see me when I was a guest on Johnny Carson's television show. That evening, I had sung an excerpt from *My Fair Lady* in Spanish. They decided then and there to approach me about making a record of popular songs, and I must say that they kept after me with great persistence. I was very busy, as usual, but I began to think their proposals over. When we finally sat down to decide on a possible repertoire, the first idea was to record 'Annie's Song', which had been a big hit first for John Denver and then for James Galway, doing it this time with all three of us. That did not pan out. Instead, Denver, who is a friend of the Okuns', came to the studio and sang me his song 'Perhaps Love', which he was then considering recording. I immediately loved it, and right there in the studio we began to sing together, harmonizing, varying the music, and so on. Milton recognized the strong possibilities of a Denver–Domingo duet. The project proceeded from there, and 'Perhaps Love' – the whole album, that is – sold over a million and a half copies in its first year and a half on the market.

Milton, besides being my producer in this venture, has been a great friend to me, advising me in an area in which I had no experience what-soever. Thanks to him, I now have a contract in CBS's Crossover as well as its Masterworks series. The success of my recordings of Latin American and North American popular music has been gratifying to me for two reasons, the first selfish and the second much broader: on the one hand, I can sing for and be appreciated by people who do not enjoy opera; and on the other, through these non-operatic recordings I am helping to stimulate interest in opera. In England especially, people have written to say that six months earlier they had never head of Plácido Domingo and had had no knowledge of opera. The record with John Denver had aroused their curiosity; they had bought tickets to hear me in *Hoffmann* at Covent Garden, and had found it such a pleasant experience that they had returned to hear other operas with other singers. 'Opera has become our great love, thanks to you.' There have been numerous letters of this sort, which means that the experiment has been successful in all ways.

Music in Spain and Mexico

There has been a mistaken notion within Spain itself that Spaniards are unmusical, or in any case that Spain is a country where music is not needed.

The musical sensitivity of the Spanish public has been very badly under-estimated. This was brought home to me in an unequivocal way in the summer of 1982, when I gave an outdoor concert at the University of Madrid. It was difficult for people to get there and uncomfortable for them when they arrived. There were seats for only 20,000 people and no grass for the others to sit on – just standing room on the hard ground. Nevertheless, over 250,000 people attended! They stood for two hours and demonstrated their enjoyment of a kind of music that a great many of them had never before been exposed to. It was not only very moving for me to have had that experience in my native city – I think it also convinced a number of powerful people that the moment had arrived to give the people of Madrid in particular and Spain in general a richer musical life.

Let us first consider the operatic situation in Madrid. The Teatro Real was at one time a magnificent theatre, but some years ago it was transformed into a concert hall. To be sure, it is a wonderful concert hall, but making the change was a mistake. Most of the world's important capitals have important theatres, but opera has not been given much priority in Spain in recent decades. For the past twenty years there have been opera seasons at the Teatro de la Zarzuela, and I myself have performed there annually since 1970. The Zarzuela has its good points, but it is too small and too poorly equipped for major productions. Until a few years ago there were only two performances of each opera at the Zarzuela, and all the tickets were expensive. I convinced the administration to offer a third performance at popular prices, and the result was so successful that people queued for days in order to get in. A second extra performance was added, and in 1982 a third, always with the most gratifying results. The enthusiasm has surpassed all expectations, with people queuing for up to twenty days!

A new concert hall is being planned for Madrid, and the Teatro Real is to be reconverted into a fine opera house. This will all take time, and I will believe it when I see it; but I have high hopes that it can become a reality by the late 1980s.

Barcelona has a great operatic tradition, and in fact many of the great nineteenth century Italian repertoire operas were given at the Teatro Liceo almost immediately after their world premières in the major Italian theatres. I, however, can only talk competently about the situation as it has existed from the mid 1960s – that is, as I myself have experienced it.

While living in Barcelona I had a very good working relationship with the Liceo. Its director, Juan Antonio Pamias, was a real man of the theatre who ran the organization out of his own pocket and lived by his wits, just as impresarios used to do a century ago. His pocket was capacious but not bottomless, with the result that there was a lack of adequate rehearsal time and that too many operas were scheduled in dangerously close succession. Pamias would programme twenty or twenty-two operas in three months, putting on titles that the greatest opera companies in the world would think twice about before doing: a *Tristan* would be followed three days later by *William Tell*; *La fanciulla del West* would find a little *Parsifal* inserted after it. Would you like to hear *Il trovatore*? All right, we'll put it on just for fun and follow it up with a novelty like Leoncavallo's *La Bohème*. And why not *Roberto Devereux* for good measure? Pamias's intention was to please the *proprietarios*, who own every seat and box in the theatre, by giving them a variegated and ever-changing repertoire.

Before things became impossible, we had a lovely time in Barcelona because so many singers were living there – Caballé, Aragall, Lavirgen, Sardinero, Pons and myself (Carreras was only getting started in those days) – and we would all reserve several weeks around Christmas to be with our families. As a result, we were able to do some wonderful productions together. There were, for instance, performances of *Ballo*, *Aida* and *Vespri siciliani* that I remember with great warmth and that I have spoken of earlier. But the situation inevitably deteriorated because of the conditions I have described. The orchestra was exhausted and sounded so, the chorus was hoarse, secondary parts were raw, and the staging rehearsals minimal, to put it mildly. Things came to a head at a performance of *L'Africaine* with Montserrat and myself. At that time, some of the Liceo's productions were being televised, and I asked Pamias not to let *L'Africaine*, which was a very low-quality production, be broadcast. I suggested that since the opera is long, some of the highlights might have been taken from it and televised as such in a show lasting about an hour. Pamias agreed to the solution, but afterwards, without telling me, they broadcast the entire opera. That disillusioned me completely, and I decided I had had enough. I did not return for several years, and meanwhile Pamias died.

Another gentleman, Luis Portabella, an industrialist and my personal friend, is the Liceo's new Maecenas. He ran the Palau de la Musica in Barcelona for many years and managed to bring off such feats as a concert performance of *Die Walküre* with Nilsson, Caballé and Vickers, as well as guest performances by outstanding international orchestras. At the Liceo he has arranged to do two different seasons each year – a regular one between November and April and a special festival season in the late spring and early summer, in which I have already participated. I believe that the resurrection of the Teatro del Liceo is under way.

There are also places like Bilbao, Oviedo, Valencia, Saragossa and Las Palmas that have annual opera seasons and bring in famous singers. Time has not allowed me to return to them in recent years. The 1982 Madrid version of *Samson et Dalila* was such a success that I suggested to García Navarro, the conductor, and to Luis Pascual, the stage director, that we reserve two months some time in the future and take a similarly well-prepared production all around Spain, thus giving the provincial theatres an idea of the standards they should be aiming for. One of my many desires for the future is to take the time to participate in such a tour.

There is a project now afoot to have a summer opera festival in Itálica, the Roman amphitheatre outside Seville, and I think it would be wonderful if it succeeded. By concentrating at least in part on the music that Seville has inspired, there would be a ready-made centre of gravity for the festival for many years to come.

On the whole I am optimistic about the future of music in Spain. I think it is gradually going to take its rightful place in the artistic life of the country. We still need a great deal of work, and some help will have to come from the government as well as from private sources. Financial contributions on the part of business and industry should be made tax deductible, as they are in the United States and elsewhere. Beyond that, the level of musical education must be raised.

Although I am a Spaniard and feel most at home in Spain, I also greatly love Mexico, where I spent thirteen important, formative years. My parents, my sister and other members of my family still live there, and I have maintained my ties. Musically, I think the country has made tremendous strides during the last few years. New orchestras and theatres have been created, and there is an abundance of musical activity in Mexico City today. The level is not always very high; but I am sure that this, too, will improve with time.

Tenors

Listening to records of the tenors of the past, especially Caruso and Gigli, was a great spur to my ambition when I was very young. What I admired and still admire most about Caruso is the way he gave of himself so completely in his interpretation of everything he sang. The power of his voice was especially impressive in the F-natural to B-flat range, while with

Gigli, the melting, plangent tone quality was the most striking feature. Jussi Bjoerling has been accused of coldness, but none of his recordings has ever left me cold. His regal sound and elegant phrasing were an inspiration to me. Miguel Fleta, my compatriot, I love particularly for his temperament, and Tito Schipa for his refinement. The recordings of Aureliano Pertile, Toscanini's favourite at La Scala in the 1920s, are remarkable first and foremost for the modernity of their style: he would feel at home on the stage of any opera house today – which is not true of many of his contemporaries.

I must stress, however, that the example of all the legendary singers of the past is a source of inspiration and challenge, not of intimidation and envy. As in other fields, each individual offers something unique. Life goes on, and we must seek our own paths.

In 1968, within a month of my Metropolitan debut, two other tenors made theirs in the same house – Luciano Pavarotti and Jaime (Giacomo) Aragall. In some respects the voices are similar – both incredibly beautiful and both possessing extreme facility in the high register. Luciano has of course gone on to become one of the most celebrated tenors of our time, while Jaime has not received all the recognition he deserves. As to the much discussed Pavarotti–Domingo 'rivalry', it exists much more vividly in the minds of certain journalists and fans than in those of the protagonists.

Like Aragall, Alfredo Kraus and José Carreras are also my compatriots. Alfredo is a great stylist and bel canto singer with incredible high notes; José I admire not only for his beautiful voice but also for his courage in following his own path, despite others' attempts to tell him what he should or should not do.

My Boys

Until recently I had hoped that at least one or two of my three sons would enter careers involving the theatre in one way or another. But because my life is so unsettled, because of the tremendous pressure I work under, and because of the stories invented by newspapers and magazines in order to make the operatic world appear to be something it is not, I have come to feel during the last two or three years that I would not want them to work in my field unless they love it so much that they can see no other path. I am grateful for and happy with the way my life has gone so far, but it is filled with personal sacrifices. I have been blessed with a steady nature and good internal equilibrium, and so neither the good nor the bad things that happen to me can alter my character or my attitude towards human beings. But why should my boys think the same way? As it is, they, like Marta, have already made many sacrifices to my career. People who are not very resilient can be badly hurt or embittered by this profession. I do not want that for my sons. I want them to enjoy their lives fully.

Pepe, who now lives in England and calls himself Joe, is mainly interested in photography, and I am encouraging him wholeheartedly. He plays the guitar for fun. He will be twenty-five when this book is published, and I am sure that he will have a productive life. Placi, who will be eighteen, and Alvaro, who will be fifteen, go to school in Switzerland. Neither of them seems to be inclined to go to university, which does not bother me in the least. Unemployment is an ever more pressing problem in the industrialized world, and university graduates are no more likely to find work than anyone else. If they do eventually demonstrate serious interest in a profession related to mine, I will do everything to help them, but I think it is good for them that their father is not, for instance, a businessman, whose way of life they could simply inherit. In music, in the theatre, you may be named Ludwig van Beethoven, Jr, or William Shakespeare, Jr, and it will do you very little good. Alvaro shows signs of interest in stage direction, and Placi has a fantastic musical gift: he can play virtually anything by ear at the piano straight off, from Verdi to the latest pop music. He has already written a song for me (I recorded it as part of my album 'My Life for a Song') and is working on others. I would not be surprised if he becomes the third Plácido Domingo in a row to make music his life, or if he and Alvaro both end up in show business. It is in their blood.

Like every parent, I can talk all I like about what I want for my children, but in the end they will go their own ways.

Future Projects

As I finish this final chapter of my book, I am preparing to sing in a new production of *Manon Lescaut* at Covent Garden (spring 1983), with Kiri Te Kanawa in the title role, Giuseppe Sinopoli conducting, and Götz Friedrich directing. In the autumn I will be appearing there in *Otello*, conducted by Sir Colin Davis, and will make my British conducting debut there in *Die Fledermaus*.

At the Met, I will be opening the hundredth anniversary season in the autumn of 1983 with Jessye Norman and Tatiana Troyanos in Berlioz's *Les Troyens*, conducted by Levine and directed by Fabrizio Melano. Later in the season I will sing in a new production of Zandonai's *Francesca da Rimini* and will take part in the company's centennial spring tour. I am scheduled to open the following season with *Lohengrin*, again under Levine's baton, with Anna Tomowa-Sintow as Elsa and Eva Marton as Ortrud. The director will be that outstanding man of the theatre, August Everding. I shall also be conducting *Bohème* at the Met in 1984.

A wonderful year at La Scala is approaching for me. I will open the Milan opera season for the fifth time in December 1983 with *Fanciulla*, co-starring Rosalind Plowright and Silvano Carroli, with Maazel on the podium and Louis Malle, the famous film director, in charge of the staging. A month later, I am scheduled to record *Il trovatore* with Giulini and the Scala company, and I will be opening the following season in *Carmen* with Abbado conducting. In an optimistic moment I 'reserved' La Scala for a performance of *Otello* on 5 February 1987, the hundredth anniversary of the world première.

Before this book appears, I will have participated in the shooting of a film of *Carmen* directed by Francesco Rosi (Maazel conducts, with Julia Migenes-Johnson as Carmen, Faith Esham as Micaela, and Ruggero Raimondi as Escamillo). I am also planning to be in Zeffirelli's film of *Aida* and Karajan's of *Turandot*, and perhaps a cinematic version of *The Merry Widow* in the reasonably near future. One of the most exciting movies in which I expect to be involved is *The Tales of Hoffmann*, to be directed by Ingmar Bergman. Seiji Ozawa, with whom I have sung only the Verdi Requiem, will be the conductor, and the rest of the cast is still to be decided upon. We are looking for shooting dates in 1984 or 1985, and Bergman has said that this will be his last film.

I love the German lied repertoire – so much so that I would not dare to attempt any of it without extremely careful preparation. That is another project for the future. For now, I am limiting my concert activities to appearances before large audiences in variegated but mainly operatic repertoire.

Preface to My Next Forty Years

My life has so far been both lucky and happy, and reliving it while working on this book has given me much pleasure. But I would like to end the tale by describing one of my dreams for the future: the founding of an outstanding opera school.

I often think back fondly on my days in Hamburg in the late 1960s, when I would spend time with conductor Nello Santi discussing vocal style, talking about how Caruso or Gigli sang certain phrases, and listening with admiration to Nello's stories of how Toscanini used to take hours to teach singers like Stabile and Valdengo the two words 'un'acciuga' (an anchovy) in Verdi's *Falstaff*. Nello and I were not undertaking such a profound study, yet what we did made me think about the singer's art in a way that I had not done – or at least not enough – before. I miss those days very much.

Today, most people blame singers and their frenetic schedules for the fact that there is rarely time for us to sit down and work properly with conductors on specifically musical points. But our schedules are only one part of the problem – and perhaps not even the most important part. Conductors, too, have full, demanding schedules that do not allow them time to go over interpretative questions with the singers.

Another source of the difficulty is that staging has come gradually to occupy the bulk of rehearsal time. Much of that time is often a waste for the singers, not so much because we over-rehearse, although that is occasionally true, as because of the hours spent sitting around. In the big opera houses today, productions are sometimes very complicated, and it is right that they be thoroughly prepared – but not at the expense of the music, which is often neglected. Many times we singers spend days and days hanging about the theatre while chorus members are taught dance steps or while scenes other than our own are being rehearsed.

One of the main purposes of this book is, as I have said, to present some of my own thoughts on preparing for a career in the lyric theatre, and my ideal school would allow me to implement those thoughts. I hope to select a group of fifteen to twenty young singers, gleaned through rigorous auditioning around the world. The final selection of the participants would be mine, and I would base my choice not just on vocal potential and musicality, which would have to be first-rate, but above all on intelligence and capacity for learning. I would have to believe that each of these singers could reach an outstandingly high level of achievement in their field. These young people would already have to be vocally trained, well instructed in related areas, and on the verge of starting their own careers. I would work with them technically for one year, preparing them to perform, and then devote a second year to rehearsing and giving performances.

The school would function in connection with an opera house, and the participants would all be there on full scholarships. Each of the two school years would last eight or nine months. The students would have to have a great desire to work, because hard labour would be their lot for those two years. Life would be beautiful for them, too, but one sign of laziness and they would have to leave.

About ten students would be in their preparatory year while the other half of the group would be involved in an active performing year. The orchestra, chorus and staff of whatever theatre is involved would be available for the productions, and each member of the second-year group would be expected to sing a total of thirty or forty times a year in several different works. Doing two performances as Susannetta one year and three as Lauretta the next is useful, but it certainly does not create a complete, finished professional singer. I believe in work; and if you are a performer, you must perform.

I want the instructors for this course to be the best possible people in their respective areas – musical coaches, language coaches, stage directors, and dancing, fencing and mime teachers. It would also be a good idea for singers to learn something about the technical side of operatic production, so that they develop a proper eye for make-up, costuming and lighting.

I want young conductors, too, to have the chance to gain experience in connection with this school. Fine opera conductors are a rarity; yet one sees so many young conductors who would like to work in opera, who have done all their homework, but who simply cannot find opportunities for acquiring practical expertise. Eventually we might even accommodate young directors, designers and others on the technical side of the profession as well. In short, I hope that this school will make a big impact on the whole world of opera.

The programme would work two ways. On the one hand, I want to be able to say to the Metropolitan or to any other major theatre, 'I see that you have a weak point – that you need another mezzo-soprano, a lyric tenor and a bass. In two years, you will have them, and they will be first-rate.' And on the other hand, if one of those houses has a young singer who is already performing but who appears to need further polishing, that person could be sent to the school for just that purpose. I think the public would be surprised to learn how many times well-established singers have come to me and to some of my colleagues to ask not just for advice but for real, concrete technical assistance. My school will be a place where such assistance will be available.

One possibly ideal location is Monaco. I mentioned the project to Princess Grace not long before her death, and she was very encouraging. Not only are Monte Carlo's climate and accessibility excellent: there is also a jewel of an opera house that is underused at present. I naturally think of my native Spain as another potential location for the school, and I have already discussed with Prince Alfonso de Hohenlohe, the moving spirit behind most activities in Marbella on the Costa del Sol, the possibility of setting it up there. Two theatre administrations, including that of the beautiful Teatro Filarmonico in Verona, have also approached me about the establishment of my programme.

There will be an additional didactic aspect to the school. In whatever city it is located, I want children and teenagers to be able to attend performances after having first been properly prepared for what they are going to see and hear. And it ought to do them good to realize that some of the people they are hearing are not many years older than themselves and are already on their way to becoming internationally known performers in their own right.

Some of my friends have told me to keep quiet about this idea until I am ready to act upon it. But at the risk of seeming vain, I must say that the most important element in the programme will be what I myself can bring to it as a result of a lifetime in the theatre. I would not and could not do all the administrative and academic work myself; but my ideas, which are already quite clear in my mind, and my participation, would be determinant. I believe that I have a nose (or an ear, in this case) for real talent. It is useless to lavish effort on people who will never be able to make the grade and, more tragically, to let real talent pass by. No one can expect to have a hundred per cent success record, but I do feel that I know enough to avoid some of the worst errors of this sort.

This is all a dream in the sense that it is an ideal goal, but it is far from being an unattainable one. In fact, if I wanted to set this programme up immediately, I could do so. But I am not in a hurry. I do not want to initiate it until my singing days are over, so that I can devote most of my time and energy to it. I hope to be conducting more then, but conducting does not require the constant concern with one's own physical well-being that singing demands.

I do ask myself sometimes just how difficult it will be for me to leave the stage when the time comes. I certainly do not want to be one of those singers of whom people say, 'My God, he's still singing! Has he no self-respect?' I can imagine myself fifteen years from now doing musical comedy – Professor Higgins in a Spanish version of *My Fair Lady*, which I love, or other roles in other classics of the genre. But I do believe that I ought not to activate my plans for the school until I get the stage bug completely out of my system. Then I will be able to divide my time between the podium and the school, and that will be all. I look forward to the future with joyful anticipation.

Plácido Domingo, March 1983

AFTERWORD
by Harvey Sachs*

'All men of every sort who have done something of excellence, or truly resembling excellence, ought, if they are honest and worthy, to describe their own life by their own hand; but such a fine enterprise should not be initiated before they have passed the age of forty.'

Benvenuto Cellini began his autobiography, over four centuries ago, with these words. In any times, the life of a man who has achieved worldly success can hardly fail to be a fascinating tale. There are, of course, potential drawbacks; Stendhal hit on an important one when, in the first chapter of one of his own autobiographical works (*Vie de Henri Brulard*), he reminded himself of the necessarily 'frightful quantity of *I*'s and *me*'s! They would be enough to put the most kind-hearted reader into a bad temper.'

Plácido Domingo expressed similar concerns when we first met to discuss this project at the end of 1980, less than a month before his fortieth birthday. He wondered what point there was in writing a book about his life when he still ought to have many active years ahead of him. Only when it occurred to him that what he has learned and done and thought about so far could be of more than passing interest did he decide the book could be of value. 'After all,' he said, 'I have spent nearly all my life in the musical theatre, one way or another, and I think I can say some important and interesting things about my roles, my profession and my world.' And so he began.

The first things that strike, or perhaps stun, anyone who has much to do with Plácido Domingo are the quantity and diversity of his undertakings. He has not yet performed in the central crater of Mount Etna, broadcast

---

* Harvey Sachs is an American-born Canadian conductor and writer. He regularly conducts orchestras in Italy, where he makes his home, and in Canada, and he is the author of two highly acclaimed books, *Toscanini* (1978) and *Virtuoso* (1982).

live from a space shuttle, or sung a benefit concert for an audience of penguins in Antarctica; but there are few things he has missed that are normally considered part of an opera singer's career and many things he has done that most singers never attempt. In addition to performing opera on four continents, he maintains a potentially crushing schedule of recording sessions, concerts, filmings, television appearances and interviews; and he manages to do it all with remarkable calm, remaining fresh and enthusiastic, and keeping his concentration level at the maximum. The source of his ability to work so much, to function so well, lies in his marvellous equilibrium. Thus he is able to deal with both the pleasant and the unpleasant results of his success without losing his perspective.

I find Domingo a wholly delightful person. His one weakness, if it is indeed a weakness, is that he is too generous with his time, too sweet-tempered, even with the reptilian element of the operatic milieu. He is even gentle with those who wish to drag famous persons into their own petty intrigues and with those who try to insert themselves, possessively, into his life. His natural gregariousness is so strong that only under the most provoking circumstances will he react negatively to another human being. He believes that it is part of his professional duty to treat with dignity those who show interest in his work, whether or not they treat him with equal thoughtfulness. Fortunately, Domingo truly enjoys most of the people with whom he works, and they truly enjoy working with him. I refer not only to his colleagues and to conductors and stage directors but also to the prompters, wardrobe staff and sub-assistant stage managers at the Met or Covent Garden or La Scala - wherever he performs. These are the people who are sometimes subjected to high-handed treatment by star performers. I have yet to meet one of them who does not take pleasure in 'having Plácido around the house'.

Although Domingo is justifiably proud of his standing in his field, it would be hard to find anyone in a similar position, in any field, less afflicted with the curse of conceit. Domingo's active sense of humour - about himself as well as others - deflects impulses towards self-satisfaction and pomposity. Naturally, he prefers good reviews to bad ones, but he does not give too much credence to either. He was touched, however, when Mstislav Rostropovich - who had read Domingo's statement that when singing he tries to imitate the sound quality and phrasing of a wonderful cello played by a wonderful cellist - said that no cello could sound as beautiful as the voice of Plácido Domingo.

Within the profession, Domingo is well known for his complete musical mastery of the roles he sings. He is a fine pianist, and his conducting experience has given him an unusually keen awareness of a role as part of a dramatic whole. He learns his parts by himself, often studying them directly from the orchestral score. Sometimes, as he has said, he works silently, without a piano, learning and absorbing the music while travelling from one engagement to another. He has paid tribute in these pages to several conductors, including Carlos Kleiber, James Levine, Carlo Maria Giulini, Claudio Abbado, Riccardo Muti, Zubin Mehta and Lorin Maazel. What he has not said is that, as a result of his outstanding and dependable musicianship, he has long been one of the favourite singers of these exacting artists. They enjoy working with him and take his ideas seriously, and the same is true of his working relationships with most of the major stage directors. His opinions are valuable because while studying a score he does not merely learn the notes and think about the type of delivery that will be most impressive vocally, but also develops a precise idea of the dramatic purpose of every phrase. He is always conscious of his movements on stage and thus, unlike some of his colleagues, he never, during stage rehearsals, resembles an ocean liner being pushed and pulled by tug-boat stage directors and their assistants.

In this book, Domingo has occasionally said that this or that production 'was a success' or that he was 'well received'. Having spent much time with him during the past two years, I find such statements amusing in their understatement. They give no idea at all of the adulation that meets this man wherever he goes. And I don't just mean the ovations he receives on stage. After a Domingo performance, his dressing-room looks like Groucho Marx's stateroom in – appropriately enough – *A Night at the Opera*. In the corridors or outside the stage door, he makes his way with difficulty through enthusiastic masses of people seeking his attention or his autograph or asking to be photographed with him. He almost always responds graciously to their requests. Some of the correspondence can be a bit harder to deal with. An unknown lady admirer, who clearly had no idea of the extent of Domingo's devotion to his family, once wrote to suggest that he ride off with her on a white horse, into Spain's Sierra Morena, to live a life of liberty – 'just like Don José and Carmen in the opera's second act', she said. On reading the letter, her idol commented, 'She has conveniently forgotten what happens to Carmen in the fourth act.'

If Domingo, in this account of his career, has not dwelt on his triumphs, his reason is not false modesty, for he is happy to have already accomplished so much. But he does not look on his work as competitive in any way, and he strongly believes that all artists have unique qualities that must be developed as fully as possible if they are to do their best for the music and thus for the public. Although Domingo is a person of great warmth, someone whom it is always fun to be with, he has a sense of privacy that does not permit him to exceed certain limits. I daresay that this is one of the few books ever written by an opera personality that contains neither malicious gossip nor personal attacks, and few rebuttals of others' attacks. Such unfortunate aspects of the theatrical environment sadden rather than anger him.

Domingo's family is as important a constant in his life as his work. Marta is his best adviser, his severest critic and his closest friend and companion. Seeing Domingo, the father, with their teenaged sons always makes me feel that his most important goal in life is for them to be able to think of him with pride and affection for the rest of their lives. And Joe, his oldest son, told me: 'My father is a great artist, but I admire him a hundred times more as a human being.'

My role in this book's creation has merely been that of scribe and organizer for Domingo, who has an extremely efficient mind and does not need a ghost writer any more than he needs a microphone to project his magnificent voice from the stages of the world's major opera houses. His astounding memory, not just for music but also for dates, names, places and faces, has facilitated the work considerably. Even without the aid of his meticulous date-books, he is able to reconstruct almost day by day much of his phenomenally busy career. The annual date-books, bound in green leather – 'green to symbolize hope', he says – were begun in 1963 and list casts, conductors, stage directors, and numbers of performances sung of a given opera at a given house. The earlier books, from his days in Tel Aviv, often contain his comments on his work – sometimes enthusiastic, sometimes not. His 19 January 1964 entry reads: 'Stupendous rehearsal of *Pearl Fishers*. Everything went very well. The "B naturals" were very secure. . . .' Four days later he wrote: 'Mediocre performance of *Pearl Fishers*. I just couldn't find my way during the first duet. The arias were so-so. . . .'

In later years, unfortunately, his diary entries were limited to simple lists of engagements because of his monumental work-load and travel schedule. I understand that Domingo's father, discussing his son's hectic pace, said: 'You get into a hotel elevator with Plácido and Marta and one of them says, "It's decided. We're going to Rome tomorrow." By the time the elevator reaches the lobby they're saying, "No, let's go to Manila after all."' And Marta says of her husband's schedule, 'Plácido is perfectly capable of singing a whole opera, attending a dinner party afterwards, going to sleep at 5 a.m. and being on stage for rehearsal at 11 a.m. He has the constitution of a horse.'

There are certain people who, despite everything, try to keep pace with this man of boundless energy. Their help in providing supplementary information and scheduling data has been essential to the book's creation. First of all, thanks are due to Paul Garner, Domingo's loyal secretary; then to his managers, Marianne and Gerard Semon of New York, Margherita Stafford of London, and Michel Glotz of Paris. Plácido Domingo also wishes to thank the public relations departments of Polygram, RCA, CBS, EMI, Phonogram and Decca recording companies for their assistance in supplying information for the Discography.

APPENDIX I: PERFORMANCE LIST

The following is a nearly complete list of Placido Domingo's appearances as an opera and concert singer from his debut in 1959 until March 1983. About half a dozen entries are missing from the pre-Tel Aviv (1959-62) section, and there is a bit of confusion in the listings for the latter half of 1966 and all of 1968. (Domingo's 1968 date-book disappeared a few years ago, and he would be very pleased if whoever may have picked it up by accident would return it to him care of this publisher.) None the less, the list does show the overwhelming majority of his performances. Not included are Domingo's appearances in zarzuela and musical comedy, most of the concerts in which he sang only one or two numbers, conducting engagements and recording sessions. In each of the listings, it is to be assumed that he sang the lead tenor role unless otherwise noted. An asterisk (*) indicates his debut in a role, a house or a city.

By a quick count, Domingo has sung on stage seventy roles in fifty-five operas, and solo parts in eight choral-orchestral works; recordings add another sixteen operas to his repertoire. Now in his forty-third year, he is approaching his seventeen hundredth performance. Include conducting, zarzuela, musical comedy and special television appearances, and the number would easily exceed two thousand.

1959

23, 25 Sept. *Rigoletto* (Borsa*), Mexico City*

21, 23 Oct. *Dialogues des Carmélites* (Chaplain*), Mexico City

1960

11 Sept. *Turandot* (Altoum*), Mexico City
1 Oct. *Turandot* (Pang*), Monterrey*
5 Oct. *Lucia* (Normanno*), Monterrey

8 Oct. *Traviata* (Gastone*), Monterrey
15 Oct. *Carmen* (Remendado*), Monterrey
17 Oct. *Otello* (Cassio*), Monterrey

1961

26 Apr. *Traviata* (Gastone), Mexico City
19 May *Traviata* (Alfredo*), Monterrey
28 May *Ultimo sueño* (Enrique*), Mexico City

28 June *Amelia Goes to the Ball* (Lover*), Mexico City
2 July *Fedora* (Désiré,* Baron*), Mexico City

8, 10 Aug. *Boris Godunov* (Shuisky,*
    Simpleton*), Mexico City
15, 17 Aug. *Andrea Chénier* (Abbé,*
    Incredibile*), Mexico City
21, 23 Aug. *Tosca* (Spoletta*), Mexico
    City
29, 31 Aug. *Traviata* (Gastone), Mexico
    City

5, 7, 9 Sept. *Carmen* (Remendado),
    Mexico City
15 Sept. *Butterfly* (Goro*), Mexico City
30 Sept. *Tosca* (Cavaradossi*), Mexico
    City
24 Oct. *Rigoletto* (Borsa), Guadalajara*
28 Oct. *Lucia* (Arturo*), Guadalajara
16, 18 Nov. *Lucia* (Arturo), Dallas*
    (American debut)

1962

25 Feb. *Tosca*, Mexico City
4 Mar. *Bohème*,* Mexico City
5 May *Cantata*,* Puebla*[1]
10 May *Così fan tutte*,* Mexico City
17 May *Adriana Lecouvreur*,* Mexico
    City
? June *Così*, Mexico City
? June *Così*, Puebla
? June *Tosca* (Spoletta), Puebla
? June *Butterfly* (Goro), Puebla
10, 12 Aug. Beethoven 9th Symphony,*
    Mexico City
? Sept. *Amelia*, Monterrey

7 Oct. *Butterfly* (Pinkerton*), Torreón*
20 Oct. *Traviata*, Guadalajara
? Oct. *Triptico francescano* (by Refice),*
    Guadalajara (?)
1 Nov. *Butterfly*, Tampa*
8,10 Nov. *Lucia* (Arturo), New
    Orleans*
19 Nov. *Otello* (Cassio), Hartford*
26, 30 Nov. *Lucia* (Edgardo*), Fort
    Worth*
29 Dec. *Bohème*, Tel Aviv* (Israeli
    debut)

[1] 100th anniversary of defeat of France by Mexico at Puebla.

1963

8 Jan. *Traviata*, Tel Aviv
9 Jan. *Bohème*, Tel Aviv
15 Jan. *Butterfly*, Tel Aviv
21, 28 Jan. *Bohème*, Tel Aviv
29 Jan. *Traviata*, Tel Aviv
6 Feb. *Bohème*, Tel Aviv
11 Feb. *Traviata*, Tel Aviv
13 Feb. *Bohème*, Tel Aviv
19 Feb. *Butterfly*, Tel Aviv
25 Feb. *Bohème*, Tel Aviv
12, 16 Mar. *Faust*,* Tel Aviv
18 Mar. *Traviata*, Tel Aviv
23, 25 Mar. *Faust*, Tel Aviv

27 Mar. *Traviata*, Tel Aviv
30 Mar. *Faust*, Tel Aviv
10 Apr. *Faust*, Tel Aviv
21, 24 Apr. *Butterfly*, Tel Aviv
25 Apr. *Traviata*, Haifa*
1, 5, 7 May *Butterfly*, Tel Aviv
9 May *Butterfly*, Beersheba*
11 May *Butterfly*, Tel Aviv
12 May *Faust*, Tel Aviv
13 May *Butterfly*, Tel Aviv
22 May *Bohème*, Tel Aviv
26 May *Faust*, Tel Aviv
1, 5, 10 June *Butterfly*, Tel Aviv

12 June *Faust*, Tel Aviv
15 June *Butterfly*, Tel Aviv
17 June *Bohème*, Tel Aviv
18, 20, 23 June *Butterfly*, Tel Aviv
25, 29 June, 1, 3, 6, 8 July *Carmen* (Don José*), Tel Aviv
14 July *Faust*, Tel Aviv
20 July *Traviata*, Tel Aviv
21 July *Butterfly*, Tel Aviv
23 July *Traviata*, Jerusalem*
28 July *Traviata*, Tel Aviv
5 Aug. *Faust*, Tel Aviv
7 Aug. *Traviata*, Tel Aviv
10 Aug. *Bohème*, Tel Aviv
14 Aug. *Traviata*, Tel Aviv
19 Aug. *Butterfly*, Tel Aviv
21 Aug. *Faust*, Tel Aviv
26 Aug. *Traviata*, Tel Aviv

27, 31 Aug. *Butterfly*, Tel Aviv
21, 23, 25, 28, 30 Sept., 3, 5 Oct. *Don Giovanni* (Ottavio*), Tel Aviv
7 Oct. *Bohème*, Tel Aviv
10, 12, 14 Oct. *Don Giovanni*, Tel Aviv
17 Oct. *Faust*, Beersheba
19 Oct. *Don Giovanni*, Tel Aviv
22 Oct. *Butterfly*, Tel Aviv
24 Oct. *Don Giovanni*, Haifa
26, 30 Oct., 2, 4 Nov. *Don Giovanni*, Tel Aviv
6 Nov. *Don Giovanni*, Jerusalem
9 Nov. *Don Giovanni*, Tel Aviv
11 Nov. *Butterfly*, Tel Aviv
13, 16, 20, 23, 25, 30 Nov., 2, 4, 7, 9, 11, 14, 18, 21, 23, 28 Dec. *Don Giovanni*, Tel Aviv
30 Dec. *Bohème*, Tel Aviv

1964

4, 6, 8, 11, 13, 18 Jan. *Don Giovanni*, Tel Aviv
21, 23, 25 Jan. *Pearl Fishers*,* Tel Aviv
27 Jan. *Don Giovanni*, Tel Aviv
29 Jan., 1, 3, 5, 8, 10, 12, 15 Feb. *Pearl Fishers*, Tel Aviv
17 Feb. *Don Giovanni*, Tel Aviv
20 Feb. *Pearl Fishers*, Haifa
22, 24, 26 Feb., 2, 4, 7, 9, 11, 14 Mar. *Pearl Fishers*, Tel Aviv
16 Mar. *Don Giovanni*, Tel Aviv
18, 21, 23, 25, 28 Mar. *Pearl Fishers*, Tel Aviv
29 Mar. *Faust*, Tel Aviv
30 Mar., 4, 20, 22, 25 Apr. *Pearl Fishers*, Tel Aviv
3 May *Traviata*, Tel Aviv
20 May *Faust*, Tel Aviv
21, 25, 27 May., 1, 7 June *Pearl Fishers*, Tel Aviv
16 June *Traviata*, Tel Aviv
17 June *Don Giovanni*, Tel Aviv
20, 22 June *Pearl Fishers*, Tel Aviv

24 June *Traviata*, Tel Aviv
28 June *Pearl Fishers*, Tel Aviv
1, 6, 9 July *Carmen*, Tel Aviv
11 July *Pearl Fishers*, Tel Aviv
14 July *Carmen*, Tel Aviv
16 July *Carmen*, Haifa
20, 22 July *Carmen*, Tel Aviv
23 July *Pearl Fishers*, Kfar Atta*
25 July *Pearl Fishers*, Tel Aviv
28 July *Carmen*, Tel Aviv
30 July *Carmen*, Kiryat Bialik*
1 Aug. *Pearl Fisher*, Tel Aviv
4 Aug. *Carmen*, Tel Aviv
8 Aug. *Pearl Fisher*, Tel Aviv
12 Aug. *Traviata*, Tel Aviv
15 Aug. *Pearl Fishers*, Tel Aviv
5, 8, 10, 12 Sept. *Eugene Onegin*,* Tel Aviv
13 Sept. *Tosca*, Tel Aviv
14, 16 Sept. *Onegin*, Tel Aviv
17 Sept. *Tosca*, Tel Aviv
19 Sept. *Onegin*, Tel Aviv
22 Sept. *Tosca*, Nahariyya*
24 Sept. *Onegin*, Haifa

28 Sept. *Pearl Fishers*, Tel Aviv
30 Sept., 3 Oct. *Onegin*, Tel Aviv
6 Oct. *Tosca*, Tel Aviv
10, 12, 14, 17, 19 Oct. *Onegin*, Tel Aviv
22 Oct. *Pearl Fishers*, Haifa
24, 27 Oct. *Onegin*, Tel Aviv
29 Oct. *Pearl Fishers*, Tel Aviv
2 Nov. *Onegin*, Tel Aviv
4 Nov. *Tosca*, Tel Aviv
11, 14 Nov. *Onegin*, Tel Aviv
16 Nov. *Carmen*, Tel Aviv

21 Nov. *Butterfly*, Tel Aviv
24, 28 Nov. *Onegin*, Tel Aviv
29 Nov. *Pearl Fishers*, Jerusalem
2, 5, 7 Dec. *Onegin*, Tel Aviv
12 Dec. *Butterfly*, Tel Aviv
14 Dec. *Faust*, Tel Aviv
19 Dec. *Pearl Fishers*, Tel Aviv
22 Dec. *Carmen*, Tel Aviv
28 Dec. *Onegin*, Tel Aviv
29 Dec. *Carmen*, Tel Aviv
30 Dec. *Pearl Fishers*, Tel Aviv

1965

3 Jan. *Carmen*, Tel Aviv
11 Jan. *Onegin*, Tel Aviv
21, 22, 25 Jan. *Cavalleria rusticana*,* Tel
        Aviv
26 Jan. *Faust*, Tel Aviv
27, 29 Jan. *Cavalleria*, Tel Aviv
31 Jan. *Carmen*, Tel Aviv
2 Feb. *Cavalleria*, Tel Aviv
4 Feb. *Cavalleria*, Haifa
5, 8, 10 Feb. *Cavalleria*, Tel Aviv
11 Feb. *Carmen*, Tel Aviv
12, 15, 17, 19, 22, 24, 26 Feb., 1, 3, 5, 8
        Mar. *Cavalleria*, Tel Aviv
11 Mar. *Cavalleria*, Haifa
12, 15, 18, 19, 22 Mar. *Cavalleria*, Tel
        Aviv
24 Mar. *Cavalleria*, Jerusalem
26, 29, 31 Mar., 3, 5, 7, 10, 12
        Apr. *Cavalleria*, Tel Aviv
13 Apr. *Traviata*, Tel Aviv
14, 17, 19, 21, 24, 26 Apr., 1, 3, 8, 10, 15,
        17, 22, 24 May *Cavalleria*, Tel
        Aviv

26 May *Cavalleria*, Kfar Atta
29, 31 May, 2, 9 June *Cavalleria*, Tel Aviv
12 June *Tosca*, Tel Aviv
14 June *Cavalleria*, Tel Aviv
8 July *Carmen*, Washington, DC*
30 July *Samson et Dalila*,* Chautauqua*
2 Aug. *Samson et Dalila*, Chautauqua
7 Sept. *Tales of Hoffmann*,* Mexico City
30 Sept. *Tosca*, Mexico City
8, 9, 15 Oct. *Butterfly*, Binghamton, NY*
17 Oct. *Butterfly*, NYC Opera,* New
        York*
21 Oct. *Carmen*, NYC Opera
23 Oct. *Butterfly*, Puebla
31 Oct. *Carmen*, NYC Opera
5, 6 Nov. *Samson et Dalila*, Milwaukee*
11, 13, 14 Nov. *Butterfly*, Marseille*
        (French and European debut)
3, 5 Dec. *Carmen*, Fort Worth
10, 12 Dec. *Messiah*,* Boston*; Handel &
        Haydn Society
14 Dec. *Hoffmann*, Philadelphia*

1966[2]

1, 4, 8 Jan. *Carlota*,* *Mulata*,* *Severino*,*
        Barcelona* (Spanish debut)
15, 16 Jan. *Tosca*, Toledo,* Ohio
22 Jan. *Tosca*, Dayton, Ohio*
22, 27 Feb. *Don Rodrigo** (US premiere),
        NYC Opera[3]

3, 5 Mar. *Chénier* (Chénier*), New Orleans
10 Mar. *Don Rodrigo*, NYC Opera
19 Mar. *Samson et Dalila*, Binghamton
25, 27 Mar. *Don Rodrigo*, NYC Opera
6, 10 Apr. *Hippolyte et Aricie*,* Boston
26 Apr. *Bohème*, Boston

[2] The record for the latter half of 1966 is incomplete.
[3] First performance by New York City Opera in the New York State Theater, Lincoln Center.

1 May *Bohème*, Boston
16, 17, 19, 21 May *Faust*, San Diego*
26 May *Elijah*,* Mexico City
29 June *Carmen*, Cincinnati*
2 July *Carmen*, Cincinnati
15, 17 July *Cavalleria*, Cincinnati
30 July Concert, Milwaukee
9 Aug. *Cavalleria* and *Pagliacci*,* New
York (Lewisohn Stadium)
13, 21 Aug. *Butterfly*, NYC Opera, Long
Island Festival
13 Sept. *Lucia*, Guadalajara
16 Sept. *Barber of Seville*,* Guadalajara
29 Sept. *Carmen*, NYC Opera

30 Sept. *Don Giovanni*, NYC Opera
4 Oct. *Carmen*, NYC Opera
13, 15 Oct. *Tosca*, New Orleans
23 Oct. *Traviata*, NYC Opera
27, 29 Oct. *Lucia*, New Orleans
30 Oct. *Carmen*, NYC Opera
3 Nov. *Tosca*, NYC Opera
5 Nov. *Carmen*, NYC Opera
9 Nov. *Hoffmann*, NYC Opera
12 Nov. *Traviata*, NYC Opera
15 Nov. *Anna Bolena** (concert form),
Carnegie Hall*; American Opera
Society
2, 4 Dec. *Butterfly*, Fort Worth

1967

8 Jan. *Tosca*, Hamburg* (German debut)
20,22 Jan. *Samson et Dalila*, Fort Worth
3, 4, 6 Feb. *Hoffmann*, Baltimore*
9, 12 Feb. *Don Rodrigo*, NYC Opera
16 Feb. *Traviata*, NYC Opera
19 Feb. *Carmen*, NYC Opera
23, 24, 25 Feb. *Creation* Mass*
2 Mar. *Creation* Mass, New Brunswick,
NJ*
4 Mar. *Creation* Mass, Carnegie Hall
5 Mar. *Butterfly*, NYC Opera
8 Mar. *Tabarro*,* NYC Opera
11 Mar. *Traviata*, NYC Opera
12, 15 Mar. *Don Rodrigo*, NYC Opera
18 Mar. *Butterfly*, NYC Opera
22 Mar. *Traviata*, NYC Opera
25 Mar. *Bohème*, NYC Opera
26 Mar. *Traviata*, NYC Opera
1 Apr. *Pagliacci*, Pasadena*
11, 14, 16 Apr. *Faust*, Houston*
21, 23, 25 Apr. *Elijah*, Lima* (Peruvian
debut)
1, 2, 4, 6 May *Tosca*, San Diego
11 May *Aida*,* Hamburg
19, 25, 28 May *Don Carlo*,* Vienna*
(Austrian debut)
31 May *Ballo*,* Berlin*

7, 9 July *Chénier*, Cincinnati
12, 15 July *Traviata*, Cincinnati
29, 30 July *Ballo*, Chicago*
16, 18, 20 Aug. *Chénier*, Santiago* (Chilean
debut)
2, 4, 6 Sept. *Carmen*, Santiago
15, 17, 24 Sept. *Traviata*, NYC Opera
28 Sept. *Pagliacci*, NYC Opera
30 Sept. *Butterfly*, NYC Opera
1 Oct. *Pagliacci*, NYC Opera
5 Oct. *Tosca*, NYC Opera
7 Oct. *Butterfly*, NYC Opera
13 Oct. *Bohème*, NYC Opera
15 Oct. *Butterfly*, NYC Opera
19 Oct. *Hoffmann*, Mexico City
24, 27, 29 Oct. *Carmen*, Mexico City
30 Oct. *Pagliacci*, NYC Opera
3 Nov. *Butterfly*, NYC Opera
4 Nov. *Traviata*, NYC Opera
11 Nov. *Tosca*, NYC Opera
17 Nov. *Don Rodrigo*, Los Angeles* (NYC
Opera tour)
18 Nov. *Traviata*, Los Angeles (NYC
Opera tour)
21, 26 Nov. *Butterfly*, Los Angeles (NYC
Opera tour)
1, 3 Dec. *Aida*, Fort Worth

4 Dec. *Don Rodrigo*, Los Angeles (NYC
       Opera tour)
22 Dec. *Bohème* dress rehearsal,[4] Hamburg

23, 25, 28 Dec. *Bohème*, Hamburg
31 Dec. Concert, Hamburg

[4] Dress rehearsal sung as a performance (full voice and before an invited public).

1968[5]

6 Jan. *Tosca*, Hamburg
7 Jan. *Bohème*, Hamburg
14, 16 Jan. *Lohengrin*,* Hamburg
22, 24, 27, 30 Jan. *Ballo*, Miami*
9, 11 Feb. *Faust*, Orlando*
15 Feb. *Manon Lescaut*,* Hartford
24 Feb. *Pagliacci*, NYC Opera
8, 10 Mar. *Manon Lescaut*, Fort Worth
14, 16 Mar. *Trovatore*,* New Orleans
? Mar. *Hoffmann*, Shreveport, Louisiana*
23 Mar. *Hoffmann*, San Antonio, Texas*
30 Mar. *Butterfly*, NYC Opera
7 Apr. *Tosca*, NYC Opera
14 Apr. *Carmen*, NYC Opera
19 Apr. *Tosca*, NYC Opera
21 Apr. *Cavalleria*, NYC Opera
1, 4, 7, 9, 11, 14 May *Tosca*, Vancouver*
       (Canadian debut)
4 June *Trovatore*, Hamburg
9 June *Bohème*, Hamburg
14 June Concert, Paris* (Salle Pleyel)

17 June *Don Carlo*, Vienna
21 June *Pagliacci*, Vienna
23 June *Butterfly*, Vienna
26 June *Faust*, Vienna
30 June *Pagliacci*, Vienna
19, 21 July *Carmen*, Cincinnati
26, 28 July *Hoffmann*, Cincinnati
10 Aug. *Carmen*, Saratoga,* N.Y.
19 Sept. *Pagliacci*, NYC Opera
20, 25 Sept. *Tabarro*, NYC Opera
27 Sept. *Pagliacci*, NYC Opera
28 Sept. *Adriana*, Met Opera*
2 Oct. *Adriana*, Met Opera
5 Oct. *Pagliacci*, NYC Opera
8 Oct. *Adriana*, Met Opera
12 Oct. *Pagliacci*, NYC Opera
16, 25 Oct. *Adriana*, Met Opera
27 Oct. *Pagliacci*, NYC Opera
14, 16 Nov. *Tabarro* and *Cavalleria*, New
      Orleans
20 Nov. *Tosca*, Met Opera

[5] The record for this entire year is incomplete.

1969

2 Jan. *Rigoletto* (Duke*), Hamburg
6, 10 Jan. *Bohème*, Hamburg
12 Jan. *Butterfly*, Hamburg
14 Jan. *Tosca*, Hamburg
18 Jan. *Forza*,* Hamburg
24 Jan. *Butterfly*, Hamburg
27 Jan. *Bohème*, Hamburg
4, 7, 9 Feb. *Don Carlo*, Houston
12 Feb. *Concert*, Scranton, Pennsylvania*
15 Feb. *Tosca*, Met Opera
15 Feb. *Butterfly* (first act only), Met
     Opera

20 Feb. *Manon*,* NYC Opera
6, 10 Mar. *Trovatore*, Met Opera
13 Mar. *Adriana*, Met Opera
17 Mar. *Trovatore*, Met Opera
20, 24 Mar. *Adriana*, Met Opera
27 Mar. *Trovatore*, Met Opera
3 Apr. *Tosca*, Met Opera
18, 19 Apr. Beethoven 9th Symphony
1, 3, 6, 8, 10, 13 May *Manon*,
     Vancouver
17 May *Trovatore*, Vienna
20 May Verdi Requiem,* London

24 May *Bohème*, Hamburg
26 May *Rigoletto*, Hamburg
2 June *Forza*, Hamburg
6 June *Tosca*, Hamburg
7 June *Bohème*, Hamburg
15 June *Rigoletto*, Hamburg
24, 28 June, 1, 5 July *Carmen* (concert
        form), Tel Aviv, Israel
        Philharmonic
16, 19, 24, 27 July *Turandot* (Calaf*),
        Verona* (Italian debut)

2, 5, 8, 13, 16 Aug. *Don Carlo*, Verona
28 Sept. TV concert, London
31 Oct. Verdi Requiem (organ
        accompaniment), Hackensack,
        NJ*
9 Nov. Concert, Allentown, Pennsylvania*
15 Nov. *Bohème*, San Francisco*
7, 11, 16 Dec. *Ernani*,* La Scala*
19 Dec. *Carmen*, Vienna
21, 27, 30 Dec. *Ernani*, La Scala

1970

4 Jan. *Forza*, Hamburg
8 Jan. *Pagliacci*, Hamburg
11 Jan. *Bohème*, Hamburg
14 Jan. *Don Carlo*, Vienna
15 Jan. *Pagliacci*, Hamburg
18 Jan. *Forza*, Hamburg
24 Jan. Concert, Philadelphia
26 Jan. *Bohème*, Hamburg
29 Jan. *Tosca*, Hamburg
2 Feb. *Forza*, Hamburg
4 Feb. *Tosca*, Hamburg
13, 18, 21 Feb. *Turandot*, Met Opera
25 Feb. Verdi Requiem, London
2 Mar. *Rigoletto*, Hamburg
5 Mar. *Forza*, Hamburg
8 Mar. *Bohème*, Hamburg
13, 15 Mar. *Ballo*, Fort Worth
19, 21 Mar. *Ballo*, New Orleans
26 Mar. *Forza*, Hamburg
30 Mar. *Cavalleria*, Hamburg
31 Mar. *Pagliacci*, Hamburg
3 Apr. *Pagliacci*, Vienna
4, 5 Apr. Beethoven 9th Symphony,
        Vienna
13, 16, 19 Apr. *Don Carlo*, La Scala
29 Apr. *Tosca*, Cleveland* (Met Opera
        tour)
5 May *Cavalleria*, Atlanta* (Met Opera
        tour)
14, 16 May *Gioconda*,* Madrid*

19 May *Tosca*, Minneapolis* (Met Opera
        tour)
23 May Missa Solemnis,* Rome* (St
        Peter's)
27 May *Lucia*, Detroit* (Met Opera tour)
1, 5 June *Lucia*, Met Opera
13 June Concert, Munich*
15 June *Trovatore*, Hamburg
20, 23, 26 June *Aida*, Hamburg
30 June TV performance, London
25, 30 July, 2, 6, 13, 17 Aug. *Manon
        Lescaut*, Verona
27 Aug. Missa Solemnis, Edinburgh*
        (Scottish debut)
15 Sept. *Cavalleria*, Met Opera
17 Sept. *Aida*, Mexico City
19, 26 Sept. *Cavalleria*, Met Opera
30 Sept. *Ballo* dress rehearsal, Met Opera
3 Oct. *Ballo*, Met Opera
7 Oct. *Chénier* dress rehearsal, Met Opera
10, 13 Oct. *Ballo*, Met Opera
15, 18, 21, 24 Oct. *Roberto Devereux*,
        NYC Opera
29 Oct. *Chénier*, Met Opera
7, 11 Nov. *Tosca*, Met Opera
15 Nov. Concert, Trenton, NJ*
20 Nov. *Devereux*, Los Angeles (NYC
        Opera tour)
22 Nov. *Tosca*, San Francisco
26 Nov. *Carmen*, San Francisco

28 Nov. *Tosca*, San Francisco
1 Dec. *Trovatore*, Philadelphia
5, 11 Dec. *Traviata*, Met Opera

17 Dec. *Tosca*, Met Opera
23, 28 Dec. *Chénier*, Met Opera

1971

5 Jan. *Chénier*, Met Opera
13 Jan. *Aida*, Met Opera
19 Jan. *Ernani*, Met Opera
22, 24 Jan. *Bohème*, Fort Worth
30 Jan. *Ballo*, Met Opera
1 Feb. Concert, Mexico City
4 Feb. *Ballo*, Met Opera
6 Feb. *Carmen*, Met Opera
9 Feb. *Forza*, Vienna
15 Feb. *Forza*, Hamburg
18 Feb. *Trovatore*, Hamburg
21 Feb. *Tosca*, Hamburg
28 Feb. *Aida*, Hamburg
7, 11, 14 Mar. *Lucia*, Hamburg
16, 18 Mar. *Bohème*, Hamburg
21, 24, 27, 30 Mar. *Lucia*, Hamburg
1 Apr. *Ballo*, Vienna
3 Apr. *Lucia*, Hamburg
6 Apr. *Tosca*, Vienna
11 Apr. *Trovatore*, Vienna
16, 18 Apr. *Carmen*, New Orleans
23 Apr. *Bohème*, La Scala
6, 9, 11, 14, 16 May *Manon Lescaut*,
Naples*
19, 21 May *Chénier*, Madrid
28, 30 May, 6, 9 June *Turandot*, Florence*

17, 20, 23 June *Carmen*, Hamburg
25 June Concert, Landau*
27 June *Forza*, Hamburg
14 Aug. *Traviata*, Los Angeles
(Hollywood Bowl)
25 Aug. Concert, Geneva* (Swiss debut)
4 Sept. *Chénier*, Mexico City
20, 25 Sept. *Don Carlo*, Met Opera
30 Sept., 1 Oct. Verdi Requiem, La Scala
4 Oct. *Faust*, Met Opera
8, 11 Oct. *Don Carlo*, Met Opera
14 Oct. *Faust*, Met Opera
19, 21 Oct. *Aida*, San Juan,* P.R.
24 Oct. Concert, El Paso, Texas*
26 Oct. *Trovatore*, San Francisco
29 Oct. *Faust*, Met Opera
4 Nov. *Luisa Miller*,* Met Opera
6 Nov. *Tosca*, Met Opera
9 Nov. *Luisa Miller*, Met Opera
13 Nov. *Tosca*, Met Opera
24, 27 Nov. *Forza*, Met Opera
29 Nov. *Luisa Miller*, Met Opera
8, 11, 15 Dec. *Tosca*, Covent Garden*
18, 22, 25 Dec. *Manon Lescaut*, Barcelona
27, 29 Dec. *Tosca*, Covent Garden

1972

1, 4, 7 Jan. *Tosca*, Covent Garden
11 Jan. *Lucia*, Piacenza*
15 Jan. *Ernani*, Amsterdam* (Dutch
debut)
22 Jan. *Bohème*, Munich
27 Jan. *Ballo*, Mantua*
30 Jan. *Tosca*, Turin*
1 Feb. *Carmen*, Hamburg
3 Feb. *Butterfly*, Hamburg
5 Feb. *Tosca*, Hamburg
8 Feb. *Butterfly*, Hamburg
10 Feb. *Forza*, Hamburg

13 Feb. *Tosca*, Turin
15 Feb. *Carmen*, Hamburg
18 Feb. *Tosca*, Belgrade* (Yugoslav debut)
20 Feb. *Tosca*, Vienna
26 Feb. *Faust*, Met Opera
29 Feb. *Pagliacci* and *Tabarro*,
Philadelphia
4 Mar. *Rigoletto*, San Antonio
6 Mar. Concert, Washington
13, 15, 18, 21 Mar. *Aida*, Miami
26 Mar. *Bohème*, Munich
7 Apr. *Aida* dress rehearsal, La Scala

10, 13, 16, 20 Apr. *Aida*, La Scala
22 Apr. Bing Gala, Met Opera
27 Apr. *Faust*, Boston (Met Opera tour)
1 May *Traviata*, Cleveland (Met Opera tour)
4 May *Faust*, Cleveland (Met Opera tour)
7 May *Aida*, La Scala
9 May *Faust*, Atlanta (Met Opera tour)
16 May *Bohème*, Memphis* (Met Opera tour)
19 May *Faust*, New Orleans (Met Opera tour)
25 May *Faust*, Minneapolis (Met Opera tour)
28 May *Adriana*, Caracas* (Venezuelan debut)
31 May *Faust*, Detroit (Met Opera tour)
3 June *Bohème*, Detroit (Met Opera tour)
4, 5 June Verdi Requiem, San Juan
12, 14 June *Turandot*, Madrid
16 June *Don Carlo*, Vienna
19 June Concert, Zurich*
27 June *Cavalleria* and *Pagliacci*, Hamburg
30 June *Carmen*, Hamburg
14, 16, 19, 22, 25 July *Forza*, Buenos Aires* (Argentine debut)
29 July *Carmen*, Mexico City
4 Sept. *Aida*, Munich (La Scala)

6 Sept. Verdi Requiem, Munich (La Scala)
7 Sept. *Aida*, Munich (La Scala)
8 Sept. Verdi Requiem, Munich (La Scala)
22 Sept. *Ballo*, Met Opera
24 Sept. *Tosca*, San Juan
28 Sept. *Ballo*, Met Opera
30 Sept. *Tosca*, San Juan
2 Oct. *Ballo*, Met Opera
12 Oct. *Tosca* dress rehearsal, San Francisco
15, 18, 21, 27, 29 Oct. *Tosca*, San Francisco
30 Oct. *Africaine** dress rehearsal, San Francisco
3, 7, 12, 15, 18 Nov. *Africaine*, San Francisco
20 Nov. *Carmen*, Los Angeles (NYC Opera tour)
22 Nov. Verdi Requiem dress rehearsal, Cleveland
24, 25 Nov. Verdi Requiem, Cleveland
5 Dec. *Ballo* dress rehearsal, La Scala
7, 11, 14 Dec. *Ballo*, La Scala
19 Dec. *Carmen*, Belgrade
21, 24 Dec. *Ballo*, La Scala
28 Dec. *Ballo*, Barcelona

1973

1 Jan. *Chénier*, Barcelona
4 Jan. *Ballo*, La Scala
6 Jan. *Chénier*, Barcelona
9, 12, 14 Jan. *Ballo*, Barcelona
16 Jan. *Tosca*, Vienna
20 Jan. Concert, Philadelphia
21 Jan. *Tabarro* and *Cavalleria*, Newark, NJ*
28 Jan. *Cavalleria* and *Pagliacci*, Hamburg
4 Feb. *Aida*, Vienna
7 Feb. *Rigoletto*, Vienna
9, 13 Feb. *Aida*, Vienna
16 Feb. *Tosca*, Budapest* (Hungarian debut)

20 Feb. *Aida*, Vienna
2, 5 Mar. *Trovatore*, Met Opera
9 Mar. *Tabarro* and *Cavalleria*, Hartford
17 Mar. *Trovatore*, Met Opera
22 Mar. *Francesca da Rimini** (concert form), Carnegie Hall
24, 29 Mar., 11 Apr. *Trovatore*, Met Opera
13, 15 Apr. *Trovatore*, Fort Worth
18, 20, 21 Apr. Verdi Requiem, San Francisco
27, 29 Apr. *Carmen*, Marseille
2 May *Bohème*, Vienna
6 May *Tosca*, Vienna

10 May *Cavalleria* and *Pagliacci*, Vienna
13 May *Aida*, Vienna
17 May *Cavalleria* and *Pagliacci*,
    Hamburg
20, 23, 26 May *Trovatore*, Paris*
29, 31 May *Trovatore*, Madrid
3 June *Samson et Dalila* (concert form),
    Royal Festival Hall, London
10 June *Trovatore*, Munich
17 June *Aida*, Hamburg
4, 7, 10, 13, 18, 21, 24, 27 July *Carmen*,
    Covent Garden

6 Sept. *Carmen*, Vienna
17, 22, 27 Sept. *Trovatore*, Met Opera
2 Oct. *Traviata*, Met Opera
5, 8 Oct. *Trovatore*, Met Opera
13 Oct. *Bohème*, Vienna
20, 27 Oct. *Trovatore*, Paris
1 Nov. *Traviata*, Met Opera
4 Nov. *Adriana*, Newark
6, 17 Nov. *Traviata*, Met Opera
29 Nov., 3, 8, 11, 14, 19 Dec. *Hoffmann*,
    Met Opera
29 Dec. *Aida*, Barcelona

1974

1, 3, 5 Jan. *Aida*, Barcelona
9, 14 Jan. *Aida*, Covent Garden
27 Jan. *Ballo*, Hamburg
6, 9, 11 Feb. *Bohème*, Covent Garden
12 Feb. Verdi Requiem, Royal Festival
    Hall, London
15 Feb. *Bohème*, Covent Garden
17 Feb. *Aida*, Vienna
19, 21 Feb. *Bohème*, Covent Garden
24 Feb. *Don Carlo*, Hamburg
26 Feb. *Bohème*, Covent Garden
2 Mar. *Bohème*, Covent Garden
6, 9, 12, 15 Mar. *Tosca*, Paris
17 Mar. *Tosca*, Vienna
24 Mar. *Chénier*, Turin
3 Apr. *Vespri siciliani** dress rehearsal,
    Paris
6 Apr. *Chénier*, Turin
9, 13, 18, 23 Apr. *Vespri*, Paris
28 Apr. *Pagliacci*, Hamburg
6, 9 May *Carmen*, La Scala
14 May *Tosca*, La Scala
16 May *Carmen*, La Scala
17 May *Tosca*, La Scala
22 May *Forza*, Valencia*
25 May *Tosca*, Saragossa*
27 May *Carmen*, Saragossa
5 June Concert, Madrid
8, 10 June *Tosca*, Moscow* (Russian
    debut) (La Scala)
12 June Concert, Moscow (Kremlin)

15 June *Tosca*, Moscow (La Scala)
18 June *Vespri*, Hamburg
22 June *Aida*, Hamburg
25 June *Forza*, Hamburg
27 June *Tosca*, Hamburg
30 June *Pagliacci*, Hamburg
14 July *Tosca*, Verona
18 July Verdi Requiem, Venice*
19, 27, 30 July *Tosca*, Verona
3 Aug. *Tosca*, Torre del Lago*
10, 14 Aug. *Aida*, Verona
17 Aug. *Carmen*, Figueras*
23 Sept. *Vespri*, Met Opera
28 Sept. *Roméo et Juliette*,* Met Opera
2 Oct. *Vespri*, Met Opera
8 Oct. *Roméo*, Met Opera
11 Oct. Concert, Grand Rapids,
    Michigan*
14 Oct. *Roméo*, Met Opera
16 Oct. *Carmen*, NYC Opera
19 Oct. *Vespri*, Met Opera
22 Oct. *Roméo*, Met Opera
26 Oct. *Vespri*, Met Opera
30 Oct. *Roméo*, Met Opera
4 Nov. *Vespri*, Met Opera
8 Nov. *Roméo*, Met Opera
10 Nov. *Turandot*, Newark, NJ
20 Nov. *Forza*, Frankfurt*
26, 29 Nov., 1, 5 Dec. *Fanciulla del West*,*
    Turin
9, 12 Dec. *Tosca*, La Scala

14 Dec. *Bohème*, Stuttgart*
17, 20 Dec. *Tosca*, La Scala
22 Dec. *Fanciulla*, Turin

28 Dec. *Vespri*, Barcelona
30 Dec. *Carmen*, Barcelona

1975

2, 5 Jan. *Vespri*, Barcelona
19 Jan. *Ballo*, Hamburg
30 Jan., 3, 5, 8, 11, 14, 17, 20 Feb. *Ballo*,
　　Covent Garden
23 Feb. *Don Carlo*, Hamburg
26 Feb. *Forza*, Hamburg
1 Mar. *Cavalleria* and *Pagliacci*, Hamburg
14, 16 Mar. *Tosca*, Barcelona
20 Mar. *Bohème*, Barcelona
23, 25 Mar. *Carmen*, San Juan
29, 31 Mar. *Carmen*, Nice*
5 Apr. *Trovatore*, Paris
7 Apr. *Adriana*, Paris
12 Apr. *Trovatore*, Paris
14 Apr. *Tosca*, La Scala
19 Apr. *Trovatore*, Paris
2 May *Forza*, Paris
5 May *Bohème*, Valencia
7, 10, 13, 16, 19 May *Forza*, Paris
21 May *Bohème*, Valencia

24 May *Forza*, Paris
1 June *Chénier*, Saragossa
4, 7 June *Carmen*, Madrid
12, 14 June *Tosca*, Madrid
16 June *Tosca*, Frankfurt
22 June *Ballo*, Caracas
26, 31 July *Turandot*, Verona
11, 16, 21 Aug. *Don Carlo*, Salzburg*
24 Aug. Verdi Requiem, Salzburg
26, 29 Aug. *Don Carlo*, Salzburg
7 Sept. *Carmen*, Elda*
14 Sept. *Bohème*, Hamburg
28 Sept., 2 Oct. *Otello* (Otello*), Hamburg
5 Oct. *Tosca*, Hamburg
9, 12, 16 Oct. *Otello*, Hamburg
5, 8, 11, 16, 21 Nov. *Chénier*, San Franciso
30 Nov. *Tosca*, Newark, NJ
2, 5, 8, 12, 15, 18 Dec. *Carmen*, Met Opera
23, 26 Dec. *Turandot*, Barcelona (Sofia
　　Opera)

1976

1 Jan. *Turandot*, Barcelona (Sofia Opera)
8, 11, 13 Jan. *Pagliacci*, Barcelona
15 Jan. *Cavalleria* and *Pagliacci*, Barcelona
4, 7, 10, 13, 16, 19 Feb. *Cavalleria* and
　　Pagliacci, Covent Garden
21 Feb. *Tosca*, Stuttgart*
24 Feb. *Pagliacci*, Covent Garden
1, 6 Mar. *Aida*, Met Opera
8 Mar. *Le Cid** (concert form), Carnegie
　　Hall
13, 16, 19, 22 Mar. *Carmen*, Met Opera
26 Mar. *Aida*, Met Opera
9 Apr. *Pagliacci*, Frankfurt
18 Apr. *Otello*, Hamburg
24 Apr. *Tosca*, Vienna
6, 9, 12, 15, 17, 19 May *Tosca*, Munich
22 May *Bohème*, Saragossa

26, 29 May *Otello*, Madrid
31 May, 2 June *Carmen*, Valencia
25, 29 June, 3, 8, 12, 17 July *Otello*, Paris
25 July *Aida*, Verona
28 July Concert, Santander*
24 Aug. *Traviata*, Hamburg
2, 5 Sept. *Cavalleria* and *Pagliacci*,
　　Tokyo* (Japanese debut)
7, 9 Sept. *Pagliacci*, Tokyo
12 Sept. *Bohème*, Elda
25, 29 Sept., 9, 12, 15 Oct. *Hoffmann*,
　　Chicago
27, 30 Oct., 5, 10, 13, 16 Nov. *Cavalleria*
　　and *Pagliacci*, San Francisco
4 Dec. *Otello* dress rehearsal, La Scala
7, 11, 15, 19, 22 Dec. *Otello*, La Scala

1977

3 Jan. *Tosca*, Vienna
8 Jan. *Ballo*, Hamburg
15 Jan. *Bohème*, Paris
17 Jan. Concert, Cologne*
18, 21, 24, 28 Jan. *Bohème*, Paris
31 Jan. *Cavalleria* and *Pagliacci*, Vienna
5, 8, 13 Feb. *Otello*, Barcelona
15, 18, 20 Feb. *Fedora*,* Barcelona
25 Feb. *Forza*, Met Opera
1 Mar. *Tosca*, Met Opera
5, 8, 12, 16, 19 Mar. *Forza*, Met Opera
26, 29 Mar., 1, 4 Apr. *Chénier*, Met Opera
11, 13, 16, 19 Apr. *Fanciulla*, Miami
24 Apr. *Tosca*, Berlin
28, 30 Apr. *Tosca*, Valencia
3, 6 May *Aida*, Madrid
24, 27 May *Fanciulla*, Covent Garden
30 May Royal Gala, Covent Garden
31 May, 3, 6, 10 June *Fanciulla*, Covent
    Garden
15 June *Tosca*, Munich
23, 27, 30 June *Aida*, Covent Garden

3 July *Otello*, Hamburg
12, 15, 18 July *Aida*, Covent Garden
23, 26 July *Cavalleria* and *Pagliacci*,
    Verona
30 July *Don Carlo*, Salzburg
3 Aug. Concert, Monte Carlo*
6, 9 Aug. *Cavalleria* and *Pagliacci*, Verona
22, 25, 28, 31 Aug., 3, 7 Sept. *Carmen*,
    Edinburgh
9 Sept. *Tosca*, Bilbao*
13 Sept. *Chénier*, Bilbao
17 Sept. *Ballo*, Hamburg
20 Sept. *Bohème*, Munich
23 Sept. *Chénier*, Oviedo*
25 Sept. *Tosca*, Oviedo
1 Oct. *Hoffmann*, Newark, NJ
12, 15, 18, 21 Oct. *Bohème*, Met Opera
31 Oct., 4, 7, 12, 16, 19 Nov. *Rigoletto*,
    Met Opera
27 Nov., 1, 3 Dec. *Africaine*, Barcelona
11 Dec. *Tosca*, Munich
18, 22, 25, 28 Dec. *Werther*,* Munich

1978

2 Jan. *Werther*, Munich
7 Jan. *Don Carlo*, La Scala
13, 16, 18, 21 Jan. *Fanciulla*, Covent
    Garden
26, 29, 31 Jan. *Carmen*, Barcelona
6 Feb. *Bohème*, Vienna
9, 12, 15, 19, 24 Feb. *Otello*, Munich
6, 8, 11 Mar. *Adriana*, Miami
14, 16 Mar. *Chénier*, San Juan
31 Mar., 5 Apr. *Cavalleria* and *Pagliacci*,
    Met Opera
8 Apr. *Tosca*, Met Opera
11, 15 Apr. *Cavalleria* and *Pagliacci*, Met
    Opera
21, 24, 27 Apr. *Manon Lescaut*, Madrid
1, 4 May *Trovatore*, Vienna
14, 17, 20, 23 May *Manon Lescaut*, La
    Scala

31 May *Tosca*, Las Palmas*
16 June *Manon Lescaut*, La Scala
30 June, 4, 8, 13, 17 July *Otello*, Paris
22 July *Samson et Dalila*, Orange*
27 Aug. *Carmen*, Bilbao
8 Sept. *Otello*, San Francisco
10 Sept. Concert, San Francisco
13, 17 Sept. *Otello*, San Francisco
19 Sept. *Tosca*, Monterrey
22, 26, 30 Sept. *Otello*, San Francisco
7, 10, 14, 18, 21 Oct. *Werther*, Met Opera
29 Oct., 4 Nov. *Trovatore*, Hamburg
13, 16, 22, 25, 28 Nov., 1 Dec. *Africaine*,
    Covent Garden
9, 12, 15, 17, 20 Dec. *Carmen*, Vienna
25, 28 Dec. *Cavalleria* and *Pagliacci*,
    Munich

1979

3 Jan. *Cavalleria* and *Pagliacci*, Munich

13, 17, 20, 24, 27 Jan. *Luisa Miller*, Met
  Opera

30 Jan., 2 Feb. *Tosca*, Met Opera

13 Feb. *Tosca*, Cologne

17 Feb. *Trovatore*, Zurich

21, 24 Feb. *Trovatore*, Frankfurt

1, 4 Mar. *Fanciulla*, Vienna

7, 10 Mar. *Lucia*, Vienna

22, 25, 28, 31 Mar. *Aida*, Munich

4, 7, 10 Apr. *Le Cid*, Hamburg

16 Apr. *Carmen*, Las Palmas

22 Apr. *Aida*, Munich

29 Apr., 2, 5, 8 May *Manon Lescaut*,
  Hamburg

13 May *Pagliacci*, San Juan

20, 24, 27 May *Tabarro* and *Pagliacci*,
  Madrid

4, 7, 12, 15, 19, 22 June *Luisa Miller*,
  Covent Garden

11 July *Tosca*, Macerata*

15, 18 July *Werther*, Munich

21 July *Tosca*, Macerata

29 July *Fanciulla*, Buenos Aires

4 Aug. Concert, Monte Carlo

8, 11 Aug. *Fanciulla*, Buenos Aires

9 Sept. *Giuramento** (concert form),
  Vienna

24, 28 Sept., 2, 6, 10 Oct. *Otello*, Met
  Opera

17, 20, 23 Oct. *Fanciulla*, San Francisco

25 Oct. *Carmen*, Monterrey

27, 31 Oct., 2 Nov. *Fanciulla*, San
  Francisco

5 Nov. *Carmen*, Guadalajara

23, 27, 30 Nov., 3, 8, 12, 15 Dec. *Chénier*,
  Chicago

20, 22 Dec. *Tosca*, Manila*

1980

12, 16, 20 Jan. *Otello*, Monte Carlo

23 Jan. *Don Carlo*, Vienna

5, 9, 12, 16, 19 Feb. *Otello*, Covent Garden

5, 8 Mar. *Ballo*, Met Opera

17, 21, 24, 29 Mar. *Manon Lescaut*, Met
  Opera

2 Apr. Concert, San Juan

9, 12, 16, 19 Apr. *Manon Lescaut*, Met
  Opera

26, 29 Apr., 3, 6 May *Otello*, La Scala

9, 12, 15 May *Carmen*, Paris

28 May *Tosca*, Vienna

8 June *Bohème*, Hamburg

12, 15 June *Carmen*, Hamburg

19, 22, 25 June *El Poeta** (world première),
  Madrid

30 June, 4, 8, 11 July *Bohème*, Paris

26 July, 6, 9, 14, 18, 22 Aug. *Hoffmann*,
  Salzburg

5, 9, 13, 18, 21, 24 Sept. *Samson et Dalila*,
  San Francisco

5, 9, 12, 16 Oct. *Hoffmann*, Cologne.

22 Oct. Verdi Requiem, Carnegie Hall

1 Nov. *Aida*, Newark, NJ

7 Nov. Concert, Buffalo,* NY

12 Nov. Concert, Los Angeles

23 Nov. *Carmen*, Hamburg

30 Nov. *Bohème*, Munich

15, 19, 23, 26, 30 Dec. *Hoffmann*, Covent
  Garden

APPENDIX I

1981

2, 6, 9 Jan. *Hoffmann*, Covent Garden
14 Jan. *Ballo*, Cologne
24, 27 Jan. *Cavalleria* and *Pagliacci*, La Scala
30 Jan., 5, 7 Feb. *Pagliacci*, La Scala
10 Feb. *Tosca*, Naples
15 Feb. *Le Cid*, Paris (Châtelet*)
23 Feb. *Ballo*, Met Opera
1 Mar. Concert, Houston
17, 21, 24, 28 Mar., 1 Apr. *Traviata*, Met Opera
6 Apr. *Otello*, Mexico City
15 Apr. Concert, Düsseldorf*
19 Apr. *Ballo*, Hamburg
30 Apr., 2, 5, 8 May *Chénier*, Vienna
20, 23, 26 May *Gioconda*, Berlin
29 May *Carmen*, Berlin
3, 6, 9, 12 June *Lucia*, Madrid

16 June *Tosca*, Met Opera (Central Park)
21, 24, 27, 30 June, 3 July *Otello*, Buenos Aires
21, 24, 28 July *Otello*, Bregenz*
6, 10, 14, 18, 21 Aug. *Hoffmann*, Salzburg
2, 5, 8 Sept. *Otello*, Tokyo (La Scala)
21, 25 Sept. *Norma*,* Met Opera
28 Sept. *Tosca*, Guadalajara
30 Sept., 3, 6 Oct. *Norma*, Met Opera
9 Oct. *Samson et Dalila*, Monterrey
25, 28, 31 Oct. *Manon Lescaut*, Munich
6, 9, 13, 16 Nov. *Tosca*, Covent Garden
19 Nov. *Aida*, Monte Carlo
21 Nov. *Tosca*, Covent Garden
23 Nov. *Aida*, Monte Carlo
27, 30 Nov. *Tosca*, Covent Garden
4, 7, 10, 13 Dec. *Carmen*, San Francisco
17 Dec. *Turandot*, Cologne

1982

3, 6 Jan. *Luisa Miller*, Hamburg
16 Jan. Concert, New York (Studio 8-H)
18, 22, 26, 30 Jan., 2 Feb. *Hoffmann*, Covent Garden
4 Feb. *Pagliacci*, Berne*
8 Feb. *Norma*, Met Opera
10 Feb. Concert, New York (St Patrick's Cathedral)
13 Feb. *Norma*, Met Opera
16 Feb. *Bohème*, Met Opera
20 Feb. Verdi Requiem, Met Opera
22 Feb. *Bohème*, Met Opera
28 Feb. Concert, Met Opera
8, 11, 15 Mar. *Hoffmann*, Met Opera
18 Mar. Concert, Pasadena
20, 24, 27, 30 Mar., 3 Apr. *Hoffmann*, Met Opera
6, 11 Apr. *Carmen*, San Juan
15, 19, 21 Apr. *Otello*, La Scala
2, 5, 7, 9 May *Tosca*, Buenos Aires

26, 30 May *Bohème*, Barcelona
2, 5, 8 June *Otello*, Vienna
12 June *Chénier*, Vienna
16 June *Carmen*, Vienna
22, 27, 30 June, 3, 6 July *Samson et Dalila*, Madrid
9 July Concert, Madrid
10, 16, 20, 24 Aug. *Hoffmann*, Salzburg
4, 7, 12 Sept. *Otello*, Vienna
25, 28 Sept., 2, 5, 9 Oct. *Gioconda*, Met Opera
13 Oct. *Gioconda* (first act only), Met Opera
16, 19, 22 Oct. *Tosca*, Chicago
24 Oct. *Pagliacci*, Guadalajara
31 Oct. Concert, Rome (Vatican)
5, 9, 12, 15, 18, 24, 27 Nov. *Fanciulla*, Covent Garden
7, 11, 14, 18, 22, 28 Dec. *Ernani*, La Scala

APPENDIX I

1983

17, 19, 22, 25 Jan. *Chénier*, Miami
30 Jan. Concert, Met Opera
5, 9, 12 Feb. *Gioconda*, Met Opera
17 Feb. *Bohème*, Met Opera

21 Feb. *Adriana*, Met Opera
7 Mar. Concert, Washington, DC
9, 12, 15, 22, 26 Mar. *Don Carlo*, Met
    Opera

APPENDIX II: DISCOGRAPHY

This is a listing of American and British releases. In the first section (Complete Operas and Other Works), dates indicate the years in which the recordings were made; in the second (Other Recordings), they indicate the years in which the records were released. The many recital albums consisting of excerpts from complete opera recordings are not listed here. A few of the items in this discography are no longer in print, while many are also available on cassette.

COMPLETE OPERAS AND OTHER WORKS

Beethoven Symphony No. 9 in D, Op. 125 (1969). Leinsdorf, Boston Symphony; Marsh, Veasey, Milnes. (US) RCA LSC 7055
  Symphony No. 9 (1980). Böhm, Vienna Philharmonic; Norman, Fassbaender, Berry. DG 2741009
Bellini *Norma* (1972). Caballé, Cossotto, Raimondi; Cillario, London Philharmonic. (US) RCA LSC 6202; (GB) RCA SER 5658-60
Berlioz *Béatrice et Bénédict* (1979). Minton, Cotrubas, Fischer-Dieskau; Barenboim, Orchestre de Paris. DG 2707130
  La Damnation de Faust (1978-9). Minton, Fischer-Dieskau, Bastin; Barenboim, Orchestre de Paris. DG 2709087
  Grande Messe des Morts (Requiem) (1979). Barenboim, Orchestre de Paris. DG 2707119
Bizet *Carmen* (1975). Troyanos, Te Kanawa, van Dam; Solti, London Philharmonic. (US) Lon. OSA 13115; (GB) Decca D11D3; excerpts (GB) Decca SET 621
  Carmen (1978). Berganza, Cotrubas, Milnes; Abbado, London Symphony. DG 2709083; excerpts DG 2537049
Boito *Mefistofele* (1973). Caballé, Ligi, Treigle; Rudel, London Symphony. (US) Ang. SCLX 3806; (GB) EMI SLS 973
Charpentier *Louise* (1976). Cotrubas, Berbié, Bacquier; Prêtre, New Philharmonia. (US) CBS M3 34207; (GB) CBS 79302
Cilèa *Adriana Lecouvreur* (1977). Scotto, Obraztsova, Milnes; Levine, Philharmonia. (US) CBS M3 34588; (GB) CBS 79310
Donizetti *L'elisir d'amore* (1977). Cotrubas, Wixell, Evans; Pritchard, Royal Opera. (US) CBS M3 34585; (GB) CBS 79210

Giordano *Andrea Chénier* (1976). Scotto, Milnes; Levine, National Philharmonic. (US) RCA ARL 3-2046; (GB) RCA RL 02046

Gounod *Faust* (1978). Freni, Allen, Ghiaurov; Prêtre, Paris Opéra. (US) Ang. SZDX 3868; (GB) EMI SLS 5170

Leoncavallo *I pagliacci* (1971). Caballé, Milnes; Santi, London Symphony. (Contains excerpts from Leoncavallo's *La bohème*, *Chatterton*, and *Zazà*.) (US) RCA LSC 7090; (GB) RCA SER 5635-6

Mascagni *Cavalleria rusticana* (1979). Scotto, Elvira; Levine, National Philharmonic. (US) RCA CRL 1-3091; (GB) RCA RL 13091

Massenet *Le Cid* (1976). Bumbry, Plishka; Queler, Opera Orchestra of NY. (US) CBS M3 34211; (GB) CBS 79300

La Navarraise (1975). Horne, Milnes, Bacquier; Lewis, London Symphony. RCA ARL 1-1114

Werther (1979). Obraztsova, Auger, Moll; Chailly, Cologne Radio Symphony. DG 2709091

Montemezzi *L'amore dei tre re* (1976). Moffo, Siepi, Elvira, Davies; Santi, London Symphony. (US) RCA ARL 2-1945; (GB) RCA RL 01945; excerpts (US) RCA ARK 1-2191

Offenbach *Les Contes d'Hoffmann* (1971). Sutherland, Tourangeau, Cuenod, Bacquier; Bonynge, Orchestre de la Suisse-Romande. (US) Lon. 13106; (GB) Decca SET 545/7; excerpts (US) Lon. 26369; (GB) Decca SET 569

Puccini *La Bohème* (1973). Caballé, Blegen, Milnes, Raimondi; Solti, London Philharmonic. (US) RCA ARL 2-0371; (GB) RCA ARL 2 0371

La fanciulla del West (1977). Neblett, Milnes; Mehta, Royal Opera. DG 2709078; excerpts DG 2537032

Gianni Schicchi (1976). Cotrubas, Gobbi; Maazel, London Symphony. (US) CBS M 34534; (GB) CBS 79312

Madama Butterfly (1978). Scotto, Wixell; Maazel, Philharmonia. (US) CBS M3 35181; (GB) CBS 79313; excerpts (US) CBS HM 45890

Manon Lescaut (1971-2). Caballé, Sardinero; Bartoletti, New Philharmonia. (US) Ang. SBLX-3782; (GB) EMI SLS 962

La rondine (1982). Te Kanawa; Maazel, National Philharmonic. (US) CBS 12M 37852; (GB) CBS D2 378527 (to be released shortly)

Il tabarro (1971). L. Price, Milnes; Leinsdorf, New Philharmonia. (US) RCA LSC 3220; (GB) RCA SER 5619

Il tabarro (1977). Scotto, Wixell; Maazel, Philharmonia. (US) CBS M 34570; (GB) CBS 79312

Tosca (1972). L. Price, Milnes; Mehta, New Philharmonia. RCA ARL 2-0105

Tosca (1980). Scotto, Bruson; Levine, Philharmonia. (US) Ang. DSBX 3919; (GB) EMI SLS 5213

Turandot (1981). Ricciarelli, Hendricks, Raimondi; Karajan, Vienna Philharmonic. DG 2741013

Le villi (1979). Scotto, Nucci; Maazel, National Philharmonic. (US) CBS 36669; (GB) CBS 76890

Saint-Saëns *Samson et Dalila* (1978). Obraztsova, Bruson, Lloyd; Barenboim, Orchestre de Paris. DG 2709095; excerpts DG 2537056

Strauss, R. *Der Rosenkavalier* (1971). Ludwig, Jones, Popp, Berry; Bernstein, Vienna Philharmonic. (US) CBS D4M 30652; (GB) CBS 77416; excerpts (US) CBS M 31959

Verdi *Aida* (1971). L. Price, Bumbry, Milnes, Raimondi; Leinsdorf, London Symphony. (US) RCA LSC 6198; (GB) RCA SER 5609-11; excerpts (US) LSC 3275

Aida (1974). Caballé, Cossotto, Cappuccilli, Ghiaurov; Muti, New Philharmonia. (US) Ang. SCLX 3815; (GB) EMI SLS 977; excerpts (US) Ang. S 37228; (GB) EMI ASD 3292

Aida (1981). Ricciarelli, Obraztsova, Nucci, Ghiaurov; Abbado, La Scala. DG 2741014

Un ballo in maschera (1975). Arroyo, Grist, Cossotto, Cappuccilli; Muti, New Philharmonia. (US) Ang. SCLX 3762; (GB) EMI SLS 984

Un ballo in maschera (1980). Ricciarelli, Gruberova, Obraztsova, Bruson; Abbado, La Scala. DG 2740251; excerpts DG 2537059

Don Carlo (1970) (in Italian). Caballé, Verrett, Milnes, Raimondi; Giulini, Royal Opera. (US) Ang. SDL 3774; (GB) EMI SLS 956; excerpts (GB) EMI ASD 2823

Don Carlos (1984) (in French). Ricciarelli, Valentini-Terrani, Nucci, Raimondi; Abbado, La Scala. DG (release number not yet assigned)

Ernani (1982). Freni, Bruson, Ghiaurov; Muti, La Scala. (US) Ang. DSCX 3942

La forza del destino (1976). L. Price, Cossotto, Milnes, Raimondi, Bacquier; Levine, London Symphony. (US) RCA ARL 4-1864; (GB) RCA RL 01864

Giovanna d'Arco (1972). Caballé, Milnes; Levine, London Symphony. (US) Ang. SCL 3791; (GB) EMI SLS 967

I lombardi (1971). Deutekom, Raimondi; Gardelli, Royal Philharmonic. Philips 6703 032

Luisa Miller (1979). Ricciarelli, Obraztsova, Bruson, Howell; Maazel, Royal Opera. DG 2709096; excerpts DG 2537055

Macbeth (1976). Verrett, Cappuccilli, Ghiaurov; Abbado, La Scala. DG 2709062

Messa da Requiem (1970). Bernstein, London Symphony; Arroyo, Veasey, Raimondi. (US) CBS M2 30060; (GB) CBS 77231

Messa da Requiem (1979). Abbado, La Scala; Ricciarelli, Verrett, Ghiaurov. DG 2707120

Messa da Requiem (1980). Mehta, New York Philharmonic; Caballé, Berini, Plishka. (US) CBS D2 36927; (GB) CBS 36927

Nabucco (1982). Dimitrova, Valentini-Terrani, Cappuccilli, Nesterenko; Sinopoli, Deutsche Oper (Berlin). DG 2741021

Otello (1978). Scotto, Milnes; Levine, National Philharmonic. (US) RCA CRL 3-2951; (GB) RCA RL 02951

Rigoletto (1979). Cotrubas, Obraztsova, Cappuccilli, Ghiaurov, Moll; Giulini, Vienna Philharmonic. DG 2740225; excerpts DG 2537057

Simon Boccanegra (1973). Ricciarelli, Cappuccilli, Raimondi; Gavazzeni, RCA Italiana. (US) RCA ARL 3-0564; (GB) RCA SER 5696-8

La traviata (1976-7). Cotrubas, Milnes; Kleiber, Bavarian State Opera. DG 2707103; excerpts DG 2537047

La traviata (1982). Stratas, MacNeil; Levine, New York Philharmonic. Elektra 60267 1T

Il trovatore (1969). L. Price, Cossotto, Milnes; Mehta, New Philharmonia. (US) RCA LSC 6194; (GB) RCA SER 5586-8; excerpts (US) RCA LSC 3203

I vespri siciliani (1973). Arroyo, Milnes, Raimondi; Levine, New Philharmonia. RCA ARL 4-0370

Wagner *Die Meistersinger* (1976). Ligendza, Ludwig, Fischer-Dieskau; Jochum, Deutsche Oper (Berlin). DG 2740149; excerpts DG 2537041

Weber *Oberon* (1970). Nilsson, Haman, Grobe, Prey; Kubelik, Bavarian Radio. DG 2726052

OTHER RECORDINGS

'Romantic Arias' (1969). Downes, Royal Philharmonic. (US) RCA LSC 3083; (GB) RCA SB 6795

'Recital of Italian Operatic Arias' (1970). Santi, Berlin Opera. (US) Lon. 26080; (GB) Decca SXL 6451

'Great Operatic Duets' (1971). Milnes; Guadagno, London Symphony. (US) RCA LSC 3182; (GB) RCA SER 5593

'Domingo Sings Caruso' (1972). Santi, London Symphony. (US) RCA AGL 1-4140; (GB) RCA SER 5613

'Domingo Conducts Milnes! Milnes Conducts Domingo!' (1973). New Philharmonia. RCA ARL 1-0122

'La voce d'oro' (1973). Santi, New Philharmonia. RCA ARL 1-0048

'Music of My Country' (zarzuela arias) (1974). García Navarro, Orquesta Sinfónica de Barcelona. (US) Lon. OS 26434; (GB) Decca SXL 6988

'The Operatic Duo of the Century' (1975). Price; Santi, New Philharmonia. RCA ARL 1-0840

'Be My Love' (1976). Loges & Peeters, London Symphony. DG 2530 700

'Great Love Duets' (1978). Ricciarelli; Gavazzeni, Santa Cecilia (Rome). (USA) RCA ARL 1-2799; (GB) SER 5672

'Romantic Opera Duets' (1978). Scotto; Adler, National Philharmonic. (US) CBS M35135; (GB) CBS 76732

'Plácido Domingo and the Vienna Choirboys' (1980). Froschauer, Vienna Symphony. (US) RCA ARL 1-3835; (GB) RL 30469

'Gala Opera Concert' (1981). Giulini, Los Angeles Philharmonic. DG 2532 009-10

'Christmas with Plácido Domingo' (1981). Holdridge, Vienna Symphony. (US) CBS 37245; (GB) CBS 73635

'Perhaps Love' (1981). With John Denver. (US) CBS 37243; (GB) CBS 73592

'Tangos' (1981). Pansera. DG 2536 416

'Adoro' (popular Mexican songs) (1982). Salazar. (US) CBS FM 37284; (GB) CBS 73652

'My Life for a Song' (1983). Holdridge. (US) CBS FM 37799; (GB) CBS 73683

INDEX